MEDITERRANEAN DIET COOKBOOK for Beginners

2000 Bold and Healthy Recipes for Lasting Weight Loss and Hormone Balancing, 30-Day Meal Plan to Help You Build Healthy Habits

Lora B. Evans

© 2024 Lora B. Evans

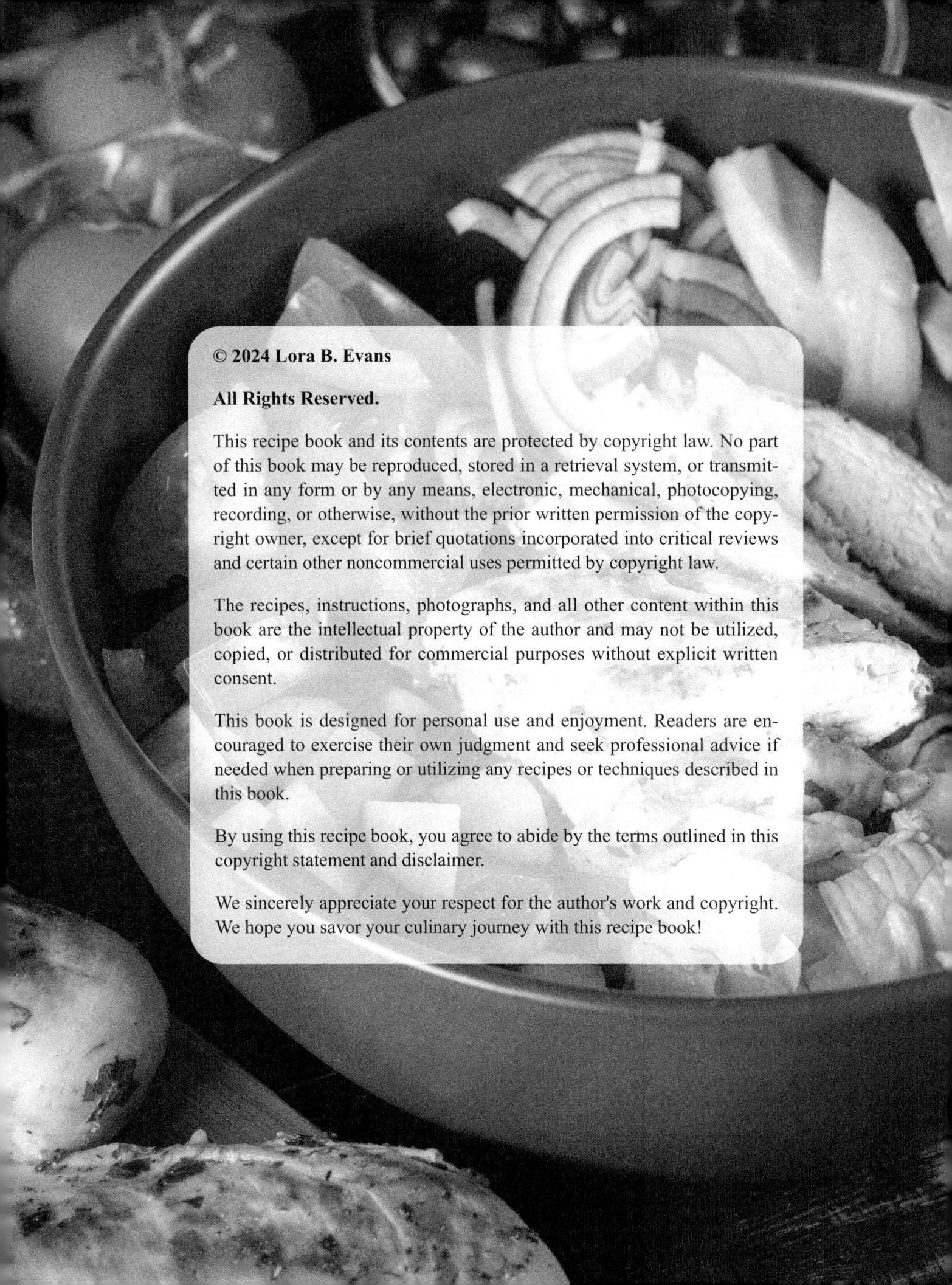

All Rights Reserved.

This recipe book and its contents are protected by copyright law. No part of this book may be reproduced, stored in a retrieval system, or transmitted in any form or by any means, electronic, mechanical, photocopying, recording, or otherwise, without the prior written permission of the copyright owner, except for brief quotations incorporated into critical reviews and certain other noncommercial uses permitted by copyright law.

The recipes, instructions, photographs, and all other content within this book are the intellectual property of the author and may not be utilized, copied, or distributed for commercial purposes without explicit written consent.

This book is designed for personal use and enjoyment. Readers are encouraged to exercise their own judgment and seek professional advice if needed when preparing or utilizing any recipes or techniques described in this book.

By using this recipe book, you agree to abide by the terms outlined in this copyright statement and disclaimer.

We sincerely appreciate your respect for the author's work and copyright. We hope you savor your culinary journey with this recipe book!

CONTENTS

INTRODUCTION — 12

What is the Mediterranean Diet? 13
The Mediterranean Diet Pyramid 13
8 Easy Ways to Follow the Mediterranean Diet for Better Health 14

30-DAY MEAL PLAN — 16

BREAKFAST RECIPES — 18

Baked Oatmeal With Cinnamon 19
Herbed Quinoa And Asparagus 19
Corn And Shrimp Salad 19
Quinoa And Potato Bowl 19
Artichokes And Cheese Omelet 19
Herbed Potatoes And Eggs 20
Couscous With Artichokes, Sun-dried Tomatoes And Feta 20
Zucchini Oats 20
Menemen 20
Stuffed Figs 21
Cheesy Caprese Style Portobellos Mushrooms 21
Tomato And Lentils Salad 21
Cranberry And Dates Squares 21
Blueberries Quinoa 21
Cauliflower Hash Brown Breakfast Bowl 22
Pumpkin Oatmeal With Spices 22
Parmesan Omelet 22
Overnight Oats With Nuts 22
Chicken Liver 23
Cheesy Thyme Waffles 23
Lemon Peas Quinoa Mix 23
Herbed Muffins 23
Fruits And Pistachios 23
Avocado Baked Eggs 24
Oregano Muffins 24
Breakfast Spanakopita 24
Mediterranean Omelet 24
Cheesy Yogurt 25
Cheesy Olives Bread 25
Avocado Toast 25
Shanklish Cheese 25

Breakfast Tostadas 25
Olive And Milk Bread.. 26
Endives, Fennel And Orange Salad 26
Creamy Chorizo Bowls.. 26

SNACK AND APPETIZER RECIPES   27

Kalamata Hummus... 28
Chickpeas And Eggplant Bowls............................ 28
Slow Cooked Cheesy Artichoke Dip 28
Creamy Eggplant Dip 28
Zucchini Cakes... 29
Peach Skewers 29
Bulgur Lamb Meatballs 29
Creamy Potato Spread... 29
Lavash Chips.. 29
Eggplant Chips... 30
Balsamic Wings 30
Goat Cheese And Chives Spread 30
Cheddar Bites... 30
Cucumber Sandwich 30
Perfect Italian Potatoes 30
Hot Squash Wedges 31
Stuffed Zucchinis 31
Multipurpose Dough 31
Popcorn-pine Nut Mix 31
Plum Wraps.. 32
Vinegar Beet Bites 32
Mediterranean-style Nachos Recipe 32
Olives And Cheese Stuffed Tomatoes..................... 32
Marinated Chickpeas 33
Feta And Roasted Red Pepper Bruschetta 33
Lemon Salmon Rolls... 33
Chickpeas Salsa 33
Lemon Endive Bites.. 33
Lentils Stuffed Potato Skins................................. 34
Pesto Dip... 34
Creamy Pepper Spread.. 34
Grilled Shrimp Kabobs 34
Cucumber Roll Ups... 34
Lime Yogurt Dip 35
Mediterranean Dip Duo 35
Roasted Seeds 35
Delicious Eggplant Caponata............................... 35

MEAT RECIPES   36

Balsamic Chicken With Roasted Tomatoes 37
Carrot Mushroom Beef Roast 37
Italian Pork Spareribs.. 37
Pork And Parsley Spread 37
Pork Chops And Cherries Mix 37
Baked Pork Chops... 38
Lamb Chops... 38
Cherry Stuffed Lamb... 38
Tender Beef In Tomato-artichoke Stew 38
Flavorful Beef Bourguignon 39
Creamy Chicken-spinach Skillet............................ 39
Italian Pork And Mushrooms................................ 39

Mediterranean Diet Cookbook

Rosemary Beef Eggplant	39
Sweet Chili Lamb	39
Beef With Beets And Broccoli	40
Upside-down Rice (makloubeh)	40
Pita Chicken Burger With Spicy Yogurt	40
Pork Shanks And Wine Sauce	41
Artichoke Beef Roast	41
Greek Chicken Stew	41
Meatball Gyro Pita Sandwich	41
Ancestral Roasted Chicken	42
Chili Lamb Meatballs	42
Shrimp And Vegetable Rice	42
Thyme Ginger Garlic Beef	43
Steaks And Greek Yogurt Mix	43
Pork Kebabs	43
Beef And Zucchini Skillet	43
Light Beef Soup	43
Sweet Pork Ribs	44
Pork And Tomato Meatloaf	44
Stuffed Squash Casserole	44
Hot Pork Meatballs	45
Italian Beef	45
Kumquat And Chicken Tagine	45
Lamb And Zucchini Mix	45

VEGETABLE RECIPES 46

Cold Veggie Udon	47
Broccoli And Leek Soup	47
Celery Carrot Brown Lentils	47
Chili Eggplant	47
Pomegranate, Squash In Quinoa Stew	48
Summer Vegetables	48
Savoy Cabbage With Coconut Cream Sauce	48
Stir Fried Eggplant	49
Zucchini Fritters	49
Roasted Brussels Sprouts And Pecans	49
Creamy Eggplants	49
Creamy Kale And Mushrooms	50
Mediterranean Diet Styled Stuffed Peppers	50
Paprika 'n Cajun Seasoned Onion Rings	50
Rosemary Sweet Potato	50
Vegetarian Cabbage Rolls	50
Braised Kale And Carrots	51
Instant Pot Artichoke Hearts	51
Instant Pot Fried Veggies	51
Flavors Basil Lemon Ratatouille	51
Eggplant With Olives	52
Ratatouille Pasta Style	52
Garlic Parmesan Artichokes	52
Refreshing Greek Salad	52
Vegetarian Bowtie Veggie Pasta	52
Sweet And Savory Couscous	53
Mushroom And Potato Mix	53
Indian Bell Peppers And Potato Stir Fry	53
Cheesy Asparagus	53
Sweet Potatoes Oven Fried	54
Cheese Onion Spread	54
Thyme Mushrooms	54
Mushroom And Zucchini Pie	54
Cold Cucumber Soup	55
Ginger Vegetable Stir Fry	55
Tomato And Palm Salad	55

Mediterranean Diet Cookbook

Chilli Broccoli..55	Cheese And Broccoli Balls 56
Orange Lettuce Salad................................55	Mushroom-cauliflower Risotto 56
Cold Watermelon Gazpacho 56	

POULTRY RECIPES 57

Curry Chicken, Artichokes And Olives 58	Turmeric Baked Chicken Breast.................62
Greek Chicken Bites 58	Chicken With Peas 62
Grilled Chicken On The Bone 58	Garlic Chicken And Endives.......................62
Creamy Coriander Chicken........................58	Chicken Pilaf...63
Chipotle Turkey And Tomatoes 59	Turkey And Salsa Verde.............................63
Sage And Nutmeg Chicken 59	Chicken And Rice 63
Herbed Almond Turkey..............................59	Chicken Roulade..63
Balsamic Chicken Tortillas 59	Chicken Skewers..64
Chicken And Lemongrass Sauce 60	Tomato Chicken And Lentils 64
Chicken And Parsley Sauce 60	Creamy Chicken And Mushrooms..............64
Slow Cooked Chicken And Capers Mix 60	Oregano Chicken And Zucchini Pan...........64
Chicken And Olives 60	Turkey And Asparagus Mix 65
Chicken And Sweet Potatoes 60	Chicken Wings And Dates Mix...................65
Chicken And Olives Bowls.........................61	Chicken Salad And Mustard Dressing 65
Chili Chicken Fillets 61	Bbq Chicken Mix..65
Duck And Tomato Sauce............................61	Chicken And Greens Salad 65
Turkey And Chickpeas 61	Stuffed Chicken..66
Chicken With Artichokes And Beans.........61	Lemony Turkey And Pine Nuts...................66
Turkey And Cranberry Sauce 62	Chicken And Sausage Mix.........................66
Paprika Chicken And Pineapple Mix..........62	

BEANS & GRAINS RECIPES 67

Pecorino Pasta With Sausage And Fresh Tomato 68	Seafood Paella With Couscous 69
Feta, Eggplant And Sausage Penne............68	Belly-filling Cajun Rice & Chicken..........69
Ricotta And Spinach Ravioli.......................68	Garbanzo And Kidney Bean Salad 69
Red Quinoa Peach Porridge.......................69	Sun-dried Tomatoes And Chickpeas........70

Leek, Bacon And Pea Risotto 70	Breakfast Salad From Grains And Fruits 75
Mediterranean Diet Pasta With Mussels 70	Cinnamon Quinoa Bars 76
Kidney Bean And Parsley-lemon Salad 71	Filling Macaroni Soup 76
Lemon Asparagus Risotto 71	Cilantro-dijon Vinaigrette On Kidney Bean Salad .. 76
Pasta Primavera Without Cream 71	Goat Cheese 'n Red Beans Salad 77
Italian White Bean Soup 72	Cucumber Olive Rice 77
Fruity Asparagus-quinoa Salad 72	Feta On Tomato-black Bean 77
Spanish Rice Casserole With Cheesy Beef 72	Baked Parmesan And Eggplant Pasta 77
Chorizo-kidney Beans Quinoa Pilaf 73	Chickpea-crouton Kale Caesar Salad 78
Delicious Pasta Primavera 73	Italian Mac & Cheese 78
Nutty And Fruity Amaranth Porridge 73	Vegan Olive Pasta 78
Lime-cilantro Rice Chipotle Style 73	Puttanesca Style Bucatini 78
Rice And Chickpea Stew 74	Escarole And Cannellini Beans On Pasta 79
Orange, Dates And Asparagus On Quinoa Salad 74	Saffron Green Bean-quinoa Soup 79
Raw Tomato Sauce & Brie On Linguine 74	Bean And Toasted Pita Salad 79
Seafood And Veggie Pasta 75	Cucumber And Tomato Salad 79
Appetizing Mushroom Lasagna 75	

LUNCH & DINNER RECIPES 80

Honey Roasted Chicken With Rosemary Potatoes .. 81	Pistachio Crusted Lamb Chops 84
Fettuccine With Spinach And Shrimp 81	Tomato Topped Eggplant Pie 84
Caramelized Onion Pasta 81	Crispy Pollock And Gazpacho 84
Beets Salad 81	Herbed Beef And Tomato Soup 84
Yogurt Marinated Pork Chops 82	Pork Fennel Meatballs 85
Shrimp Pancakes 82	Sesame Turkey Fillets With Fresh Greens 85
Ratatouille Spaghetti 82	Turkey Fritters And Sauce 85
Parsley Beef Stew 82	Chorizo Broiled Mussels 85
Stuffed Eggplants 83	Fig And Prosciutto Pita Bread Pizza 86
Lentil Tabbouleh And Haloumi 83	Mediterranean-style Salmon Fillet 86
Cherry Braised Lamb Shanks 83	Mint Chicken Soup 86
Chicken Breasts Mediterranean-style With Avocado Tapenade 83	Basil Rice Soup 86
	Tomato Roasted Feta 86

Quinoa Chicken Casserole 87	Veggie And Pasta Soup 89
Bean And Beef Chili 87	Garlic Butter Seafood 89
Parmesan Penne 87	Beef Stuffed Bell Peppers 89
Garlicky Roasted Chicken 87	Mediterranean Flounder 89
Kalamata Olives Penne 88	Mussels And Shrimp In Wine Sauce And Garlic Crostini 90
Fish Parcels 88	
Sage Pork And Beans Stew 88	Raisin Stuffed Lamb 90
Layered Potato Chicken Casserole 88	

FISH AND SEAFOOD RECIPES — 91

Honey Halibut 92	Greek Trout Spread 97
Orange Herbed Sauced White Bass 92	Salmon And Green Beans 97
Shrimp And Yogurt Sauce 92	Salsa Fish Fillets 97
Baked Tilapia 92	Stewed Mussels & Scallops 97
Kale, Beets And Cod Mix 93	Leftover Salmon Salad Power Bowls 98
Salmon And Zucchini Rolls 93	Easy Fish Curry 98
Fried Salmon 93	Minty Sardines Salad 98
Baked Sea Bass 93	Dill Calamari 98
Dijon Mustard And Lime Marinated Shrimp 93	Shrimp And Lemon Sauce 98
Shrimp And Calamari Mix 94	Walnut Salmon Mix 99
Lemon-garlic Baked Halibut 94	Lemon Swordfish 99
Tuna Risotto 94	Warm Caper Tapenade On Cod 99
Fish And Orzo 94	One-pot Seafood Chowder 99
Smoked Trout Tartine 95	Crab Stew 100
Leeks And Calamari Mix 95	Easy Broiled Lobster Tails 100
Italian Tuna Pasta 95	Trout And Tzatziki Sauce 100
Parmesan Salmon Balls 95	Creamy Curry Salmon 100
Crazy Saganaki Shrimp 96	Mustard Cod 101
Creamy Bacon-fish Chowder 96	Garlic Roasted Shrimp With Zucchini Pasta 101
Avocado Peach Salsa On Grilled Swordfish 96	Delicious Fish Tacos 101
Salmon And Peach Pan 96	Shrimp Scampi 101
Mahi Mahi And Pomegranate Sauce 97	

Mediterranean Diet Cookbook

SALADS & SIDE DISHES RECIPES — 102

- Garden Salad With Grapes ... 103
- Tangy Citrus Salad With Grilled Cod ... 103
- Dill Cucumber Salad ... 103
- Easy Quinoa & Pear Salad ... 103
- Barley And Chicken Salad ... 104
- Chickpeas, Corn And Black Beans Salad ... 104
- Sweet And Sour Spinach Salad ... 104
- Cardamom Apples ... 104
- Cucumber Salad Japanese Style ... 104
- Cheesy Barley ... 105
- Mediterranean-style fish soup ... 105
- Quinoa Salad ... 105
- Summer Bean Salad And Smoked Trout ... 105
- Chickpea Salad Recipe ... 106
- Quick Arugula Salad ... 106
- Fennel Salad With Lemon, Toasted Almonds, And Mint ... 106
- Lamb Stew With Apricots And Moroccan Mint Tea ... 106
- Mediterranean Potato Salad ... 107
- Tuna-dijon Salad ... 107
- Tomato-mozzarella With Balsamic Dressing ... 108
- Lime Beans Salad ... 108
- Lemony Lentil Salad With Salmon ... 108
- Healthy Detox Salad ... 108
- Herbed Tomato-arugula Salad With Chicken ... 108
- Parmesan Polenta ... 109
- Roasted Eggplant Salad ... 109
- Spiced Parsley Salad ... 109
- Tabbouleh- Arabian Salad ... 109
- Yogurt Peppers Mix ... 109
- Avocado And Onion Mix ... 110
- Dill Beets Salad ... 110
- Warm Shrimp Salad With Feta And Honeydew ... 110
- Dandelion Greens ... 110
- Chives Rice Mix ... 111
- Bacon And Tomato Pasta ... 111
- Spiced Meat And Rice ... 111
- Spring Soup Recipe With Poached Egg ... 111
- Minty Cauliflower Mix ... 111
- Lemon Endives ... 111
- Tomato Salad With Olives, Feta, And Mint ... 112
- Balsamic Asparagus ... 112
- Greek Antipasto Salad ... 112
- Anchovy And Orange Salad ... 112

OTHER MEDITERRANEAN RECIPES — 113

- Fresh Gazpacho ... 114
- Buffalo Chicken Crust Pizza ... 114
- Mediterranean Father's Day Chicken Burgers ... 114
- Bbq Chicken Pizza ... 115
- Parmesan Zucchini Soup ... 115
- Veal Shank Barley Soup ... 115
- Creamy Bell Pepper Soup With Cod Fillets ... 115
- Santorini Sunrise ... 116
- Minty Green Pea Soup ... 116
- Curried Veggies And Poached Eggs ... 116
- Cooked Beef Mushroom Egg ... 116
- Tuscan White Bean Soup ... 117

Open Face Egg And Bacon Sandwich	117
Mediterranean-style Lamb Leg With Potatoes	117
Eggs Benedict And Artichoke Hearts	118
Spicy Tortilla Soup	118
Roasted Vegetable Soup	118
Chicken Green Bean Soup	119
Leek And Potato Soup	119
Breakfast Egg On Avocado	119
Mediterranean Dip	119
Neufchatel Cheese Mediterranean Dip	120
Potato Rosti	120
Italian Vegetable Soup	120
Jew's Mallow Stew (mulukhiya)	120
Breakfast Egg-artichoke Casserole	121
Light Tartar Dill Sauce	121
Yogurt Fish Soup	121
Spiced Lentil Stew	121
Lentil And Swiss Chard Soup	122
St. Valentine's Mediterranean Pancakes	122
Okra Stew (bamya)	122
French Baked Brie Recipe With Figs, Walnuts And Pistachios	122
Egg And Ham Breakfast Cup	123
Spicy Red Lentil Soup	123
Arrabbiata White Bean Soup	123
Veggie Hash	123
Easy Butternut Squash With Quinoa And Lentils	124
Pink Lady Mediterranean Drink	124
Toasted Bagels	124
Mediterranean Last-minute Feta Cheese Dip	124
Sweet And Sour Rhubarb Lentil Soup	125
Tomato Haddock Soup	125
Kale Gazpacho	125

DESSERT RECIPES 126

Lime Grapes And Apples	127
Mediterranean Doughnuts	127
Five Berry Mint Orange Infusion	127
Shredded Phyllo And Sweet Cheese Pie (knafe)	127
Peach Tart	128
Cinnamon Pear Jam	128
Apple Dates Mix	128
Minty Tart	128
Greek Raisins And Vanilla Cream	128
Spiced Cookies	129
Vanilla Apple Pie	129
Yogurt Mousse With Sour Cherry Sauce	129
Grapes Stew	129
Healthy Zucchini Pudding	129
Watermelon Cream	130
Chocolate Cups	130
Banana Cinnamon Cupcakes	130
Yogurt Parfait	130
Peanut Banana Yogurt Bowl	130
Cinnamon Banana And Semolina Pudding	130
Lime Vanilla Fudge	131
Cranberries And Pears Pie	131
Delicious Apple Pear Cobbler	131
Warm Peach Compote	131
Pasta Flora Or Greek Tart With Apricot Jam	131
Hazelnut Pudding	132

Cocoa Yogurt Mix 132	Blackberry Pie 134
Red Wine Poached Pears 132	Cherry Compote 134
Almond Tea Biscuits 132	Cocoa Brownies 134
Baklava 132	Mango And Honey Cream 134
Mediterranean Stuffed Custard Pancakes 133	Blueberry Muffins 135
Cinnamon Pears 133	Mandarin Cream 135
Almond Peaches Mix 133	Beetroot Apple Smoothie 135
Honey Fruit Compote 133	Papaya Cream 135
Almond Pudding 134	Raw Truffles 135

SHOPPING LIST — 137

APPENDIX A: MEASUREMENT CONVERSIONS — 138

APPENDIX B: RECIPES INDEX — 140

INTRODUCTION

Hello, I'm Lora B. Evans, and I'm thrilled to welcome you to my Mediterranean Diet Cookbook. As an author with a deep passion for food and a background in nutrition and culinary arts, I am excited to share my knowledge and love for the Mediterranean diet with you.

The Mediterranean diet is not just a way of eating; it's a way of life. It's a dietary pattern that is rich in fruits, vegetables, whole grains, lean proteins, and heart-healthy fats. It has been scientifically proven to promote good health, reduce the risk of chronic diseases, and even enhance longevity. I have personally witnessed its positive impact on countless individuals, and I am passionate about helping others embrace this lifestyle for themselves.

The purpose of this cookbook is to make the Mediterranean diet accessible and achievable for everyone. Whether you're a seasoned home cook or just starting your culinary journey, my goal is to provide you with a comprehensive resource that not only explains the principles of the Mediterranean diet but also offers practical guidance on how to incorporate it into your daily life.

Inside this cookbook, you will find a wide variety of delicious recipes, each accompanied by step-by-step instructions, detailed shopping lists, estimated cooking times, and practical tips to make the cooking process as easy and enjoyable as possible. Whether you're whipping up a quick weeknight meal or preparing a special dinner for guests, I've got you covered.

I believe that food should be a source of pleasure and nourishment, and my hope is that this cookbook will inspire you to savor the flavors of the Mediterranean while reaping the health benefits it has to offer. So, grab your apron, head to the kitchen, and let's embark on this culinary journey together. Here's to your health and happiness through the Mediterranean diet!

What is the Mediterranean Diet?

The Mediterranean diet is a style of eating that emphasizes minimally processed, plant-based foods. It includes fruits, vegetables, nuts, beans, whole grains including whole-grain pasta and breads, olive oil, red wine, and small amounts of fish, eggs, dairy, and meats.

As the name implies, the Mediterranean diet is inspired by the traditional eating habits of people living in countries bordering the Mediterranean Sea, particularly the olive-growing cultures of Southern Italy and Greece.

There is no single Mediterranean diet. The details of what characterizes Mediterranean-style eating can shift from country to country due to differences in culture, ethnic background, religion, economy, geography, and agricultural production. However, the various versions of a Mediterranean diet share common features such as:

plentiful vegetables and fruits, whole grains, legumes, fish, nuts, seeds, and olive oil

low to modest amounts of meat and dairy

very limited processed foods or sugars.

The Mediterranean Diet Pyramid

The Mediterranean diet pyramid is a graphical representation of the Mediterranean diet designed to improve understanding and increase adherence to this way of eating. It was created in 1993 by Oldways, an American nonprofit, with support from the Harvard School of Public Health and The World Health Organization. The pyramid was designed as a healthier option than the U.S. Department of Agriculture's original food pyramid, which was popular then.

The pyramid shows the food groups in the Mediterranean diet and their ideal frequency, resting on a base of physical activity and communal meals. Water and red wine are displayed beside the pyramid as healthy drinks.

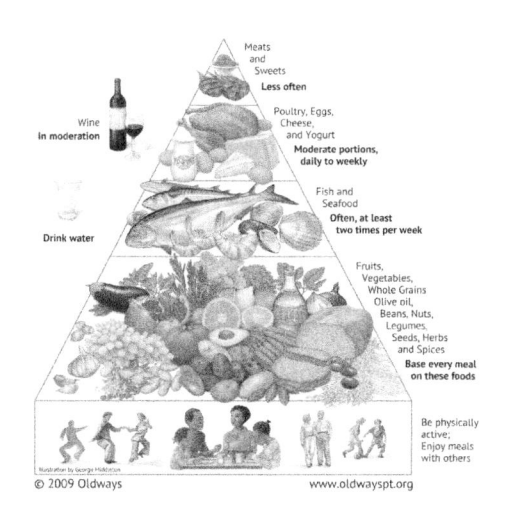

Mediterranean Diet Cookbook

8 Easy Ways to Follow the Mediterranean Diet for Better Health

1. Rethink Your Plate

While you may normally decide on a central protein first and then choose a vegetable and a starch to accompany it, try choosing a vegetable or grain first. Instead of a main dish with sides, you will be serving more equal "small plates." You don't necessarily need to make more dishes than you normally would—just approach the composition of the meal and your planning differently.

2. Moderation Is Key

No matter what you're eating, make sure to moderate your intake. Portions are smaller in the Mediterranean diet. A pound of pasta serves six people, not four, and pieces of chicken and meat are in the 4- to 6-ounce range and may be highlighted by a small amount of a light and flavorful sauce. A Mediterranean-style meal is composed of appropriate portions of multiple dishes.

3. Eat What's Fresh and In Season

Eat lots of vegetables and fruits every day. Much of Mediterranean meal planning is based on what vegetables are available and celebrates seasonality. By figuring out what is seasonal and local, you will get better-quality produce that is worthy of being the centerpiece of a meal. Farmers' markets are an excellent source of inspiration. If fresh produce isn't available, we've found that there are certain substitutes that are of reliable quality year-round, such as jarred artichokes, varieties of small tomatoes like cherry and grape, and frozen fava beans and peas.

4. Eat Beans and Whole Grains Every Day

Since meat and poultry are used more sparingly in the Mediterranean diet, beans, lentils, nuts, and whole grains are major sources of daily protein. They can be the starring ingredient in soups and stews, salads, and heartier dishes when combined with meat or fish but they can also play a supporting role in vegetable and pasta dishes. Whole grains contain a number of key nutrients, such as antioxidants.

Mediterranean Diet Cookbook

5. Eat More Fish and Less Red Meat

Consuming fresh seafood has long been important in the countries along the Mediterranean Sea. The health benefits of eating fish and shellfish include that they are low in calories and saturated fat and rich in omega-3 fatty acids. Some Mediterranean fish aren't well known in the United States, but there are available substitutes for most of them. Fish like sardines and mackerel have the added benefit of being less expensive than many other types of fresh fish. Fish can be pan-roasted, baked, broiled, braised, and grilled and doesn't always have to be an entrée. It can be served as a starter, as part of a composed salad, in soups, and in pasta dishes.

6. Use Meat as a Flavoring

Dishes that contain small amounts of meat are common throughout the Mediterranean, since traditionally this was a way to stretch pricey meat further by combining it with less expensive grains or beans. Cook with flavorful cuts of meat such as lamb shanks and shoulder chops, and cured meats like Italian pancetta, Spanish chorizo, and the Turkish sausage sujuk, so that a smaller amount can have a bigger impact.

7. Serve Fresh Fruit and Carefully Chosen Sweets for Dessert

It is customary in many parts of the region to have a piece of fresh fruit as the ending to a meal. Cakes and cookies are not eaten on a daily basis but are often saved for special family gatherings and celebrations. To keep with the Mediterranean diet's emphasis on eliminating as much saturated fat as possible, try to replace the butter in your cakes, cookies, and pastries with olive oil.

8. Embrace Variety

Balance and diversity are hallmarks of Mediterranean meals, so try to serve an array of dishes with different tastes, textures, and temperatures. Many dishes taste great whether they are warm, at room temperature, or even cold out of the fridge. This helps to reduce the pressure to get a completely hot meal on the table. The Mediterranean diet's emphasis on diversity of ingredients will help you become a more versatile cook.

30-Day Meal Plan

DAY	BREAKFAST	LUNCH	DINNER
1	Baked Oatmeal With Cinnamon 19	Pecorino Pasta With Sausage And Fresh Tomato 68	Honey Roasted Chicken With Rosemary Potatoes 81
2	Herbed Quinoa And Asparagu 19	Feta, Eggplant And Sausage Penne 68	Fettuccine With Spinach And Shrimp 81
3	Corn And Shrimp Salad 19	Red Quinoa Peach Porridge 69	Caramelized Onion Pasta 81
4	Quinoa And Potato Bowl 19	Ricotta And Spinach Ravioli 68	Yogurt Marinated Pork Chops 82
5	Artichokes And Cheese Omelet 19	Seafood Paella With Couscous 69	Shrimp Pancakes 8
6	Herbed Potatoes And Eggs 20	Belly-filling Cajun Rice & Chicken 69	Ratatouille Spaghetti 82
7	Couscous With Artichokes, Sun-dried Tomatoes And Feta 20	Sun-dried Tomatoes And Chickpeas 70	Parsley Beef Stew 82
8	Zucchini Oats 20	Leek, Bacon And Pea Risotto 70	Stuffed Eggplants 83
9	Menemen 20	Mediterranean Diet Pasta With Mussels 70	Lentil Tabbouleh And Haloumi 83
10	Stuffed Figs 21	Garbanzo And Kidney Bean Salad 69	Cherry Braised Lamb Shanks 83
11	Cheesy Caprese Style Portobellos Mushrooms 21	Kidney Bean And Parsley-lemon Salad 71	Chicken Breasts Mediterranean-style With Avocado Tapenade 83
12	Tomato And Lentils Salad 21	Lemon Asparagus Risotto 71	Pistachio Crusted Lamb Chops 84
13	Cranberry And Dates Squares 21	Pasta Primavera Without Cream 71	Tomato Topped Eggplant Pie 84
14	Blueberries Quinoa 21	Italian White Bean Soup 72	Crispy Pollock And Gazpacho 84
15	Cauliflower Hash Brown Breakfast Bowl 22	Fruity Asparagus-quinoa Salad 72	Herbed Beef And Tomato Soup 84

Mediterranean Diet Cookbook

DAY	BREAKFAST	LUNCH	DINNER
16	Pumpkin Oatmeal With Spices 22	Spanish Rice Casserole With Cheesy Beef 72	Pork Fennel Meatballs 85
17	Parmesan Omelet 22	Chorizo-kidney Beans Quinoa Pilaf 73	Sesame Turkey Fillets With Fresh Greens 85
18	Overnight Oats With Nuts 22	Delicious Pasta Primavera 73	Turkey Fritters And Sauce 85
19	Chicken Liver 23	Nutty And Fruity Amaranth Porridge 73	Chorizo Broiled Mussels 85
20	Cheesy Thyme Waffles 23	Rice And Chickpea Stew 74	Fig And Prosciutto Pita Bread Pizza 86
21	Lemon Peas Quinoa Mix 23	Orange, Dates And Asparagus On Quinoa Salad 74	Mediterranean-style Salmon Fillet 86
22	Herbed Muffins 23	Lime-cilantro Rice Chipotle Style 73	Mint Chicken Soup 86
23	Fruits And Pistachios 23	Raw Tomato Sauce & Brie On Linguine 74	Basil Rice Soup 86
24	Avocado Baked Eggs 24	Seafood And Veggie Pasta 75	Tomato Roasted Feta 86
25	Oregano Muffins 24	Appetizing Mushroom Lasagna 75	Quinoa Chicken Casserole 87
26	Breakfast Spanakopita 24	Breakfast Salad From Grains And Fruits 75	Bean And Beef Chili 87
27	Mediterranean Omelet 24	Cinnamon Quinoa Bars 76	Parmesan Penne 87
28	Cheesy Yogurt 25	Filling Macaroni Soup 76	Garlicky Roasted Chicken 87
29	Cheesy Olives Bread 25	Cilantro-dijon Vinaigrette On Kidney Bean Salad 76	Kalamata Olives Penne 88
30	Avocado Toast 25	Goat Cheese 'n Red Beans Salad 77	Fish Parcels 88

Mediterranean Diet Cookbook

Breakfast Recipes

Breakfast Recipes

Baked Oatmeal With Cinnamon
Servings: 4 | Cooking Time: 25 Minutes

Ingredients:
- 1 cup oatmeal
- 1/3 cup milk
- 1 pear, chopped
- 1 teaspoon vanilla extract
- 1 tablespoon Splenda
- 1 teaspoon butter
- ½ teaspoon ground cinnamon
- 1 egg, beaten

Directions:
1. In the big bowl mix up together oatmeal, milk, egg, vanilla extract, Splenda, and ground cinnamon.
2. Melt butter and add it in the oatmeal mixture.
3. Then add chopped pear and stir it well.
4. Transfer the oatmeal mixture in the casserole mold and flatten gently. Cover it with the foil and secure edges.
5. Bake the oatmeal for 25 minutes at 350F.

Nutrition Info:
- Calories 151, fat 3.9, fiber 3.3, carbs 23.6, protein 4.9

Herbed Quinoa And Asparagus
Servings: 4 | Cooking Time: 0 Minutes

Ingredients:
- 3 cups asparagus, steamed and roughly chopped
- 1 tablespoon olive oil
- 3 tablespoons balsamic vinegar
- 1 and ¾ cups quinoa, cooked
- 2 teaspoons mustard
- Salt and black pepper to the taste
- 5 ounces baby spinach
- ½ cup parsley, chopped
- 1 tablespoon thyme, chopped
- 1 tablespoon tarragon, chopped

Directions:
1. In a salad bowl, combine the asparagus with the quinoa, spinach and the rest of the ingredients, toss and keep in the fridge for 10 minutes before serving for breakfast.

Nutrition Info:
- calories 323, fat 11.3, fiber 3.4, carbs 16.4, protein 10

Corn And Shrimp Salad
Servings: 4 | Cooking Time: 10 Minutes

Ingredients:
- 4 ears of sweet corn, husked
- 1 avocado, peeled, pitted and chopped
- ½ cup basil, chopped
- A pinch of salt and black pepper
- 1 pound shrimp, peeled and deveined
- 1 and ½ cups cherry tomatoes, halved
- ¼ cup olive oil

Directions:
1. Put the corn in a pot, add water to cover, bring to a boil over medium heat, cook for 6 minutes, drain, cool down, cut corn from the cob and put it in a bowl.
2. Thread the shrimp onto skewers and brush with some of the oil.
3. Place the skewers on the preheated grill, cook over medium heat for 2 minutes on each side, remove from skewers and add over the corn.
4. Add the rest of the ingredients to the bowl, toss, divide between plates and serve for breakfast.

Nutrition Info:
- calories 371, fat 22, fiber 5, carbs 25, protein 23

Quinoa And Potato Bowl
Servings: 4 | Cooking Time: 20 Minutes

Ingredients:
- 1 sweet potato, peeled, chopped
- 1 tablespoon olive oil
- ½ teaspoon chili flakes
- ½ teaspoon salt
- 1 cup quinoa
- 2 cups of water
- 1 teaspoon butter
- 1 tablespoon fresh cilantro, chopped

Directions:
1. Line the baking tray with parchment.
2. Arrange the chopped sweet potato in the tray and sprinkle it with chili flakes, salt, and olive oil.
3. Bake the sweet potato for 20 minutes at 355F.
4. Meanwhile, pour water in the saucepan.
5. Add quinoa and cook it over the medium heat for 7 minutes or until quinoa will absorb all liquid.
6. Add butter in the cooked quinoa and stir well.
7. Transfer it in the bowls, add baked sweet potato and chopped cilantro.

Nutrition Info:
- Per Servingcalories 221, fat 7.1, fiber 3.9, carbs 33.2, protein 6.6

Artichokes And Cheese Omelet
Servings: 1 | Cooking Time: 8 Minutes

Ingredients:
- 1 teaspoon avocado oil
- 1 tablespoon almond milk
- 2 eggs, whisked
- A pinch of salt and black pepper
- 2 tablespoons tomato, cubed
- 2 tablespoons kalamata olives, pitted and sliced

Mediterranean Diet Cookbook

- 1 artichoke heart, chopped
- 1 tablespoon tomato sauce
- 1 tablespoon feta cheese, crumbled

Directions:
1. In a bowl, combine the eggs with the milk, salt, pepper and the rest of the ingredients except the avocado oil and whisk well.
2. Heat up a pan with the avocado oil over medium-high heat, add the omelet mix, spread into the pan, cook for 4 minutes, flip, cook for 4 minutes more, transfer to a plate and serve.

Nutrition Info:
- calories 303, fat 17.7, fiber 9.9, carbs 21.9, protein 18.2

Herbed Potatoes And Eggs
Serves:1 Cup | Cooking Time:32 Minutes

Ingredients:
- 2 large potatoes
- 4 large eggs, at room temperature
- 1 tsp. salt
- 1/2 tsp. ground black pepper
- 2 TB. fresh parsley, chopped
- 2 whole green onions, finely chopped

Directions:
1. In a large saucepan, add potatoes along with enough water to cover potatoes by 1 inch. Set over medium heat, bring to a simmer, and cook for 25 minutes.
2. Pour off water, and set potatoes aside to slightly cool.
3. Add eggs to a medium saucepan, pour in enough water to cover eggs, and set over medium heat. Bring to a boil, cook for 2 minutes, and remove from heat. Cover, and set aside for 15 minutes.
4. Remove eggs, place in a bowl of cold water, and let sit for 10 minutes.
5. Peel potatoes and eggs, and place in a large bowl. Season with salt and black pepper, and mash using a potato masher for about 1 minute or until the texture resembles medium chunks.
6. Add parsley and green onions, and toss well.
7. Serve warm with pita bread and Greek yogurt.

Couscous With Artichokes, Sun-dried Tomatoes And Feta
Servings: 6 | Cooking Time:15 Minutes

Ingredients:
- 3 cups chicken breast, cooked, chopped
- 2 1/3 cups water, divided
- 2 jars (6-ounces each) marinated artichoke hearts, undrained
- 1/4 teaspoon black pepper, freshly ground
- 1/2 cup tomatoes, sun-dried
- 1/2 cup (2 ounces) feta cheese, crumbled
- 1 cup flat-leaf parsley, fresh, chopped
- 1 3/4 cups whole-wheat Israeli couscous, uncooked
- 1 can (14 1/2 ounces) vegetable broth

Directions:
1. In a microwavable bowl, combine 2 cups of the water and the tomatoes. Microwave on HIGH for about 3 minutes or until the water boils. When water is boiling, remove from the microwave, cover, and let stand for about 3 minutes or until the tomatoes are soft; drain, chop, and set aside.
2. In a large saucepan, place the vegetable broth and the remaining 1/3 cup of water; bring to boil. Stir in the couscous, cover, reduce heat, and simmer for about 8 minutes or until tender. Remove the pan from the heat; add the tomatoes and the remaining ingredients. Stir to combine.

Nutrition Info:
- Per Serving:419 Cal, 14.1 g total fat (3.9 g sat. fat, 0.8 g poly. Fat, 1.4 g mono), 64 mg chol.,677 mg sodium, 42.5 g carb.,2.6 g fiber, 30.2 g protein.

Zucchini Oats
Servings: 4 | Cooking Time: 10 Minutes

Ingredients:
- 2 cups rolled oats
- 2 cups of water
- ½ teaspoon salt
- 1 tablespoon butter
- 1 zucchini, grated
- ¼ teaspoon ground ginger

Directions:
1. Pour water in the saucepan.
2. Add rolled oats, butter, and salt.
3. Stir gently and start to cook the oats for 4 minutes over the high heat.
4. When the mixture starts to boil, add ground ginger and grated zucchini. Stir well.
5. Cook the oats for 5 minutes more over the medium-low heat.

Nutrition Info:
- Calories 189, fat 5.7, fiber 4.7, carbs 29.4, protein 6

Menemen
Servings: 4 | Cooking Time: 15 Minutes

Ingredients:
- 2 tomatoes, chopped
- 2 eggs, beaten
- 1 bell pepper, chopped
- 1 teaspoon tomato paste
- ¼ cup of water
- 1 teaspoon butter
- ½ white onion, diced
- ½ teaspoon chili flakes
- 1/3 teaspoon sea salt

Directions:
1. Put butter in the pan and melt it.
2. Add bell pepper and cook it for 3 minutes over the medium heat. Stir it from time to time.
3. After this, add diced onion and cook it for 2 minutes more.
4. Stir the vegetables and add tomatoes.
5. Cook them for 5 minutes over the medium-low heat.
6. Then add water and tomato paste. Stir well.
7. Add beaten eggs, chili flakes, and sea salt.
8. Stir well and cook menemen for 4 minutes over the medium-low heat.

Mediterranean Diet Cookbook

9. The cooked meal should be half runny.

Nutrition Info:
- Calories 67, fat 3.4, fiber 1.5, carbs 6.4, protein 3.8

Stuffed Figs
Servings: 2 | Cooking Time: 15 Minutes

Ingredients:
- 7 oz fresh figs
- 1 tablespoon cream cheese
- ½ teaspoon walnuts, chopped
- 4 bacon slices
- ¼ teaspoon paprika
- ¼ teaspoon salt
- ½ teaspoon canola oil
- ½ teaspoon honey

Directions:
1. Make the crosswise cuts in every fig.
2. In the shallow bowl mix up together cream cheese, walnuts, paprika, and salt.
3. Fill the figs with cream cheese mixture and wrap in the bacon.
4. Secure the fruits with toothpicks and sprinkle with honey.
5. Line the baking tray with baking paper.
6. Place the prepared figs in the tray and sprinkle them with olive oil gently.
7. Bake the figs for 15 minutes at 350F.

Nutrition Info:
- Calories 299, fat 19.4, fiber 2.3, carbs 16.7, protein 15.2

Cheesy Caprese Style Portobellos Mushrooms
Servings: 2 | Cooking Time: 15 Minutes

Ingredients:
- 2 large caps of Portobello mushroom, gills removed
- 4 tomatoes, halved
- Salt and freshly cracked black pepper, to taste
- ¼ cup fresh basil
- 4 tbsp olive oil
- ¼ cup shredded Mozzarella cheese

Directions:
1. Switch on the oven, then set its temperature to 400°F and let it preheat.
2. Meanwhile, prepare mushrooms, and for this, brush them with olive oil and set aside until required.
3. Place tomatoes in a bowl, season with salt and black pepper, add basil, drizzle with oil and toss until mixed.
4. Distribute cheese evenly in the bottom of each mushroom cap and then top with prepared tomato mixture.
5. Take a baking sheet, line it with aluminum foil, place prepared mushrooms on it and bake for 15 minutes until thoroughly cooked.
6. Serve straight away.

Nutrition Info:
- Calories 315, Total Fat 29.2g, Total Carbs 14.2g, Protein 4.7g, Sugar 10.4g, Sodium 55mg

Tomato And Lentils Salad
Servings: 4 | Cooking Time: 35 Minutes

Ingredients:
- 2 yellow onions, chopped
- 4 garlic cloves, minced
- 2 cups brown lentils
- 1 tablespoon olive oil
- A pinch of salt and black pepper
- ½ teaspoon sweet paprika
- ½ teaspoon ginger, grated
- 3 cups water
- ¼ cup lemon juice
- ¾ cup Greek yogurt
- 3 tablespoons tomato paste

Directions:
1. Heat up a pot with the oil over medium-high heat, add the onions and sauté for 2 minutes.
2. Add the garlic and the lentils, stir and cook for 1 minute more.
3. Add the water, bring to a simmer and cook covered for 30 minutes.
4. Add the lemon juice and the remaining ingredients except the yogurt. toss, divide the mix into bowls, top with the yogurt and serve.

Nutrition Info:
- calories 294, fat 3, fiber 8, carbs 49, protein 21

Cranberry And Dates Squares
Servings: 10 | Cooking Time: 0 Minutes

Ingredients:
- 12 dates, pitted and chopped
- 1 teaspoon vanilla extract
- ¼ cup honey
- ½ cup rolled oats
- ¾ cup cranberries, dried
- ¼ cup almond avocado oil, melted
- 1 cup walnuts, roasted and chopped
- ¼ cup pumpkin seeds

Directions:
1. In a bowl, mix the dates with the vanilla, honey and the rest of the ingredients, stir well and press everything on a baking sheet lined with parchment paper.
2. Keep in the freezer for 30 minutes, cut into 10 squares and serve for breakfast.

Nutrition Info:
- calories 263, fat 13.4, fiber 4.7, carbs 14.3. protein 3.5

Blueberries Quinoa
Servings: 4 | Cooking Time: 0 Minutes

Ingredients:
- 2 cups almond milk
- 2 cups quinoa, already cooked
- ½ teaspoon cinnamon powder
- 1 tablespoon honey
- 1 cup blueberries
- ¼ cup walnuts, chopped

Directions:
1. In a bowl, mix the quinoa with the milk and the rest of the ingredients, toss, divide into smaller bowls and serve for breakfast.

Nutrition Info:
- calories 284, fat 14.3, fiber 3.2, carbs 15.4, protein 4.4

Cauliflower Hash Brown Breakfast Bowl
Servings: 2 | Cooking Time: 30 Minutes

Ingredients:
- 1 tablespoon lemon juice
- 1 egg
- 1 avocado
- 1 teaspoon garlic powder
- 2 tablespoons extra virgin olive oil
- 2 oz mushrooms, sliced
- ½ green onion, chopped
- ¼ cup salsa
- ¾ cup cauliflower rice
- ½ small handful baby spinach
- Salt and black pepper, to taste

Directions:
1. Mash together avocado, lemon juice, garlic powder, salt and black pepper in a small bowl.
2. Whisk eggs, salt and black pepper in a bowl and keep aside.
3. Heat half of olive oil over medium heat in a skillet and add mushrooms.
4. Sauté for about 3 minutes and season with garlic powder, salt, and pepper.
5. Sauté for about 2 minutes and dish out in a bowl.
6. Add rest of the olive oil and add cauliflower, garlic powder, salt and pepper.
7. Sauté for about 5 minutes and dish out.
8. Return the mushrooms to the skillet and add green onions and baby spinach.
9. Sauté for about 30 seconds and add whisked eggs.
10. Sauté for about 1 minute and scoop on the sautéed cauliflower hash browns.
11. Top with salsa and mashed avocado and serve.

Nutrition Info:
- Calories: 400 Carbs: 15.8g Fats: 36.7g Proteins: 8g Sodium: 288mg Sugar: 4.2g

Pumpkin Oatmeal With Spices
Servings: 6 | Cooking Time: 13 Minutes

Ingredients:
- 2 cups oatmeal
- 1 cup of coconut milk
- 1 cup milk
- 1 teaspoon Pumpkin pie spices
- 2 tablespoons pumpkin puree
- 1 tablespoon Honey
- ½ teaspoon butter

Directions:
1. Pour coconut milk and milk in the saucepan. Add butter and bring the liquid to boil.
2. Add oatmeal, stir well with the help of a spoon and close the lid.
3. Simmer the oatmeal for 7 minutes over the medium heat.
4. Meanwhile, mix up together honey, pumpkin pie spices, and pumpkin puree.
5. When the oatmeal is cooked, add pumpkin puree mixture and stir well.
6. Transfer the cooked breakfast in the serving plates.

Nutrition Info:
- Calories 232, fat 12.5, fiber 3.8, carbs 26.2, protein 5.9

Parmesan Omelet
Servings: 2 | Cooking Time: 10 Minutes

Ingredients:
- 1 tablespoon cream cheese
- 2 eggs, beaten
- ¼ teaspoon paprika
- ½ teaspoon dried oregano
- ¼ teaspoon dried dill
- 1 oz Parmesan, grated
- 1 teaspoon coconut oil

Directions:
1. Mix up together cream cheese with eggs, dried oregano, and dill.
2. Place coconut oil in the skillet and heat it up until it will coat all the skillet.
3. Then pour the egg mixture in the skillet and flatten it.
4. Add grated Parmesan and close the lid.
5. Cook omelet for 10 minutes over the low heat.
6. Then transfer the cooked omelet in the serving plate and sprinkle with paprika.

Nutrition Info:
- Calories 148, fat 11.5, fiber 0.3, carbs 1.4, protein 10.6

Overnight Oats With Nuts
Servings: 2 | Cooking Time: 8 Hours

Ingredients:
- ½ cup oats
- 2 teaspoons chia seeds, dried
- 1 tablespoon almond, chopped
- ½ teaspoon walnuts, chopped
- 1 cup skim milk
- 2 teaspoons honey
- ½ teaspoon vanilla extract

Directions:
1. In the big bowl mix up together chia seeds, oats, honey, and vanilla extract.
2. Then add skim milk, walnuts, and almonds. Stir well.
3. Transfer the prepared mixture into the mason jars and close with lids.
4. Put the mason jars in the fridge and leave overnight.
5. Store the meal in the fridge up to 2 days.

Nutrition Info:
- Calories 202, fat 5.4, fiber 4.9, carbs 29.4, protein 8.7

Chicken Liver

Serves: ¼ Cup | Cooking Time: 7 Minutes

Ingredients:
- 2 lb. chicken liver
- 3 TB. extra-virgin olive oil
- 3 TB. minced garlic
- 1 tsp. salt
- 1/2 tsp. ground black pepper
- 1 cup fresh cilantro, finely chopped
- 1/4 cup fresh lemon juice

Directions:
1. Cut chicken livers in half, rinse well, and pat dry with paper towels.
2. Preheat a large skillet over medium heat. Add extra-virgin olive oil and garlic, and cook for 2 minutes.
3. Add chicken liver and salt, and cook, tossing gently, for 5 minutes. Remove the skillet from heat, and spoon liver onto a plate.
4. Add black pepper, cilantro, and lemon juice. Lightly toss, and serve warm.

Cheesy Thyme Waffles

Servings: 2 | Cooking Time: 15 Minutes

Ingredients:
- ½ cup mozzarella cheese, finely shredded
- ¼ cup Parmesan cheese
- ¼ large head cauliflower
- ½ cup collard greens
- 1 large egg
- 1 stalk green onion
- ½ tablespoon olive oil
- ½ teaspoon garlic powder
- ¼ teaspoon salt
- ½ tablespoon sesame seed
- 1 teaspoon fresh thyme, chopped
- ¼ teaspoon ground black pepper

Directions:
1. Put cauliflower, collard greens, spring onion and thyme in a food processor and pulse until smooth.
2. Dish out the mixture in a bowl and stir in rest of the ingredients.
3. Heat a waffle iron and transfer the mixture evenly over the griddle.
4. Cook until a waffle is formed and dish out in a serving platter.

Nutrition Info:
- Calories: 144 Carbs: 8.5g Fats: 9.4g Proteins: 9.3g Sodium: 435mg Sugar: 3g

Lemon Peas Quinoa Mix

Servings: 4 | Cooking Time: 20 Minutes

Ingredients:
- 1 and ½ cups quinoa, rinsed
- 1 pound asparagus, steamed and chopped
- 3 cups water
- 2 tablespoons parsley, chopped
- 2 tablespoons lemon juice
- 1 teaspoon lemon zest, grated
- ½ pound sugar snap peas, steamed
- ½ pound green beans, trimmed and halved
- A pinch of salt and black pepper
- 3 tablespoons pumpkin seeds
- 1 cup cherry tomatoes, halved
- 2 tablespoons olive oil

Directions:
1. Put the water in a pot, bring to a boil over medium heat, add the quinoa, stir and simmer for 20 minutes.
2. Stir the quinoa, add the parsley, lemon juice and the rest of the ingredients, toss, divide between plates and serve for breakfast.

Nutrition Info:
- calories 417, fat 15, fiber 9, carbs 58, protein 16

Herbed Muffins

Servings: 4 | Cooking Time: 15 Minutes

Ingredients:
- 3 oz ham, chopped
- 4 eggs, beaten
- 2 tablespoons coconut flour
- ½ teaspoon dried oregano
- ¼ teaspoon dried cilantro
- Cooking spray

Directions:
1. Spray the muffin's molds with cooking spray from inside.
2. In the bowl mix up together beaten eggs, coconut flour, dried oregano, cilantro, and ham.
3. When the liquid is homogenous, pour it in the prepared muffin molds.
4. Bake the muffins for 15 minutes at 360F.
5. Chill the cooked meal well and only after this remove from the molds.

Nutrition Info:
- Per Servingcalories 128, fat 7.2, fiber 2.9, carbs 5.3, protein 10.1

Fruits And Pistachios

Servings: 12 | Cooking Time: 7 Minutes

Ingredients:
- 1 1/2 cups pistachios, unsalted, roasted
- 1/2 cup dried apricots, chopped (preferably Blenheim)
- 1/2 teaspoon cinnamon
- 1/4 cup dried cranberries or pomegranate seeds
- 1/4 teaspoon nutmeg, regular ground or freshly grated
- 1/4 teaspoon ground allspice
- 2 teaspoons sugar

Directions:
1. Preheat oven to 350F.
2. Spread the pistachios into a rimmed baking sheet; bake for about 7 minutes or until lightly toasted. Cool completely.
3. In a bowl, toss the pistachios with the apricots, pomegranate seeds, cinnamon, nutmeg, allspice, and sugar until well coated.

Nutrition Info:
- Per Serving:116 Cal, 7.1 g total fat (0.9 g sat. fat), 0.0 mg chol., 2.4 mg sodium, 11 g carb.,2.1 g fiber, 3.5 g protein.

Avocado Baked Eggs
Servings: 2 | Cooking Time: 25 Minutes

Ingredients:
- 2 eggs
- 1 medium sized avocado, halved and pit removed
- ¼ cup cheddar cheese, shredded
- Kosher salt and black pepper, to taste

Directions:
1. Preheat oven to 425 degrees and grease a muffin pan.
2. Crack open an egg into each half of the avocado and season with salt and black pepper.
3. Top with cheddar cheese and transfer the muffin pan in the oven.
4. Bake for about 15 minutes and dish out to serve.

Nutrition Info:
- Calories: 210 Carbs: 6.4g Fats: 16.6g Proteins: 10.7g Sodium: 151mg Sugar: 2.2g

Oregano Muffins
Servings: 4 | Cooking Time: 21 Minute

Ingredients:
- 4 kalamata olives, chopped
- ½ cup wheat flour, whole grain
- ½ teaspoon baking powder
- ¼ teaspoon of sea salt
- 1 teaspoon dried oregano
- 3 eggs, beaten
- 2 tablespoons cream cheese

Directions:
1. In the mixing bowl whisk together eggs, cream cheese, dried oregano, sea salt, and baking powder.
2. Add wheat flour and whisk until homogenous.
3. After this, add kalamata olives and stir well with the help of the spoon/fork.
4. Leave the muffin batter for 10 minutes to rest.
5. Meanwhile, prepare the non-sticky muffin molds.
6. Stir the batter gently and pour it in the muffin molds. Fill ½ part of every mold.
7. Preheat the oven to 360F.
8. Place the muffins in the preheated oven and bake them for 21 minutes.
9. Then chill the cooked muffins well and remove from the molds.

Nutrition Info:
- Per Servingcalories 128, fat 5.7, fiber 0.7, carbs 13.1, protein 6.2

Breakfast Spanakopita
Servings: 6 | Cooking Time: 1 Hour

Ingredients:
- 2 cups spinach
- 1 white onion, diced
- ½ cup fresh parsley
- 1 teaspoon minced garlic
- 3 oz Feta cheese, crumbled
- 1 teaspoon ground paprika
- 2 eggs, beaten
- 1/3 cup butter, melted
- 2 oz Phyllo dough

Directions:
1. Separate Phyllo dough into 2 parts.
2. Brush the casserole mold with butter well and place 1 part of Phyllo dough inside.
3. Brush its surface with butter too.
4. Put the spinach and fresh parsley in the blender. Blend it until smooth and transfer in the mixing bowl.
5. Add minced garlic, Feta cheese, ground paprika, eggs, and diced onion. Mix up well.
6. Place the spinach mixture in the casserole mold and flatten it well.
7. Cover the spinach mixture with remaining Phyllo dough and pour remaining butter over it.
8. Bake spanakopita for 1 hour at 350F.
9. Cut it into the servings.

Nutrition Info:
- Calories 190, fat 15.4, fiber 1.1, carbs 8.4, protein 5.4

Mediterranean Omelet
Serves:1 Omelet

Cooking Time:10 Minutes

Ingredients:
- 2 TB. extra-virgin olive oil
- 2 TB. yellow onion, finely chopped
- 1 small clove garlic, minced
- 1/2 tsp. salt
- 1 cup fresh spinach, chopped
- 1/2 medium tomato, diced
- 2 large eggs
- 2 TB. whole or 2 percent milk
- 4 kalamata olives, pitted and chopped
- 1/2 tsp. ground black pepper
- 3 TB. crumbled feta cheese
- 1 TB. fresh parsley, finely chopped

Directions:
1. In a nonstick pan over medium heat, cook extra-virgin olive oil, yellow onion, and garlic for 3 minutes.
2. Add salt, spinach, and tomato, and cook for 4 minutes.
3. In a small bowl, whisk together eggs and whole milk.
4. Add kalamata olives and black pepper to the pan, and pour in eggs over sautéed vegetables.
5. Using a rubber spatula, slowly push down edges of eggs, letting raw egg form a new layer, and continue for about 2 minutes or until eggs are cooked.
6. Fold omelet in half, and slide onto a plate. Top with feta cheese and fresh parsley, and serve warm.

Cheesy Yogurt
Servings: 4 | Cooking Time: 0 Minutes

Ingredients:
- 1 cup Greek yogurt
- 1 tablespoon honey
- ½ cup feta cheese, crumbled

Directions:
1. In a blender, combine the yogurt with the honey and the cheese and pulse well.
2. Divide into bowls and freeze for 4 hours before serving for breakfast.

Nutrition Info:
- calories 161, fat 10, fiber 0, carbs 11.8, protein 6.6

Cheesy Olives Bread
Servings: 10 | Cooking Time: 30 Minutes

Ingredients:
- 4 cups whole-wheat flour
- 3 tablespoons oregano, chopped
- 2 teaspoons dry yeast
- ¼ cup olive oil
- 1 and ½ cups black olives, pitted and sliced
- 1 cup water
- ½ cup feta cheese, crumbled

Directions:
1. In a bowl, mix the flour with the water, the yeast and the oil, stir and knead your dough very well.
2. Put the dough in a bowl, cover with plastic wrap and keep in a warm place for 1 hour.
3. Divide the dough into 2 bowls and stretch each ball really well.
4. Add the rest of the ingredients on each ball and tuck them inside well kneading the dough again.
5. Flatten the balls a bit and leave them aside for 40 minutes more.
6. Transfer the balls to a baking sheet lined with parchment paper, make a small slit in each and bake at 425 degrees F for 30 minutes.
7. Serve the bread as a Mediterranean breakfast.

Nutrition Info:
- calories 251, fat 7.3, fiber 2.1, carbs 39.7, protein 6.7

Avocado Toast
Servings: 2 | Cooking Time: 0 Minutes

Ingredients:
- 1 tablespoon goat cheese, crumbled
- 1 avocado, peeled, pitted and mashed
- A pinch of salt and black pepper
- 2 whole wheat bread slices, toasted
- ½ teaspoon lime juice
- 1 persimmon, thinly sliced
- 1 fennel bulb, thinly sliced
- 2 teaspoons honey
- 2 tablespoons pomegranate seeds

Directions:
1. In a bowl, combine the avocado flesh with salt, pepper, lime juice and the cheese and whisk.
2. Spread this onto toasted bread slices, top each slice with the remaining ingredients and serve for breakfast.

Nutrition Info:
- calories 348, fat 20.8, fiber 12.3, carbs 38.7, protein 7.1

Shanklish Cheese
Serves: 1 Cheese Ball | Cooking Time: 15 Minutes

Ingredients:
- 6 cups Greek yogurt
- 1/2 tsp. salt
- 1/2 tsp. cayenne
- 1/2 cup dried thyme
- 1 medium tomato, finely diced
- 1/2 medium yellow onion, finely chopped
- 2 TB. extra-virgin olive oil

Directions:
1. In a large saucepan over low heat, bring Greek yogurt to a light boil. You'll see yogurt begin to curdle, and curd and whey will separate.
2. Lay two pieces of cheesecloth over a strainer, pour yogurt into the cheesecloth, and pour off excess moisture. Bring together the ends of the cheesecloth, and place the strainer over a bowl. Refrigerate for 2 days.
3. Remove cheese from the cheesecloth, and transfer to a bowl. Add salt and cayenne, and stir to combine.
4. Lay a double layer of paper towels on a plate. Form cheese into 2-inch balls, roll balls in thyme to cover completely, and place cheese on the paper towels. Cover with another layer of paper towels, and refrigerate for 24 hours to dry.
5. Store cheese in olive oil, or wrap in a paper towel and refrigerate for up to 2 weeks. When ready to serve, crumble cheese on a plate with tomatoes and yellow onion and drizzled with extra-virgin olive oil.

Breakfast Tostadas
Servings: 6 | Cooking Time: 6 Minutes

Ingredients:
- ½ white onion, diced
- 1 tomato, chopped
- 1 cucumber, chopped
- 1 tablespoon fresh cilantro, chopped
- ½ jalapeno pepper, chopped
- 1 tablespoon lime juice
- 6 corn tortillas
- 1 tablespoon canola oil
- 2 oz Cheddar cheese, shredded
- ½ cup white beans, canned, drained
- 6 eggs
- ½ teaspoon butter
- ½ teaspoon Sea salt

Directions:
1. Make Pico de Galo: in the salad bowl combine together diced white onion, tomato, cucumber, fresh cilantro, and jalapeno pepper.
2. Then add lime juice and a ½ tablespoon of canola oil. Mix

up the mixture well. Pico de Galo is cooked.
3. After this, preheat the oven to 390F.
4. Line the tray with baking paper.
5. Arrange the corn tortillas on the baking paper and brush with remaining canola oil from both sides.
6. Bake the tortillas for 10 minutes or until they start to be crunchy.
7. Chill the cooked crunchy tortillas well.
8. Meanwhile, toss the butter in the skillet.
9. Crack the eggs in the melted butter and sprinkle them with sea salt.
10. Fry the eggs until the egg whites become white (cooked). Approximately for 3-5 minutes over the medium heat.
11. After this, mash the beans until you get puree texture.
12. Spread the bean puree on the corn tortillas.
13. Add fried eggs.
14. Then top the eggs with Pico de Galo and shredded Cheddar cheese.

Nutrition Info:
- Calories 246, fat 11.1, fiber 4.7, carbs 24.5, protein 13.7

Olive And Milk Bread
Servings: 6 | Cooking Time: 50 Minutes

Ingredients:
- 1 cup black olives, pitted, chopped
- 1 tablespoon olive oil
- ½ teaspoon fresh yeast
- ½ cup milk, preheated
- ½ teaspoon salt
- 1 teaspoon baking powder
- 2 cup wheat flour, whole grain
- 2 eggs, beaten
- 1 teaspoon butter, melted
- 1 teaspoon sugar

Directions:
1. In the big bowl combine together fresh yeast, sugar, and milk. Stir it until yeast is dissolved.
2. Then add salt, baking powder, butter, and eggs. Stir the dough mixture until homogenous and add 1 cup of wheat flour. Mix it up until smooth.
3. Add olives and remaining flour. Knead the non-sticky dough.
4. Transfer the dough into the non-sticky dough mold.
5. Bake the bread for 50 minutes at 350 F.
6. Check if the bread is cooked with the help of the toothpick. Is it is dry, the bread is cooked.
7. Remove the bread from the oven and let it chill for 10-15 minutes.
8. Remove it from the loaf mold and slice.

Nutrition Info:
- Per Servingcalories 238, fat 7.7, fiber 1.9, carbs 35.5, protein 7.2

Endives, Fennel And Orange Salad
Servings: 4 | Cooking Time: 0 Minutes

Ingredients:
- 1 tablespoon balsamic vinegar
- 2 garlic cloves, minced
- 1 teaspoon Dijon mustard
- 2 tablespoons olive oil
- 1 tablespoon lemon juice
- Sea salt and black pepper to the taste
- ½ cup black olives, pitted and chopped
- 1 tablespoon parsley, chopped
- 7 cups baby spinach
- 2 endives, shredded
- 3 medium navel oranges, peeled and cut into segments
- 2 bulbs fennel, shredded

Directions:
1. In a salad bowl, combine the spinach with the endives, oranges, fennel and the rest of the ingredients, toss and serve for breakfast.

Nutrition Info:
- calories 97, fat 9.1, fiber 1.8, carbs 3.7, protein 1.9

Creamy Chorizo Bowls
Servings: 4 | Cooking Time: 15 Minutes

Ingredients:
- 9 oz chorizo
- 1 tablespoon almond butter
- ½ cup corn kernels
- 1 tomato, chopped
- ¾ cup heavy cream
- 1 teaspoon butter
- ¼ teaspoon chili pepper
- 1 tablespoon dill, chopped

Directions:
1. Chop the chorizo and place in the skillet.
2. Add almond butter and chili pepper.
3. Roast the chorizo for 3 minutes.
4. After this, add tomato and corn kernels.
5. Add butter and chopped the dill. Mix up the mixture well. Cook for 2 minutes.
6. Close the lid and simmer the meal for 10 minutes over the low heat.
7. Transfer the cooked meal into the serving bowls.

Nutrition Info:
- Per Servingcalories 422, fat 36.2, fiber 1.2, carbs 7.3, protein 17.6

Mediterranean Diet Cookbook

Snack And Appetizer Recipes

Snack And Appetizer Recipes

Kalamata Hummus
Servings: 4-6 | Cooking Time: 10 Minutes

Ingredients:
- 1 1/2 cups garbanzo beans, rinsed and drained
- 1 small red bell pepper, seeded and sliced
- 1 teaspoon cayenne (1/4 teaspoon reserved for topping)
- 1 teaspoon ground cumin, 1/4 teaspoon reserved for topping
- 1/4 cup fresh lemon juice
- 1/4 cup tahini
- 2 garlic cloves
- 2 tablespoons capers
- 3 tablespoons fresh parsley, 1 tablespoon reserved for topping
- 3/4 cup Kalamata olive
- 4 tablespoons olive oil, 2 tablespoons reserved for topping

Directions:
1. Put all of ingredients in a food processor; puree, adding just enough cold water to achieve spreadable consistency.
2. Transfer the puree into a shallow plate, smooth the top using a spoon. Drizzle with the remaining olive oil. Garnish with the remaining parsley. Sprinkle the cayenne and the cumin, making a start pattern.
3. Serve with vegetables and warm pita.

Nutrition Info:
- Per Serving: 357.7 cal., 24.8 total fat (3.4 g sat., fat), 0 mg chol., 596.9 mg sodium, 29.4 total carbs., 7 g fiber, 1.3 g sugar, and 8 g protein.

Chickpeas And Eggplant Bowls
Servings: 4 | Cooking Time: 10 Minutes

Ingredients:
- 2 eggplants, cut in half lengthwise and cubed
- 1 red onion, chopped
- Juice of 1 lime
- 1 tablespoon olive oil
- 28 ounces canned chickpeas, drained and rinsed
- 1 bunch parsley, chopped
- A pinch of salt and black pepper
- 1 tablespoon balsamic vinegar

Directions:
1. Spread the eggplant cubes on a baking sheet lined with parchment paper, drizzle half of the oil all over, season with salt and pepper and cook at 425 degrees F for 10 minutes.
2. Cool the eggplant down, add the rest of the ingredients, toss, divide between appetizer plates and serve.

Nutrition Info:
- calories 263, fat 12, fiber 9.3, carbs 15.4, protein 7.5

Slow Cooked Cheesy Artichoke Dip
Servings: 6 | Cooking Time: 60 Minutes

Ingredients:
- 10 oz can artichoke hearts, drained and chopped
- 4 cups spinach, chopped
- 8 oz cream cheese
- 3 tbsp sour cream
- 1/4 cup mayonnaise
- 3/4 cup mozzarella cheese, shredded
- 1/4 cup parmesan cheese, grated
- 3 garlic cloves, minced
- 1/2 tsp dried parsley
- Pepper
- Salt

Directions:
1. Add all ingredients into the inner pot of instant pot and stir well.
2. Seal the pot with the lid and select slow cook mode and set the timer for 60 minutes. Stir once while cooking.
3. Serve and enjoy.

Nutrition Info:
- Calories 226 Fat 19.3 g Carbohydrates 7.5 g Sugar 1.2 g Protein 6.8 g Cholesterol 51 mg

Creamy Eggplant Dip
Servings: 4 | Cooking Time: 20 Minutes

Ingredients:
- 1 eggplant
- 1/2 tsp paprika
- 1 tbsp olive oil
- 1 tbsp fresh lime juice
- 2 tbsp tahini
- 1 garlic clove
- 1 cup of water
- Pepper
- Salt

Directions:
1. Add water and eggplant into the instant pot.
2. Seal pot with the lid and select manual and set timer for 20 minutes.
3. Once done, release pressure using quick release. Remove lid.
4. Drain eggplant and let it cool.
5. Once the eggplant is cool then remove eggplant skin and transfer eggplant flesh into the food processor.
6. Add remaining ingredients into the food processor and process until smooth.
7. Serve and enjoy.

Nutrition Info:
- Calories 108 Fat 7.8 g Carbohydrates 9.7 g Sugar 3.7 g Protein 2.5 g Cholesterol 0 mg

Zucchini Cakes

Servings: 4 | Cooking Time: 10 Minutes

Ingredients:
- 1 zucchini, grated
- ¼ carrot, grated
- ¼ onion, minced
- 1 teaspoon minced garlic
- 3 tablespoons coconut flour
- 1 teaspoon Italian seasonings
- 1 egg, beaten
- 1 teaspoon coconut oil

Directions:
1. In the mixing bowl combine together grated zucchini, carrot, minced onion, and garlic.
2. Add coconut flour, Italian seasoning, and egg.
3. Stir the mass until homogenous.
4. Heat up coconut oil in the skillet.
5. Place the small zucchini fritters in the hot oil. Make them with the help of the spoon.
6. Roast the zucchini fritters for 4 minutes from each side.

Nutrition Info:
- Per Servingcalories 65, fat 3.3, fiber 3, carbs 6.3, protein 3.3

Peach Skewers

Servings: 2 | Cooking Time: 0 Minutes

Ingredients:
- 1 peach
- 4 Mozzarella balls, cherry size
- ½ teaspoon pistachio, chopped
- 1 teaspoon honey

Directions:
1. Cut the peach on 4 cubes.
2. Then skewer peach cubes and Mozzarella balls on the skewers.
3. Sprinkle them with honey and chopped pistachio.

Nutrition Info:
- Per Servingcalories 202, fat 14.3, fiber 1.2, carbs 10, protein 10.8

Bulgur Lamb Meatballs

Servings: 6 | Cooking Time: 15 Minutes

Ingredients:
- 1 and ½ cups Greek yogurt
- ½ teaspoon cumin, ground
- 1 cup cucumber, shredded
- ½ teaspoon garlic, minced
- A pinch of salt and black pepper
- 1 cup bulgur
- 2 cups water
- 1 pound lamb, ground
- ¼ cup parsley, chopped
- ¼ cup shallots, chopped
- ½ teaspoon allspice, ground
- ½ teaspoon cinnamon powder
- 1 tablespoon olive oil

Directions:
1. In a bowl, combine the bulgur with the water, cover the bowl, leave aside for 10 minutes, drain and transfer to a bowl.
2. Add the meat, the yogurt and the rest of the ingredients except the oil, stir well and shape medium meatballs out of this mix.
3. Heat up a pan with the oil over medium-high heat, add the meatballs, cook them for 7 minutes on each side, arrange them all on a platter and serve as an appetizer.

Nutrition Info:
- calories 300, fat 9.6, fiber 4.6, carbs 22.6, protein 6.6

Creamy Potato Spread

Servings: 6 | Cooking Time: 15 Minutes

Ingredients:
- 1 lb sweet potatoes, peeled and chopped
- 3/4 tbsp fresh chives, chopped
- 1/2 tsp paprika
- 1 tbsp garlic, minced
- 1 cup tomato puree
- Pepper
- Salt

Directions:
1. Add all ingredients except chives into the inner pot of instant pot and stir well.
2. Seal pot with lid and cook on high for 15 minutes.
3. Once done, allow to release pressure naturally for 10 minutes then release remaining using quick release. Remove lid.
4. Transfer instant pot sweet potato mixture into the food processor and process until smooth.
5. Garnish with chives and serve.

Nutrition Info:
- Calories 108 Fat 0.3 g Carbohydrates 25.4 g Sugar 2.4 g Protein 2 g Cholesterol 0 mg

Lavash Chips

Servings: 4 | Cooking Time: 10 Minutes

Ingredients:
- 1 lavash sheet, whole grain
- 1 tablespoon canola oil
- 1 teaspoon paprika
- ½ teaspoon chili pepper
- ½ teaspoon salt

Directions:
1. In the shallow bowl whisk together canola oil, paprika, chili pepper, and salt.
2. Then chop lavash sheet roughly (in the shape of chips).
3. Sprinkle lavash chips with oil mixture and arrange in the tray to get one thin layer.
4. Bake the lavash chips for 10 minutes at 365F. Flip them on another side from time to time to avoid burning.
5. Cool the cooked chips well.

Nutrition Info:
- Per Servingcalories 73, fat 4, fiber 0.7, carbs 8.4, protein 1.6

Eggplant Chips
Servings: 4-6 | Cooking Time: 5 Hours

Ingredients:
- 6 pieces baby eggplants, sliced lengthwise into thin pieces
- 1/2 teaspoon garlic powder
- Kosher salt, generous amount
- 1 teaspoon smoked paprika
- 1/2 teaspoon oregano
- Freshly ground black pepper, generous amount
- 1/4 cup extra-virgin olive oil
- 1/4 teaspoon cayenne pepper

Directions:
1. Place the slices of eggplant in a large-sized bowl.
2. Add the oil and the spices; gently toss using tongs, making sure each slice is coated with the spices.
3. Place the spiced slices on dehydrator trays; dehydrate on fruit/vegetable setting (135F) for about 4 to 5 hours or until they are fully crispy and dried. Check them around 3 to 4 hours. The thinner slices will be done sooner. Let cool completely. Serve or store in a container.

Nutrition Info:
- Per Serving: 140 cal, 11 g total fat (1.5 g sat. fat), 0 mg chol., 160 mg sodium, 430 mg pot., 11 total carbs., 6 g fiber, 4 g sugar, 2 g protein, 8% vitamin A, 8% vitamin C, 2% calcium, and 2% iron.

Balsamic Wings
Servings: 3 | Cooking Time: 20 Minutes

Ingredients:
- 3 chicken wings, boneless
- 1 teaspoon chili pepper, minced
- 1 tablespoon olive oil
- 1 teaspoon minced garlic
- 2 tablespoons balsamic vinegar
- ½ teaspoon salt

Directions:
1. Make the chicken sauce: whisk together minced chili pepper, olive oil, minced garlic, balsamic vinegar, and salt.
2. Preheat the oven to 360F.
3. Line the baking tray with parchment.
4. Rub the chicken wings with chicken sauce generously and transfer in the tray.
5. Bake the poultry for 20 minutes. Flip them onto another side after 10 minutes of cooking.

Nutrition Info:
- Per Serving calories 138, fat 11, fiber 0.2, carbs 3.8, protein 5.9

Goat Cheese And Chives Spread
Servings: 4 | Cooking Time: 0 Minutes

Ingredients:
- 2 ounces goat cheese, crumbled
- ¾ cup sour cream
- 2 tablespoons chives, chopped
- 1 tablespoon lemon juice
- Salt and black pepper to the taste
- 2 tablespoons extra virgin olive oil

Directions:
1. In a bowl, mix the goat cheese with the cream and the rest of the ingredients and whisk really well.
2. Keep in the fridge for 10 minutes and serve as a party spread.

Nutrition Info:
- calories 220, fat 11.5, fiber 4.8, carbs 8.9, protein 5.6

Cheddar Bites
Servings: 8 | Cooking Time: 15 Minutes

Ingredients:
- 3 Phyllo sheets
- ½ cup Cheddar cheese
- 2 eggs, beaten
- 1 tablespoon butter

Directions:
1. Mix up together Cheddar cheese with eggs.
2. Spread the round springform pan with butter.
3. Place 2 Phyllo sheets inside the springform pan.
4. Place Cheddar cheese mixture over the Phyllo sheets and cover it with the remaining Phyllo dough sheet.
5. Preheat the oven to 365F.
6. Cut the Phyllo dough pie onto 8 pieces and bake for 15 minutes.

Nutrition Info:
- Per Serving calories 113, fat 5.4, fiber 0.4, carbs 11.4, protein 5

Cucumber Sandwich
Servings: 2 | Cooking Time: 0 Minutes

Ingredients:
- 1 large cucumber, trimmed
- 2 teaspoons hummus
- ½ teaspoon chives, chopped
- ¾ teaspoon chili flakes
- ¼ teaspoon lemon juice

Directions:
1. Slice the cucumber on 4 thin circles.
2. Spread 2 cucumber circles with hummus from one side.
3. Then add chives and chili flakes.
4. Drizzle the cucumber with lemon juice.
5. Top the hummus with remaining cucumber circles and pin with a toothpick.

Nutrition Info:
- Per Serving calories 31, fat 0.6, fiber 1.1, carbs 6.2, protein 1.4

Perfect Italian Potatoes
Servings: 6 | Cooking Time: 7 Minutes

Ingredients:
- 2 lbs baby potatoes, clean and cut in half
- 3/4 cup vegetable broth
- 6 oz Italian dry dressing mix

Directions:
1. Add all ingredients into the inner pot of instant pot and stir

well.
2. Seal pot with lid and cook on high for 7 minutes.
3. Once done, allow to release pressure naturally for 3 minutes then release remaining using quick release. Remove lid.
4. Stir well and serve.

Nutrition Info:
- Calories 149 Fat 0.3 g Carbohydrates 41.6 g Sugar 11.4 g Protein 4.5 g Cholesterol 0 mg

Hot Squash Wedges
Servings: 6 | Cooking Time: 25 Minutes

Ingredients:
- 6 tablespoons olive oil
- 2 tablespoons chili paste
- 3 butternut squash, peeled and cut into wedges
- 2 tablespoons balsamic vinegar
- 1 tablespoon chives, chopped

Directions:
1. In a bowl, mix the squash wedges with the chili paste and the rest of the ingredients, toss, spread them on a baking sheet lined with parchment paper and bake at 400 degrees F for 25 minutes, flipping them from time to time.
2. Divide the wedges into bowls and serve as a snack.

Nutrition Info:
- calories 180, fat 4.2, fiber 4.4, carbs 6.5, protein 1.4

Stuffed Zucchinis
Servings: 6 | Cooking Time: 40 Minutes

Ingredients:
- 6 zucchinis, halved lengthwise and insides scooped out
- 2 garlic cloves, minced
- 2 tablespoons oregano, chopped
- Juice of 2 lemons
- Salt and black pepper to the taste
- 2 tablespoons olive oil
- 8 ounces feta cheese, crumbed

Directions:
1. Arrange the zucchini halves on a baking sheet lined with parchment paper, divide the cheese and the rest of the ingredients in each zucchini half and bake at 450 degrees F for 40 minutes.
2. Arrange the stuffed zucchinis on a platter and serve as an appetizer.

Nutrition Info:
- calories

Multipurpose Dough
Serves: 1 Roll | Cooking Time: 20 Minutes

Ingredients:
- 1 1/2 TB. active dry yeast
- 1 1/2 cups warm water
- 1 tsp. sugar
- 6 TB. extra-virgin olive oil
- 1 tsp. salt
- 3 cups all-purpose flour
- 2 TB. cornmeal

Directions:
1. In a large bowl, combine yeast, warm water, and sugar, and set aside for 5 minutes.
2. Add 3 tablespoons extra-virgin olive oil, salt, and 1 cup all-purpose flour, and stir to combine. Add another 1 cup all-purpose flour, and begin to knead dough. Add remaining 1 cup all-purpose flour, and knead for about 3 minutes or until dough comes together in a ball. If you're using an electric stand mixer, use the dough attachment to knead dough.
3. Remove dough from the bowl, and grease the bowl with 1 tablespoon extra-virgin olive oil. Return dough to the bowl, and turn over to coat dough in oil. Cover the bowl with plastic wrap and a thick towel, and set aside to rise for 2 hours.
4. Preheat the oven to 420ºF. Dust a baking sheet with cornmeal.
5. Uncover the bowl, and gently pull dough together into a ball. Divide dough into 16 pieces, lightly dust with flour, and place on the baking sheet about 2 inches apart. Bake for 20 minutes or until golden brown.
6. Transfer rolls to a plate, and brush with remaining 2 tablespoons extra-virgin olive oil.
7. Serve immediately or store in an airtight container.

Popcorn-pine Nut Mix
Servings: 10 | Cooking Time: 10 Minutes

Ingredients:
- 1 tablespoon olive oil
- 1/2 cup pine nuts
- 1/2 teaspoon Italian seasoning
- 1/4 cup popcorn, white kernels, popped
- 1/4 teaspoon salt
- 2 tablespoons honey
- 1/2 lemon zest

Directions:
1. Place the popped corn in a medium bowl.
2. In a dry pan or skillet over low heat, toast the pine nuts, stirring frequently for about 4 to 5 minutes, until fragrant and some begin to brown; remove from the heat.
3. Stir the oil in; add honey, the Italian seasoning, the lemon zest, and the salt. Stir to mix and pour over the popcorn; toss the ingredients to coat the popcorn kernels with the honey syrup.
4. It's alright if most of the nuts sink in the bowl bottom.
5. Let the mixture sit for about 2 minutes to allow the honey to cool and to get stickier.
6. Transfer the bowl contents into a Servings: bowl so the nuts are on the top. Gently stir and serve.

Nutrition Info:
- Per Serving:80 cal, 6 g total fat (0.5 g sat. fat), 0 mg chol., 105 mg sodium, 60 mg pot., 5 total carbs., <1 g fiber, 4 g sugar, 2 g protein, 2% vitamin A, 8% vitamin C, 4% calcium, and 4% iron.

Mediterranean Diet Cookbook

Plum Wraps
Servings: 4 | Cooking Time: 10 Minutes

Ingredients:
- 4 plums
- 4 prosciutto slices
- ¼ teaspoon olive oil

Directions:
1. Preheat the oven to 375F.
2. Wrap every plum in prosciutto slice and secure with a toothpick (if needed).
3. Place the wrapped plums in the oven and bake for 10 minutes.

Nutrition Info:
- Per Servingcalories 62, fat 2.2, fiber 0.9, carbs 8, protein 4.3

Vinegar Beet Bites
Servings: 4 | Cooking Time: 30 Minutes

Ingredients:
- 2 beets, sliced
- A pinch of sea salt and black pepper
- 1/3 cup balsamic vinegar
- 1 cup olive oil

Directions:
1. Spread the beet slices on a baking sheet lined with parchment paper, add the rest of the ingredients, toss and bake at 350 degrees F for 30 minutes.
2. Serve the beet bites cold as a snack.

Nutrition Info:
- calories 199, fat 5.4, fiber 3.5, carbs 8.5, protein 3.5

Mediterranean-style Nachos Recipe
Servings: 12 | Cooking Time: 15 Minutes

Ingredients:
- 6 pieces whole-wheat pita breads
- Cooking spray
- 1/2 teaspoon ground cumin
- 1/2 teaspoon ground coriander
- 1/2 teaspoon paprika
- 1/2 teaspoon pepper
- 1/2 teaspoons salt
- 1/2 cup hot water
- 1/2 teaspoon beef stock concentrate
- 1 pound ground lamb or beef
- 2 garlic cloves, minced
- 1 teaspoon cornstarch
- 2 medium cucumbers, peeled, seeded, grated
- 2 cups Greek yogurt, plain
- 2 tablespoons lemon juice
- 1/4 teaspoon grated lemon peel
- 1 teaspoon salt, divided
- 1/4 teaspoon pepper
- 1/2 cup pitted Greek olives, sliced
- 4 green onions, thinly sliced
- 1/2 cup crumbled feta cheese
- 2 cups torn romaine lettuce
- 2 medium tomatoes, seeded and chopped

Directions:
1. In a colander set over a bowl, toss the cucumbers with 1/2 teaspoon of the salt; let stand for 30 minutes, then squeeze and pat dry. Set aside.
2. In a small-sized bowl, combine the coriander, cumin, 1/2 teaspoon pepper, paprika, and 1/2 teaspoon salt; set aside.
3. Cut each pita bread into 8 wedges. Arrange them in a single layer on ungreased baking sheets. Sprits both sides of the wedges with cooking spray. Sprinkle with 3/4 teaspoon of the seasoning mix. Broil 3-4 inches from the heat source for about 3-4 minutes per side, or until golden brown. Transfer to wire racks, let cool.
4. Whisk hot water and beef stock cube in a 1-cup liquid measuring cup until blended. In a large-sized skillet, cook the lamb, seasoning with the remaining seasoning mix, over medium heat until the meat is no longer pink. Add the garlic; cook for 1 minute. Drain.
5. Stir in the cornstarch into the broth; mix until smooth. Gradually stir into the skillet; bring to a boil and cook, stirring, for 2 minutes or until thick.
6. In a small-sized bowl, combine the cucumbers, yogurt, lemon peel, lemon juice, and the remaining salt and 1/4 teaspoon pepper.
7. Arrange the pita wedges on a serving platter. Layer with the lettuce, lamb mixture, tomatoes, onions, olives, and cheese; serve immediately with the cucumber sauce.

Nutrition Info:
- Per Serving:232 cal, 6.7 g total fat (2.9 g sat. fat), 42 mg chol., 630 mg sodium, 412 mg pot., 24 total carbs., 3.3 g fiber, 4.1 g sugar, 20.2 g protein, 8% vitamin A, 12% vitamin C, 11% calcium, and 15% iron.

Olives And Cheese Stuffed Tomatoes
Servings: 24 | Cooking Time: 0 Minutes

Ingredients:
- 24 cherry tomatoes, top cut off and insides scooped out
- 2 tablespoons olive oil
- ¼ teaspoon red pepper flakes
- ½ cup feta cheese, crumbled
- 2 tablespoons black olive paste
- ¼ cup mint, torn

Directions:
1. In a bowl, mix the olives paste with the rest of the ingredients except the cherry tomatoes and whisk well.
2. Stuff the cherry tomatoes with this mix, arrange them all on a platter and serve as an appetizer.

Nutrition Info:
- calories 136, fat 8.6, fiber 4.8, carbs 5.6, protein 5.1

Marinated Chickpeas
Servings: 4 | Cooking Time: 10 Minutes

Ingredients:
- 1 can (15 ounce) chickpeas (or garbanzo beans), drained, rinsed
- 1 tablespoon fresh oregano, chopped
- 1 tablespoon lemon juice
- 1 tablespoon lemon zest
- 1 teaspoon fresh parsley, chopped
- 1/4 teaspoon minced garlic
- 3 tablespoons olive oil
- Sea salt, to taste

Directions:
1. Place the chickpeas in a bowl. Add the rest of the ingredients; toss to mix well. Marinate the chickpeas for 8 hours or overnight in the refrigerator.

Nutrition Info:
- Per Serving:176 cal., 11 g total fat (1.5 sat. fat), 0 mg chol., 290 mg sodium, 16.6 g total carbs., 3.3 g fiber, 0.2 g sugar, and 3.6 g protein.

Feta And Roasted Red Pepper Bruschetta
Servings:24 | Cooking Time:15 Minutes

Ingredients:
- 6 Kalamata olives, pitted, chopped
- 2 tablespoons green onion, minced
- 1/4 cup Parmesan cheese, grated, divided
- 1/4 cup extra-virgin olive oil brushing, or as needed
- 1/4 cup cherry tomatoes, thinly sliced
- 1 teaspoon lemon juice
- 1 tablespoon extra-virgin olive oil
- 1 tablespoon basil pesto
- 1 red bell pepper, halved, seeded
- 1 piece (12 inch) whole-wheat baguette, cut into 1/2-inch thick slices
- 1 package (4 ounce) feta cheese with basil and sun-dried tomatoes, crumbled
- 1 clove garlic, minced

Directions:
1. Preheat the oven broiler. Place the oven rack 6 inches from the source of heat.
2. Brush both sides of the baguette slices, with the 1/4 cup olive oil. Arrange the bread slices on a baking sheet; toast for about 1 minute each side, carefully watching to avoid burning. Remove the toasted slices, transferring into another baking sheet.
3. With the cut sides down, place the red peppers in a baking sheet; broil for about 8 to 10 minutes or until the skin is charred and blistered. Transfer the roasted peppers into a bowl; cover with plastic wrap. Let cool, remove the charred skin. Discard skin and chop the roasted peppers.
4. In a bowl, mix the roasted red peppers, cherry tomatoes, feta cheese, green onion, olives, pesto, 1 tablespoon olive oil, garlic, and lemon juice.
5. Top each bread with 1 tablespoon of the roasted pepper mix, sprinkle lightly with the Parmesan cheese.
6. Return the baking sheet with the topped bruschetta; broil for about 1-2 minutes or until the topping is lightly browned.

Nutrition Info:
- Per Serving:73 cal., 4.8 g total fat (1.4 sat. fat), 5 mg chol., 138 mg sodium, 5.3 g total carbs., 0.4 g fiber, 0.6 g sugar, and 2.1 g protein.

Lemon Salmon Rolls
Servings:6 | Cooking Time: 0 Minutes

Ingredients:
- 6 wonton wrappers
- 7 oz salmon, grilled
- 6 lettuce leaves
- 1 carrot, peeled
- 1 cucumber, trimmed
- 1 tablespoon lemon juice
- 1 teaspoon olive oil
- ¼ teaspoon dried oregano

Directions:
1. Cut the carrot and cucumber onto the wedges.
2. Then chop the grilled salmon.
3. Arrange the salmon, carrot and cucumber wedges, and lettuce leaves on 6 wonton wraps.
4. In the shallow bowl whisk together dried oregano, olive oil, and lemon juice.
5. Sprinkle the roll mixture with oil dressing and wrap.

Nutrition Info:
- Per Servingcalories 90, fat 3.4, fiber 0.7, carbs 7.7, protein 7.7

Chickpeas Salsa
Servings: 6 | Cooking Time: 0 Minutes

Ingredients:
- 4 spring onions, chopped
- 1 cup baby spinach
- 15 ounces canned chickpeas, drained and rinsed
- Salt and black pepper to the taste
- 2 tablespoons olive oil
- 2 tablespoons lemon juice
- 1 tablespoon cilantro, chopped

Directions:
1. In a bowl, mix the chickpeas with the spinach, spring onions and the rest of the ingredients, toss, divide into small cups and serve as a snack.

Nutrition Info:
- calories 224, fat 5.1, fiber 1, carbs 9.9, protein 15.1

Lemon Endive Bites
Servings:10 | Cooking Time: 0 Minutes

Ingredients:
- 6 oz endive
- 2 pears, chopped
- 4 oz Blue cheese, crumbled
- 1 teaspoon olive oil
- 1 teaspoon lemon juice
- ¾ teaspoon ground cinnamon

Directions:
1. Separate endive into the spears (10 spears).
2. In the bowl combine together chopped pears, olive oil, lemon juice, ground cinnamon, and Blue cheese.
3. Fill the endive spears with cheese mixture.

Nutrition Info:
- Per Servingcalories 72, fat 3.8, fiber 1.9, carbs 7.4, protein 2.8

Lentils Stuffed Potato Skins
Servings: 8 | Cooking Time: 30 Minutes

Ingredients:
- 16 red baby potatoes
- ¾ cup red lentils, cooked and drained
- 2 tablespoons olive oil
- 2 garlic cloves, minced
- 1 tablespoon chives, chopped
- ½ teaspoon hot chili sauce
- Salt and black pepper to the taste

Directions:
1. Put potatoes in a pot, add water to cover them, bring to a boil over medium low heat, cook for 15 minutes, drain, cool them down, cut in halves, remove the pulp, transfer it to a blender and pulse it a bit.
2. Add the rest of the ingredients to the blender, pulse again well and stuff the potato skins with this mix.
3. Arrange the stuffed potatoes on a baking sheet lined with parchment paper, introduce them in the oven at 375 degrees F and bake for 15 minutes.
4. Arrange on a platter and serve as an appetizer.

Nutrition Info:
- calories 300, fat 9.3, fiber 14.5, carbs 22.5, protein 8.5

Pesto Dip
Servings: 6 | Cooking Time: 0 Minutes

Ingredients:
- 1 cup cream cheese, soft
- 3 tablespoons basil pesto
- Salt and black pepper to the taste
- 1 cup heavy cream
- 1 tablespoon chives, chopped

Directions:
1. In a bowl, mix the cream cheese with the pesto and the rest of the ingredients and whisk well.
2. Divide into small cups and serve as a party dip.

Nutrition Info:
- calories 230, fat 14.5, fiber 4.8, carbs 6.5, protein 5.4

Creamy Pepper Spread
Servings: 4 | Cooking Time: 15 Minutes

Ingredients:
- 1 lb red bell peppers, chopped and remove seeds
- 1 1/2 tbsp fresh basil
- 1 tbsp olive oil
- 1 tbsp fresh lime juice
- 1 tsp garlic, minced
- Pepper
- Salt

Directions:
1. Add all ingredients into the inner pot of instant pot and stir well.
2. Seal pot with lid and cook on high for 15 minutes.
3. Once done, allow to release pressure naturally for 10 minutes then release remaining using quick release. Remove lid.
4. Transfer bell pepper mixture into the food processor and process until smooth.
5. Serve and enjoy.

Nutrition Info:
- Calories 41 Fat 3.6 g Carbohydrates 3.5 g Sugar 1.7 g Protein 0.4 g Cholesterol 0 mg

Grilled Shrimp Kabobs
Servings: 4 | Cooking Time: 4 Minutes

Ingredients:
- 1 1/2 cups whole-wheat dry breadcrumbs
- 1 clove garlic, finely minced or pressed
- 1 teaspoon dried basil leaves
- 1/4 cup olive oil
- 2 pounds shrimp, peeled, deveined, leaving the tails on
- 2 tablespoons vegetable oil
- 2 teaspoons dried parsley flakes
- Salt and pepper
- 16 skewers, soaked for at least 20 minutes in water or until ready to use if using wooden

Directions:
1. Rinse the shrimps and dry.
2. Put the vegetable and the olive oil in a re-sealable plastic bag; add the shrimp and toss to coat with the oil mixture.
3. Add the breadcrumbs, parsley, garlic, basil, salt, and pepper; toss to coat with the dry mix.
4. Seal the bag, refrigerate for 1 hour. Thread the shrimps on the skewers.
5. Grill on preheated grill for about 2 minutes each side or until golden, making sure not to overcook.

Nutrition Info:
- per serving: 502.7 cal., 24.8 g total fat (3.5 sat. fat), 285.8 mg chol., 1581.8 mg sodium, 31.7 g total carbs., 2 g fiber, 2.5 g sugar, and 36.4 g protein.

Cucumber Roll Ups
Servings: 6 | Cooking Time: 15 Minutes

Ingredients:
- 1 large cucumber
- 1/8 teaspoon ground black pepper
- 6 tablespoons feta, crumbled
- 6 tablespoons roasted garlic hummus
- 6 tablespoons roasted red pepper, chopped

Directions:
1. With a vegetable peeler, shave off long thin cucumber slices. Alternatively, you can use a sharp knife to cut the cucumber into thin slices. Do not use the inner part of the cucumber that is full of seeds. You should be able to get 12 slices.

2. Sprinkle each slice with a pinch of black pepper. Evenly spread about 1 1/2 teaspoon of hummus on each slice. Sprinkle with the red pepper and with 1 1/2 teaspoon of feta over each slice.
3. Pick one end and roll each cucumber around the filling, making sure not to roll them too tightly or the filling will squeeze out. With the seam on the bottom, place each rolling a serving plate. Secure each piece by sticking a toothpick through the center of each roll.

Nutrition Info:
- Per Serving:64 cal, 5 g total fat (1.9 sat. fat), 3.4 g carbs, 0.7 g fiber, and 2.5 g protein.

Lime Yogurt Dip
Servings:4 | Cooking Time: 0 Minutes

Ingredients:
- 1 large cucumber, trimmed
- 3 oz Greek yogurt
- 1 teaspoon olive oil
- 3 tablespoons fresh dill, chopped
- 1 tablespoon lime juice
- ¾ teaspoon salt
- 1 garlic clove, minced

Directions:
1. Grate the cucumber and squeeze the juice from it.
2. Then place the squeezed cucumber in the bowl.
3. Add Greek yogurt, olive oil, dill, lime juice, salt, and minced garlic.
4. Mix up the mixture until homogenous.
5. Store tzaziki in the fridge up to 2 days.

Nutrition Info:
- Per Servingcalories 44, fat 1.8, fiber 0.7, carbs 5.1, protein 3.2

Mediterranean Dip Duo
Servings:4-6 | Cooking Time: 10 Minutes

Ingredients:
- 4 ounces olives, ripe, less or more to taste
- 4 ounces feta cheese, crumbled
- 2 tablespoons olive oil
- 1/2 medium cucumber
- 1/2 cup red onion, chopped
- 1 teaspoon Italian seasoning, any kind
- 1 plum tomato
- 1 garlic clove
- For the hummus:
- 8 ounces hummus
- 8 ounces sour cream
- Baked whole-wheat pita chips

Directions:
1. For the Mediterranean salsa:
2. Place the cucumber, tomatoes, onion, and olives in a bowl.
3. Stir in the garlic press, olive oil, and the seasoning mix.
4. Gently stir in the crumbled feta.
5. For the hummus:
6. Whisk together the hummus and the sour cream.
7. Serve the salsa and the hummus in separate bowl. Serve with the baked pita chips.

Nutrition Info:
- Per Serving:413.6 cal., 34.4 g total fat (14.5 g sat. fat), 53.1 mg chol., 846.1 mg sodium, 0 mg pot., 18 g total carbs., 5 g fiber, 3.2 g sugar, and 11.5 g protein.

Roasted Seeds
Servings:6 | Cooking Time: 5 Minutes

Ingredients:
- 4 oz pumpkin seeds
- ½ teaspoon ground black pepper
- ¾ teaspoon salt
- 1 tablespoon sunflower oil

Directions:
1. Heat up sunflower oil in the skillet.
2. Add pumpkin seeds and roast them for 2 minutes. Stir them from time to time.
3. After this, sprinkle the seeds with salt and ground black pepper. Mix up well.
4. Roast the pumpkin seeds for 3 minutes more.

Nutrition Info:
- Per Servingcalories 123, fat 11, fiber 0.8, carbs 3.5, protein 4.7

Delicious Eggplant Caponata
Servings: 8 | Cooking Time: 5 Minutes

Ingredients:
- 1 eggplant, cut into 1/2-inch chunks
- 1 lb tomatoes, diced
- 1/2 cup tomato puree
- 1/4 cup dates, chopped
- 2 tbsp vinegar
- 1/2 cup fresh parsley, chopped
- 2 celery stalks, chopped
- 1 small onion, chopped
- 2 zucchini, cut into 1/2-inch chunks
- Pepper
- Salt

Directions:
1. Add all ingredients into the inner pot of instant pot and stir well.
2. Seal pot with lid and cook on high for 5 minutes.
3. Once done, release pressure using quick release. Remove lid.
4. Stir well and serve.

Nutrition Info:
- Calories 60 Fat 0.4 g Carbohydrates 14 g Sugar 8.8 g Protein 2.3 g Cholesterol 0.4 mg

Meat Recipes

Meat Recipes

Balsamic Chicken With Roasted Tomatoes
Servings: 2 | Cooking Time: 20 Minutes

Ingredients:
- ½ medium onion, chopped
- 1 cup mushrooms, chopped
- 1 tablespoon honey
- 1-pint cherry tomatoes, halved
- 2 chicken thighs, skins removed
- 2 tablespoon extra-virgin olive oil
- 3 tablespoon balsamic vinegar
- Fresh parsley, chopped
- Salt and pepper to taste

Directions:
1. Preheat the oven to 400oF.
2. In a greased baking sheet, place the tomatoes and drizzle with honey and oil. Season with salt and pepper and cook in the oven for 20 minutes.
3. Meanwhile, heat 1 tablespoon of olive oil in a skillet. Sauté the mushrooms and onions for 12 minutes until softened. Add the chicken then season with salt and pepper. Add the balsamic glaze and reduce the heat to low. Let it simmer for 15 minutes or until the chicken is cooked through.
4. Assemble by placing tomatoes in the plate, add a chicken thigh and spoon the mushroom and pan drippings.
5. Garnish with parsley.

Nutrition Info:
- Calories per Serving: 217.7; Carbs: 39.2g; Protein: 6.0g; Fat: 4.1g

Carrot Mushroom Beef Roast
Servings: 4 | Cooking Time: 40 Minutes

Ingredients:
- 1 1/2 lbs beef roast
- 1 tsp paprika
- 1/4 tsp dried rosemary
- 1 tsp garlic, minced
- 1/2 lb mushrooms, sliced
- 1/2 cup chicken stock
- 2 carrots, sliced
- Pepper
- Salt

Directions:
1. Add all ingredients into the inner pot of instant pot and stir well.
2. Seal pot with lid and cook on high for 40 minutes.
3. Once done, allow to release pressure naturally for 10 minutes then release remaining using quick release. Remove lid.
4. Slice and serve.

Nutrition Info:
- Calories 345 Fat 10.9 g Carbohydrates 5.6 g Sugar 2.6 g Protein 53.8 g Cholesterol 152 mg

Italian Pork Spareribs
Servings: 4 | Cooking Time: 1 Hour And 30 Minutes

Ingredients:
- 2 pork spareribs
- 2 teaspoons basil, dried
- 1 teaspoon rosemary, dried
- 2 teaspoons smoked paprika
- Salt and black pepper to the taste
- 4 garlic cloves, minced
- 6 tablespoons sherry vinegar
- ¼ cup olive oil

Directions:
1. In a bowl, mix the ribs with the rest of the ingredients, toss and keep in the fridge for 10 minutes.
2. Heat up your grill over medium-high heat, add the spareribs, cover your grill and cook them for 1 hour and 30 minutes flipping from time to time.
3. Divide between plates and serve with a side salad.

Nutrition Info:
- calories 344, fat 21, fiber 12.2, carbs 19.9, protein 23.2

Pork And Parsley Spread
Servings:4 | Cooking Time: 0 Minutes

Ingredients:
- 1 garlic clove, peeled
- ½ white onion, peeled
- 1 tablespoon fresh parsley
- 9 oz pork loin, roasted, shredded
- ½ lemon
- 1 tablespoon butter, softened
- 1 teaspoon olive oil
- ¼ teaspoon chili powder

Directions:
1. Place the garlic clove, onion, parsley, olive oil, and chili powder in the blender.
2. Squeeze the juice of a lemon and add it in the blender.
3. Blend the vegetables for 1 minute.
4. Then add shredded pork loin.
5. Blend the mixture for 3 minutes at maximum speed or until the mass is smooth and soft.
6. Then add butter and pulse it for 30 seconds more.
7. Transfer the cooked pate in the bowl.

Nutrition Info:
- Per Servingcalories 199, fat 13, fiber 0.6, carbs 2.4, protein 17.8

Pork Chops And Cherries Mix
Servings: 4 | Cooking Time: 12 Minutes

Ingredients:
- 4 pork chops, boneless
- Salt and black pepper to the taste
- ½ cup cranberry juice
- 1 and ½ teaspoons spicy mustard
- ½ cup dark cherries, pitted and halved
- Cooking spray

Directions:
1. Heat up a pan greased with the cooking spray over medium-high heat, add the pork chops, cook them for 5 minutes on each side and divide between plates.
2. Heat up the same pan over medium heat, add the cranberry juice and the rest of the ingredients, whisk, bring to a simmer, cook for 2 minutes, drizzle over the pork chops and serve.

Nutrition Info:
- calories 262, fat 8, fiber 1, carbs 16, protein 30

Baked Pork Chops
Servings: 4 | Cooking Time: 30 Minutes

Ingredients:
- 4 pork loin chops, boneless
- A pinch of salt and black pepper
- 1 tablespoon sweet paprika
- 2 tablespoons Dijon mustard
- Cooking spray

Directions:
1. In a bowl, mix the pork chops with salt, pepper, paprika and the mustard and rub well.
2. Grease a baking sheet with cooking spray, add the pork chops, cover with tin foil, introduce in the oven and bake at 400 degrees F for 30 minutes.
3. Divide the pork chops between plates and serve with a side salad.

Nutrition Info:
- calories 167, fat 5, fiber 0, carbs 2, protein 25

Lamb Chops
Serves: 1 Chop

Cooking Time: 6 Minutes

Ingredients:
- 6 (3/4-in.-thick) lamb chops
- 2 TB. fresh rosemary, finely chopped
- 3 TB. minced garlic
- 1 tsp. salt
- 1 tsp. ground black pepper
- 3 TB. extra-virgin olive oil

Directions:
1. In a large bowl, combine lamb chops, rosemary, garlic, salt, black pepper, and extra-virgin olive oil until chops are evenly coated. Let chops marinate at room temperature for at least 25 minutes.
2. Preheat a grill to medium heat.
3. Place chops on the grill, and cook for 3 minutes per side for medium well.
4. Serve warm.

Cherry Stuffed Lamb
Servings: 2 | Cooking Time: 40 Minutes

Ingredients:
- 9 oz lamb loin
- 1 oz pistachio, chopped
- 1 teaspoon cherries, pitted
- ½ teaspoon olive oil
- ¼ teaspoon dried thyme
- 1 teaspoon dried rosemary
- 1 garlic clove, minced
- ¼ teaspoon liquid honey

Directions:
1. Rub the lamb loin with dried thyme and rosemary.
2. Then make a lengthwise cut in the meat.
3. Mix up together pistachios, minced garlic, and cherries.
4. Fill the meat with this mixture and secure the cut with the toothpick.
5. Then brush the lamb loin with liquid honey and olive oil.
6. Wrap the meat in the foil and bake at 365F for 40 minutes.
7. When the meat is cooked, remove it from the foil.
8. Let the meat chill for 10 minutes and then slice it.

Nutrition Info:
- Per Servingcalories 353, fat 20.4, fiber 1.8, carbs 6, protein 36.9

Tender Beef In Tomato-artichoke Stew
Servings: 6 | Cooking Time: 2 Hours

Ingredients:
- 1 (14 ounce) can artichoke hearts, drained and halved
- 1 (14.5 ounce) can diced tomatoes
- 1 (15 ounce) can tomato sauce
- 1 (32 fluid ounce) container beef broth
- 1 bay leaf
- 1 onion, diced
- 1 tablespoon grapeseed oil
- 1 teaspoon dried basil
- 1 teaspoon dried oregano
- 1 teaspoon dried parsley
- 1/2 cup pitted and roughly chopped
- 1/2 teaspoon ground cumin
- 2 pounds stewing beef
- 4 cloves garlic, chopped or more to taste
- Kalamata olives (optional)

Directions:
1. Place a pot on medium high fire and heat for 3 minutes. Add oil and heat for 2 minutes.
2. Brown beef and cook for 15 minutes.
3. Add all ingredients, deglaze pot, and mix well.
4. Once boiling, lower fire to a simmer, cover, and cook for 60 minutes. Occasionally stirring pot.
5. If needed cook for 30 minutes more to desired beef tenderness.
6. Adjust seasoning if needed.
7. Serve and enjoy.

Nutrition Info:
- Calories per Serving: 416; Carbs: 14.1g; Protein: 29.9g;

Mediterranean Diet Cookbook

Fats: 26.2g

Flavorful Beef Bourguignon

Servings: 4 | Cooking Time: 20 Minutes

Ingredients:
- 1 1/2 lbs beef chuck roast, cut into chunks
- 2/3 cup beef stock
- 2 tbsp fresh thyme
- 1 bay leaf
- 1 tsp garlic, minced
- 8 oz mushrooms, sliced
- 2 tbsp tomato paste
- 2/3 cup dry red wine
- 1 onion, sliced
- 4 carrots, cut into chunks
- 1 tbsp olive oil
- Pepper
- Salt

Directions:
1. Add oil into the instant pot and set the pot on sauté mode.
2. Add meat and sauté until brown. Add onion and sauté until softened.
3. Add remaining ingredients and stir well.
4. Seal pot with lid and cook on high for 12 minutes.
5. Once done, allow to release pressure naturally. Remove lid.
6. Stir well and serve.

Nutrition Info:
- Calories 744 Fat 51.3 g Carbohydrates 14.5 g Sugar 6.5 g Protein 48.1 g Cholesterol 175 mg

Creamy Chicken-spinach Skillet

Servings: 4 | Cooking Time: 17 Minutes

Ingredients:
- 1 lb. boneless skinless chicken breast sliced into cutlets
- 1 medium onion diced
- 12 oz roasted red peppers finely diced
- 2 1/2 cups chicken stock divided
- 2 cups fresh baby spinach leaves
- 2 cups freshly cooked pasta
- 2 Tbs butter
- 4 garlic cloves minced
- 7 oz cream cheese try to find an herb/garlic flavored one!
- Salt and pepper

Directions:
1. Place a saucepan on medium high fire and heat for 2 minutes. Add butter and melt for a minute, swirling to coat pan.
2. Add chicken to pan, season with pepper and salt to taste. Cook chicken on high fire for 3 minutes per side.
3. Lower fire to medium and stir in onions, red peppers, and garlic. Sauté for 5 minutes and deglaze pot with a little bit of stock.
4. Whisk in chicken stock and cream cheese. Cook and mix until thoroughly combined.
5. Stir in spinach and adjust seasoning to taste. Cook for 2 minutes or until spinach is wilted.
6. Serve and enjoy.

Nutrition Info:
- Calories per Serving: 484; Carbs: 33.0g; Protein: 36.0g; Fats: 22.0g

Italian Pork And Mushrooms

Servings: 4 | Cooking Time: 7 Hours

Ingredients:
- 2 pounds pork stew meat, cubed
- Salt and black pepper to the taste
- 2 cups veggie stock
- 2 tablespoons olive oil
- 1 yellow onion, chopped
- 2 tablespoons thyme, chopped
- 4 garlic cloves, minced
- 1 pound white mushrooms, chopped
- 2 cups tomatoes, crushed
- ½ cup parsley, chopped

Directions:
1. In your slow cooker, combine meat with salt, pepper, the stock and the rest of the ingredients, put the lid on and cook on Low for 7 hours.
2. Divide the mix between plates and serve right away.

Nutrition Info:
- calories 328, fat 16.7, fiber 9.5, carbs 11.6, protein 15.7

Rosemary Beef Eggplant

Servings: 4 | Cooking Time: 30 Minutes

Ingredients:
- 1 lb beef stew meat, cubed
- 2 tbsp green onion, chopped
- 1/4 tsp red pepper flakes
- 1/2 tsp dried rosemary
- 1/2 tsp paprika
- 1 cup chicken stock
- 1 onion, chopped
- 1 eggplant, cubed
- 2 tbsp olive oil
- Pepper
- Salt

Directions:
1. Add oil into the instant pot and set the pot on sauté mode.
2. Add meat and onion and sauté for 5 minutes.
3. Add remaining ingredients and stir well.
4. Seal pot with lid and cook on high for 25 minutes.
5. Once done, allow to release pressure naturally. Remove lid.
6. Serve and enjoy.

Nutrition Info:
- Calories 315 Fat 14.5 g Carbohydrates 10 gSugar 4.9 g Protein 36.1 g Cholesterol 101 mg

Sweet Chili Lamb

Servings: 4 | Cooking Time: 25 Minutes

Ingredients:
- 1 tablespoon olive oil
- 1 pound lamb stew meat, cubed
- ½ cup sweet chili sauce

39 | Mediterranean Diet Cookbook

- 1 cup carrot, chopped
- ½ cup veggie stock
- 1 tablespoon cilantro, chopped
- Salt and black pepper to the taste

Directions:
1. Heat up a pan with the oil over medium-high heat, add the lamb and brown for 5 minutes.
2. Add the rest of the ingredients, bring to a simmer and cook over medium heat for 20 minutes more.
3. Divide everything between plates and serve.

Nutrition Info:
- calories 287, fat 21.1, fiber 11.8, carbs 25.1, protein 18.9

Beef With Beets And Broccoli
Servings:4 | Cooking Time: 35 Minutes

Ingredients:
- 2 tablespoons capers
- 1/3 cup green olives, chopped
- 1 tomato, chopped
- 1 sweet pepper, chopped
- 9 oz beef shank, chopped
- 3 oz beetroot, chopped
- ¼ cup broccoli, chopped
- 2 cups chicken stock
- 1 teaspoon dried oregano
- 1 teaspoon salt
- 1 teaspoon dried cilantro
- 1 teaspoon butter

Directions:
1. Melt the butter in the pan and add chopped beef shank.
2. Roast it for 5 minutes over the high heat.
3. Then add tomato, capers, green olives, sweet pepper, broccoli, dried oregano, salt, and dried cilantro.
4. Mix up the saute well and add chicken stock.
5. Close the lid and simmer the meal for 30 minutes over the low heat.

Nutrition Info:
- Per Servingcalories 179, fat 7.7, fiber 1.8, carbs 6.2, protein 21

Upside-down Rice (makloubeh)
Serves: 1 Cup | Cooking Time:1½ Hours

Ingredients:
- 1 large eggplant
- 2 tsp. salt
- 2 cups cauliflower florets
- Olive oil spray
- 1/2 lb. ground lamb
- 1 medium yellow onion, finely chopped
- 4 TB. extra-virgin olive oil
- 1 1/2 cups long-grain rice, rinsed
- 1 tsp. seven spices
- 1/2 tsp. ground cinnamon
- 1/2 tsp. ground nutmeg
- 1/2 tsp. ground cardamom
- 4 cups water
- 1/3 cup pine nuts
- 1/3 cup sliced almonds
- 1/4 cup fresh Italian parsley, chopped

Directions:
1. Preheat the oven to 450ºF. Lightly coat a baking sheet with olive oil spray.
2. Cut eggplant into 1/4-inch slices, sprinkle with 1/2 teaspoon salt, and let drain in a strainer for 20 minutes. Pat dry.
3. Spread eggplant and cauliflower florets on the prepared baking sheet, lightly coat with olive oil spray, and bake for 20 minutes. Set aside.
4. In a medium skillet over medium heat, brown lamb for 5 minutes, breaking up lumps with a wooden spoon.
5. Add yellow onion and 2 tablespoons extra-virgin olive oil, and cook for 5 minutes.
6. Transfer lamb and onions to a large bowl, and stir in long-grain rice, seven spices, cinnamon, nutmeg, cardamom, and remaining 11/2 teaspoons salt.
7. In a large, 3-quart pot, add a layer of eggplant, 1/2 of rice mixture, 1/2 of cauliflower, another layer of eggplant, remaining rice mixture, and a final layer of cauliflower. Slowly pour in water, cover, and cook over low heat for 40 minutes. Let rice rest for 15 minutes after cooking.
8. In a small saucepan over low heat, heat remaining 2 tablespoons extra-virgin olive oil. Add pine nuts and almonds, and toast for 3 minutes. Remove from heat.
9. Carefully place a plate over the rice pot, and carefully flip over the pot. Give the pot a few taps and a little jiggle, and slowly lift up the pot.
10. Distribute toasted almonds around the plate, sprinkle Italian parsley over top of rice, and serve warm.

Pita Chicken Burger With Spicy Yogurt
Servings: 4 | Cooking Time: 15 Minutes

Ingredients:
- ½ cup chopped green onions
- ½ cup diced tomato
- ½ cup plain low-fat yogurt
- ½ tsp coarsely ground black pepper
- 1 ½ tsp chopped fresh oregano
- 1 lb ground chicken
- 1 tbsp olive oil
- 1 tbsp Greek or Moroccan seasoning blend
- 1/3 cup Italian seasoned breadcrumbs
- 2 cups shredded lettuce
- 2 large egg whites, lightly beaten
- 2 tsps grated lemon rind, divided
- 4 pcs of 6-inch pitas, cut in half

Directions:
1. Mix thoroughly the ground chicken, 1 tsp lemon rind, egg whites, black pepper, Greek or Moroccan seasoning and green onions. Equally separate into eight parts and shaping each part into ¼ inch thick patty.
2. Put fire on medium high and place a large skillet. Fry the patties until browned or for two mins each side. Then slow the fire to medium, cover the skillet and continue cooking for another four minutes.

Mediterranean Diet Cookbook

3. In a small bowl, mix thoroughly the oregano, yogurt and 1 tsp lemon rind.
4. To serve, spread the mixture on the pita, add cooked patty, 1 tbsp tomato and ¼ cup lettuce.

Nutrition Info:
- Calories per Serving: 434.3; Carbs: 44g; Protein: 30.6g; Fat: 15.1g

Pork Shanks And Wine Sauce
Servings:5 | Cooking Time: 45 Minutes

Ingredients:
- 1-pound pork shank, trimmed
- 2 oz bacon, sliced
- ¼ cup red wine
- 1 red onion, chopped
- 1 tablespoon lemon juice
- 1 tablespoon orange juice
- 1 teaspoon garlic, diced
- 1 teaspoon ground black pepper
- 1 teaspoon kosher salt
- 1 teaspoon olive oil
- 1 teaspoon cayenne pepper
- ½ cup of water
- 1 oz celery root, roughly chopped

Directions:
1. Mix up together ground black pepper, kosher salt, and cayenne pepper.
2. Sprinkle the pork shank with the spice mixture and roast it in the hot olive oil for 3 minutes from each side. Chill the beef shank to room temperature and wrap in the bacon.
3. After this, pour water in the pan.
4. Add beef shank, onion, lemon juice, orange juice, garlic, and simmer for 5 minutes.
5. Add red wine, celery root, and close the lid.
6. Cook the meat over the low heat for 35 minutes.

Nutrition Info:
- Per Servingcalorie 358, fat 24, fiber 0.8, carbs 4.1, protein 27.7

Artichoke Beef Roast
Servings: 6 | Cooking Time: 45 Minutes

Ingredients:
- 2 lbs beef roast, cubed
- 1 tbsp garlic, minced
- 1 onion, chopped
- 1/2 tsp paprika
- 1 tbsp parsley, chopped
- 2 tomatoes, chopped
- 1 tbsp capers, chopped
- 10 oz can artichokes, drained and chopped
- 2 cups chicken stock
- 1 tbsp olive oil
- Pepper
- Salt

Directions:
1. Add oil into the instant pot and set the pot on sauté mode.
2. Add garlic and onion and sauté for 5 minutes.
3. Add meat and cook until brown.
4. Add remaining ingredients and stir well.
5. Seal pot with lid and cook on high for 35 minutes.
6. Once done, allow to release pressure naturally. Remove lid.
7. Serve and enjoy.

Nutrition Info:
- Calories 344 Fat 12.2 g Carbohydrates 9.2 g Sugar 2.6 g Protein 48.4 g Cholesterol 135 mg

Greek Chicken Stew
Servings: 8 | Cooking Time: 1 Hour And 15minutes

Ingredients:
- 10 smalls shallots, peeled
- 1 cup olive oil
- 2 teaspoons butter
- 1 (4 pound) whole chicken, cut into pieces
- 2 cloves garlic, finely chopped
- ½ cup red wine
- 1 cup tomato sauce
- 2 tablespoons chopped fresh parsley
- salt and ground black pepper to taste
- 1 pinch dried oregano, or to taste
- 2 bay leaves
- 1 ½ cups chicken stock, or more if needed

Directions:
1. In a large pot, fill half full of water and bring to a boil. Lightly salt the water and once boiling add shallots and boil uncovered for 3 minutes. Drain and quickly place on an ice bath for 5 minutes. Drain well.
2. In same pot, heat for 3 minutes and add oil and butter. Heat for 3 minutes.
3. Add chicken and shallots. Cook 15 minutes.
4. Add chopped garlic and cook for another 3 minutes or until garlic starts to turn golden.
5. Add red wine and tomato sauce. Deglaze pot.
6. Stir in bay leaves, oregano, pepper, salt, and parsley. Cook for 3 minutes.
7. Stir in chicken stock.
8. Cover and simmer for 40 minutes while occasionally stirring pot.
9. Serve and enjoy while hot with a side of rice if desired.

Nutrition Info:
- Calories per Serving: 574; Carbs: 6.8g; Protein: 31.8g; Fats: 45.3g

Meatball Gyro Pita Sandwich
Servings: 4 | Cooking Time: 30 Minutes

Ingredients:
- 1 cup Greek yogurt
- 1/4 cup cucumber, grated
- 4 teaspoons minced garlic, divided
- 1 teaspoon extra-virgin olive oil
- 1 tablespoon fresh dill
- 1 teaspoon sea salt, divided and more to taste
- 1/2 teaspoon cracked black pepper, divided and more to taste

- 1 tablespoon fresh lemon juice
- 1-pound ground chuck
- 1/4 cup Italian breadcrumbs
- 1 large egg
- 3 tablespoons chopped flat leaf Italian parsley, divided
- 1/2 teaspoon ground cumin
- 1 cup cucumbers, diced finely
- 1 cup finely diced tomatoes
- 1/2 cup finely diced red onion
- 4 flatbreads

Directions:
1. First make the tzatziki sauce by combining ¼ tsp pepper, ½ tsp salt, 1 tbsp fresh dill, 1 tsp olive oil, 1 tsp minced garlic, ¼ cup grated cucumber, 1 tbsp fresh lemon juice, and 1 cup Greek yogurt. Mix well in a Ball jar, adjust seasoning to taste if needed, cover, and refrigerate until ready to use. Best when made at least a day ahead.
2. Preheat the oven to 425°F.
3. In a large mixing bowl, combine 1-pound ground chuck, 1/4 cup dry Italian breadcrumbs, 1 large egg, 2 tablespoons chopped fresh flat-leaf Italian parsley, 1 tablespoon freshly minced garlic, 1/2 teaspoon ground cumin, 1/2 teaspoon sea salt, and 1/4 teaspoon freshly cracked black pepper.
4. Mix well to combine and then form into 16 equal sized meatballs.
5. Place meatballs on a lightly greased baking sheet and bake in the pre-heated oven for 16 minutes or until cooked through and no longer pink inside. When done, remove from oven and let it rest for 5 minutes.
6. While the meatballs are cooking, mix well a tbsp of parsley, red onions, tomatoes, and cucumbers in a bowl. Season with pepper and salt.
7. Toast flatbread in toaster oven for 5 minutes.
8. To assemble, place about 4 meatballs down the center of each flatbread. Spoon a generous amount of Tzatziki sauce on the center next to the meatballs and top with a heaping spoonful of the tomato-cucumber salad. Wrap up and enjoy!

Nutrition Info:
- Calories per Serving: 540; Carbs: 51.0g; Protein: 33.0g; Fats: 22.0g

Ancestral Roasted Chicken
Servings: 8 | Cooking Time: 60 Minutes

Ingredients:
- ½ tbsp. salt
- ½ tsp black pepper
- ½ tsp thyme
- 1 bay leaf
- 1 liter of cooking wine
- 1 whole chicken (3 lbs. preferred)
- 3 cloves garlic
- 4 tbsp orange peel, chopped coarsely

Directions:
1. Prepare chicken by placing in room temperature for at least an hour.
2. With paper towels, pat dry chicken inside and out.
3. As you begin preparing chicken seasoning, preheat oven to 450oF.
4. In a small bowl, mix thyme, pepper and salt.
5. Get 1/3 of the seasoning and wipe inside the chicken. Also place inside of the chicken the bay leaf, citrus peel and garlic.
6. Tuck the wing tips and tie chicken legs together. Spread remaining seasoning all over and around the chicken. Then place on a roasting pan.
7. Pop in the oven and bake for 50-60 minutes or until chicken is a golden brown, juices run clear or chicken things or breasts register a 160oF temperature.
8. Remove from oven and let it sit for 15 minutes more before cutting up and serving the roasted chicken.

Nutrition Info:
- Calories per Serving: 383.2; Carbs: 7.9g; Protein: 29.4g; Fat: 26.0g

Chili Lamb Meatballs
Servings:4 | Cooking Time: 10 Minutes

Ingredients:
- 1 cup lamb mince
- 1 teaspoon chili pepper
- 1 teaspoon garlic powder
- 1 teaspoon dried cilantro
- ½ teaspoon salt
- ¾ cup of water
- 1 tablespoon sunflower oil

Directions:
1. Mix up together lamb minced, chili pepper, garlic powder, dried cilantro, and salt.
2. Then add water and stir the meat mixture until homogenous.
3. Make the small meatballs with the help of the fingertips and press them gently.
4. Roast the lamb kofte in the hot sunflower oil for 4 minutes from each side.

Nutrition Info:
- Per Servingcalories 138, fat 10.5, fiber 0.1, carbs 0.6, protein 10.8

Shrimp And Vegetable Rice
Serves: 1 Cup | Cooking Time:48 Minutes

Ingredients:
- 3 TB. extra-virgin olive oil
- 1 medium yellow onion, finely chopped
- 1 TB. minced garlic
- 1 cup green peas
- 2 medium carrots, shredded (1 cup)
- 4 cups water
- 2 tsp. salt
- 10 strands saffron
- 1 tsp. turmeric
- 1/2 tsp. black pepper
- 2 cups brown rice

Directions:
1. 1/2 lb. medium raw shrimp (18 to 20), shells and veins removed

Mediterranean Diet Cookbook

2. In a large, 3-quart pot over medium heat, heat extra-virgin olive oil. Add yellow onion, and cook for 5 minutes.
3. Add garlic, green peas, and carrots, and cook for 3 minutes.
4. Add water, salt, saffron, turmeric, and black pepper; bring to a boil; and cook for about 3 minutes.
5. Add brown rice, cover, reduce heat to low, and cook for 30 minutes.
6. Gently fold shrimp into rice, cover, and cook for 10 minutes.
7. Remove from heat, fluff with a fork, cover, and set aside for 10 minutes. Serve warm.

Thyme Ginger Garlic Beef
Servings: 2 | Cooking Time: 45 Minutes

Ingredients:
- 1 lb beef roast
- 2 whole cloves
- 1/2 tsp ginger, grated
- 1/2 cup beef stock
- 1/2 tsp garlic powder
- 1/2 tsp thyme
- 1/4 tsp pepper
- 1/4 tsp salt

Directions:
1. Mix together ginger, cloves, thyme, garlic powder, pepper, and salt and rub over beef.
2. Place meat into the instant pot. Pour stock around the meat.
3. Seal pot with lid and cook on high for 45 minutes.
4. Once done, release pressure using quick release. Remove lid.
5. Shred meat using a fork and serve.

Nutrition Info:
- Calories 452 Fat 15.7 g Carbohydrates 5.2 g Sugar 0.4 g Protein 70.1 g Cholesterol 203 mg

Steaks And Greek Yogurt Mix
Servings:2 | Cooking Time: 10 Minutes

Ingredients:
- 8 oz beef steak (4 oz each steak)
- 2 teaspoons Greek yogurt
- 1 teaspoon dried oregano
- 1 teaspoon salt
- 1 teaspoon paprika
- 1 teaspoon garlic powder
- 1 tablespoon olive oil

Directions:
1. Make a marinade for steaks: whisk together Greek yogurt, dried oregano, salt, paprika, and garlic powder.
2. Rub the beef steaks with the yogurt mixture and leave to marinate for 20 minutes.
3. Preheat grill to 385F.
4. Cook the beef steaks in the grill for 5 minutes from each side.

Nutrition Info:
- Per Servingcalories 284, fat 14.4, fiber 0.9, carbs 2.5, protein 35.2

Pork Kebabs
Servings: 6 | Cooking Time: 14 Minutes

Ingredients:
- 1 yellow onion, chopped
- 1 pound pork meat, ground
- 3 tablespoons cilantro, chopped
- 1 tablespoon lime juice
- 1 garlic clove, minced
- 2 teaspoon oregano, dried
- Salt and black pepper to the taste
- A drizzle of olive oil

Directions:
1. In a bowl, mix the pork with the other ingredients except the oil, stir well and shape medium kebabs out of this mix.
2. Divide the kebabs on skewers, and brush them with a drizzle of oil.
3. Place the kebabs on your preheated grill and cook over medium heat for 7 minutes on each side.
4. Divide the kebabs between plates and serve with a side salad.

Nutrition Info:
- calories 229, fat 14, fiber 8.3, carbs 15.5, protein 12.4

Beef And Zucchini Skillet
Servings:2 | Cooking Time: 20 Minutes

Ingredients:
- 2 oz ground beef
- ½ onion, sliced
- ½ bell pepper, sliced
- 1 tablespoon butter
- ½ teaspoon salt
- 1 tablespoon tomato sauce
- 1 small zucchini, chopped
- ½ teaspoon dried oregano

Directions:
1. Place the ground beef in the skillet.
2. Add salt, butter, and dried oregano.
3. Mix up the meat mixture and cook it for 10 minutes.
4. After this, transfer the cooked ground beef in the bowl.
5. Place zucchini, bell pepper, and onion in the skillet (where the ground meat was cooking) and roast the vegetables for 7 minutes over the medium heat or until they are tender.
6. Then add cooked ground beef and tomato sauce. Mix up well.
7. Cook the beef toss for 2-3 minutes over the medium heat.

Nutrition Info:
- Per Servingcalories 182, fat 8.7, fiber 0.1, carbs 0.3, protein 24.1

Light Beef Soup
Servings: 8 | Cooking Time: 1 Hour And 10 Minutes

Ingredients:
- 1 tablespoon olive oil
- 1 large onion, chopped
- 2 cloves of garlic, minced
- 2 stalks celery, sliced

- 1-pound beef chuck, bones removed and cut into cubes
- salt and pepper to taste
- 2 carrots, peeled and diced
- 8 ounces mushrooms, sliced
- ½ teaspoon dried thyme
- 2 cups beef broth
- 2 cups chicken broth
- 2 cups water
- 1 bay leaf

Directions:
1. Heat the oil in a pot and sauté the onion, garlic, and celery until fragrant.
2. Stir in the beef chuck and season with salt and pepper.
3. Add the rest of the ingredients.
4. Close the lid and bring to a boil.
5. Allow to simmer for 60 minutes until the beef is soft.
6. Place in individual containers.
7. Put a label and store in the fridge.
8. Allow to thaw at room temperature before heating in the microwave oven.

Nutrition Info:
- Calories per serving: 252; Carbs: 10.5g; Protein: 17.2g; Fat: 15.7g

Sweet Pork Ribs
Servings:5 | Cooking Time: 35 Minutes

Ingredients:
- 1 tablespoon apple cider vinegar
- ½ cup chicken stock
- 1 oz scallions, chopped
- ¼ teaspoon sugar
- 1 tablespoon lemon juice
- 1-pound pork short ribs, chopped
- 1 cup water, for cooking
- 1 tablespoon olive oil

Directions:
1. Place pork ribs in the skillet.
2. Add olive oil and roast them for 10 minutes over the medium heat. Flip them on another side from time to time to avoid burning.
3. After this, add scallions, lemon juice, and apple cider vinegar.
4. Sprinkle the short ribs with sugar and mix up well.
5. Then add water and chicken stock.
6. Close the lid and cook the short ribs for 20 minutes over the medium heat.

Nutrition Info:
- Per Servingcalories 277, fat 19, fiber 0.2, carbs 0.8, protein 24.2

Pork And Tomato Meatloaf
Servings:8 | Cooking Time: 55 Minutes

Ingredients:
- 2 cups ground pork
- 1 egg, beaten
- ¼ cup crushed tomatoes
- 1 teaspoon salt
- 1 teaspoon ground black pepper
- 1 oz Swiss cheese, grated
- 1 teaspoon minced garlic
- 1/3 onion, diced
- ¼ cup black olives, chopped
- 1 jalapeno pepper, chopped
- 1 teaspoon dried basil
- Cooking spray

Directions:
1. Spray the loaf mold with cooking spray.
2. Then combine together ground pork, egg, crushed tomatoes, salt, ground black pepper. Grated Swiss cheese, minced garlic, onion, olives, jalapeno pepper, and dried basil.
3. Stir the mass until it is homogenous and transfer it in the prepared loaf mold.
4. Flatten the surface of meatloaf well and cover with foil.
5. Bake the meatloaf for 40 minutes at 375F.
6. Then discard the foil and bake the meal for 15 minutes more.
7. Chill the cooked meatloaf to the room temperature and then remove it from the loaf mold.
8. Slice it on the servings.

Nutrition Info:
- Per Servingcalories 265, fat 18.3, fiber 0.6, carbs 1.9, protein 22.1

Stuffed Squash Casserole
Serves: 2 Stuffed Squash | Cooking Time:50 Minutes

Ingredients:
- 10 light green summer zucchini
- 4 TB. extra-virgin olive oil
- 1 lb. ground beef
- 1 large yellow onion, finely chopped
- 1/2 cup pine nuts
- 2 tsp. salt
- 1 tsp. ground black pepper
- 1 tsp. seven spices
- 1 (16-oz.) can tomato sauce
- 1 cup water
- 1/2 tsp. garlic powder
- 1/2 tsp. onion powder
- 1/2 tsp. dried oregano

Directions:
1. Preheat the oven to 425ºF.
2. Trim off top and core out zucchini. Place zucchini on a baking sheet, and drizzle outsides with 2 tablespoons extra-virgin olive oil. Bake for 15 to 20 minutes, and set aside.
3. In a large skillet over medium heat, brown beef for 5 minutes, breaking up chunks with a wooden spoon.
4. Add yellow onion, pine nuts, remaining 2 tablespoons extra-virgin olive oil, 1 teaspoon salt, 1/2 teaspoon black pepper, and seven spices, and cook for 5 minutes.
5. In a 2-quart pot over medium heat, combine tomato sauce, water, remaining 1 teaspoon salt, remaining 1/2 teaspoon black pepper, garlic powder, onion powder, and oregano, and simmer for 10 minutes.

6. Stuff zucchini with about 3 tablespoons beef mixture each. Place stuffed zucchini in a casserole dish, gently pour tomato sauce over zucchini, and bake for 30 minutes.
7. Serve warm with a side of brown rice.

Hot Pork Meatballs
Servings: 2 | Cooking Time: 10 Minutes

Ingredients:
- 4 oz pork loin, grinded
- ½ teaspoon garlic powder
- ¼ teaspoon chili powder
- ¼ teaspoon cayenne pepper
- ¼ teaspoon ground black pepper
- ¼ teaspoon white pepper
- 1 tablespoon water
- 1 teaspoon olive oil

Directions:
1. Mix up together grinded meat, garlic powder, cayenne pepper, ground black pepper, white pepper, and water.
2. With the help of the fingertips make the small meatballs.
3. Heat up olive oil in the skillet.
4. Arrange the kofte in the oil and cook them for 10 minutes totally. Flip the kofte on another side from time to time.

Nutrition Info:
- Per Servingcalories 162, fat 10.3, fiber 0.3, carbs 1, protein 15.7

Italian Beef
Servings: 4 | Cooking Time: 35 Minutes

Ingredients:
- 1 lb ground beef
- 1 tbsp olive oil
- 1/2 cup mozzarella cheese, shredded
- 1/2 cup tomato puree
- 1 tsp basil
- 1 tsp oregano
- 1/2 onion, chopped
- 1 carrot, chopped
- 14 oz can tomatoes, diced
- Pepper
- Salt

Directions:
1. Add oil into the instant pot and set the pot on sauté mode.
2. Add onion and sauté for 2 minutes.
3. Add meat and sauté until browned.
4. Add remaining ingredients except for cheese and stir well.
5. Seal pot with lid and cook on high for 35 minutes.
6. Once done, release pressure using quick release. Remove lid.
7. Add cheese and stir well and cook on sauté mode until cheese is melted.
8. Serve and enjoy.

Nutrition Info:
- Calories 297 Fat 11.3 g Carbohydrates 11.1 g Sugar 6.2 g Protein 37.1 g Cholesterol 103 mg

Kumquat And Chicken Tagine
Servings: 6 | Cooking Time: 1 Hour And 20 Minutes

Ingredients:
- ½ tsp ground pepper
- ½ tsp salt
- ¾ tsp ground cinnamon
- 1 ½ tbsp honey
- 1 14-oz can vegetable broth
- 1 15-oz can chickpeas, rinsed
- 1 tbsp extra virgin olive oil
- 1 tbsp minced fresh ginger
- 1 tsp ground coriander
- 1 tsp ground cumin
- 1/8 tsp ground cloves
- 12-oz kumquats, seeded and roughly chopped
- 2 lbs. boneless, skinless chicken thighs, trimmed of fat and cut into 2-inch pieces
- 2 onions, thinly sliced
- 4 cloves garlic, slivered

Directions:
1. Preheat oven to 375oF.
2. On medium fire, place a heatproof casserole and heat oil.
3. Add onions and sauté for 4 minutes or until soft.
4. Add ginger and garlic, sauté for another minute.
5. Add chicken and sauté for 8 minutes.
6. Season with cloves, pepper, salt, cinnamon, cumin, and coriander. Sauté for a minute or until aromatic.
7. Add honey, chickpeas, kumquats, and broth. Bring to a boil and turn off fire.
8. Cover casserole and pop in the oven. Bake for an hour while stirring every after 15-minute intervals.

Nutrition Info:
- Calories per Serving: 412.6; Carbs: 32.1g; Protein: 43.0g; Fat: 18.7g

Lamb And Zucchini Mix
Servings: 4 | Cooking Time: 4 Hours

Ingredients:
- 2 pounds lamb stew meat, cubed
- 1 and ½ tablespoons avocado oil
- 3 zucchinis, sliced
- 1 brown onion, chopped
- 3 garlic cloves, minced
- 1 tablespoon thyme, dried
- 2 teaspoons sage, dried
- 1 cup chicken stock
- 2 tablespoons tomato paste

Directions:
1. In a slow cooker, combine the lamb with the oil, zucchinis and the rest of the ingredients, toss, put the lid on and cook on High for 4 hours.
2. Divide the mix between plates and serve right away.

Nutrition Info:
- calories 272, fat 14.5, fiber 10.1, carbs 20.3, protein 13.3

Vegetable Recipes

Vegetable Recipes

Cold Veggie Udon

Servings: 2 | Cooking Time: 10 Minutes

Ingredients:
- 2 cups Jicama, spiral
- 1/3 cup Mentsuyu, diluted 2-3 times depending on preference
- wasabi
- ¼ tsp roasted white sesame seeds
- 4 grape tomatoes, halved
- 1 soft hardboiled egg
- ½ cup tenkasu/agedama - optional
- 2 –inch daikon radish, peeled, grated and excess water squeezed
- 1 Japanese cucumber, peeled, sliced thinly and diagonally, then julienned
- 1 green onion, sliced thinly
- 2 tsp wakame seaweed
- ½ package of medium firm tofu, cut into ½ inch cubes

Directions:
1. Bring a pot of water to boil.
2. Meanwhile, in a small bowl, soak for 15 minutes the wakame seaweed in water. Once done, squeeze out water and put aside.
3. Then boil Jicama noodles and tofu for a minute or two, strain and discard hot water. Place in an ice bath until totally cold before straining again.
4. Then in a separate bowl, dilute Mentsuyu with 1/3 to 2/3s cup of water to taste. Add 3-4 ice cubes to keep Mentsuyu cold.
5. To serve, arrange noodles and tofu into two bowls. Garnish with 4 slices tomatoes, half of cucumber, half of seaweed, half of egg, half of green onion, half of sesame seeds, half of radish and half of tenkasu if using per bowl.
6. Serve with Mentsuyu on the side.

Nutrition Info:
- Calories per serving: 324; Carbs: 38.9g; Protein: 24.8g; Fat: 10.1g

Broccoli And Leek Soup

Servings: 2 | Cooking Time: 5 Minutes

Ingredients:
- 1 tbsp lemon juice
- 1 tbsp tamari
- 1 avocado, peeled and pitted
- 1 medium-sized leek, chopped
- 2 cups water
- 1 head broccoli, chopped

Directions:
1. Bring a pot of water to a boil. Add broccoli and cook for 5 minutes. Drain and cool.
2. Place all ingredients in a blender and pulse until smooth.
3. Place in a bowl and top with broccoli and leek stalks.

Nutrition Info:
- Calories per Serving: 221; Carbs: 20.9g; Protein: 5.8g; Fat: 15.2g

Celery Carrot Brown Lentils

Servings: 6 | Cooking Time: 25 Minutes

Ingredients:
- 2 cups dry brown lentils, rinsed and drained
- 2 1/2 cups vegetable stock
- 2 tomatoes, chopped
- 1/2 tsp red pepper flakes
- 1/2 tsp ground cinnamon
- 1 bay leaf
- 1 tbsp tomato paste
- 2 celery stalks, diced
- 2 carrots, grated
- 1 tbsp garlic, minced
- 2 onions, chopped
- 1/4 cup olive oil
- Pepper
- Salt

Directions:
1. Add oil into the inner pot of instant pot and set the pot on sauté mode.
2. Add celery, carrot, garlic, onion, pepper, and salt and sauté for 3 minutes.
3. Add remaining ingredients and stir everything well.
4. Seal pot with lid and cook on high for 22 minutes.
5. Once done, release pressure using quick release. Remove lid.
6. Stir well and serve.

Nutrition Info:
- Calories 137 Fat 8.8 g Carbohydrates 12.3 g Sugar 4.7 g Protein 3.1 g Cholesterol 0 mg

Chili Eggplant

Servings:3 | Cooking Time: 30 Minutes

Ingredients:
- 1 eggplant, chopped
- 1 zucchini, chopped
- 1 onion, chopped
- ½ cup of water
- 1 teaspoon olive oil
- 1 teaspoon tomato paste
- 1 teaspoon salt
- ½ teaspoon chili powder
- 1 teaspoon paprika
- 2 tomatoes, chopped

Directions:

1. Heat up olive oil in the skillet and add eggplants.
2. Roast the eggplants for 3 minutes over the medium heat and transfer them in the saucepan.
3. Then add zucchini in the skillet and roast them for 3 minutes too.
4. Add the roasted zucchini in the saucepan.
5. After this, roast onion for 4 minutes and add it in the saucepan with vegetables.
6. Add water in the saucepan.
7. Then add tomato paste, salt, chili powder, paprika, and tomatoes.
8. Close the lid and simmer the saute for 20 minutes over the low heat.

Nutrition Info:
- Per Servingcalories 104, fat 2.4, fiber 9.4, carbs 20.5, protein 3.9

Pomegranate, Squash In Quinoa Stew
Servings: 4 | Cooking Time: 65 Minutes

Ingredients:
- 1 tbsp finely chopped ginger
- 1 garlic clove, chopped
- 1 large onion, thinly sliced
- 2 tbsp olive oil
- 1 small butternut squash, deseeded and cubed
- Small handful of mint leaves
- Seeds from 1 pomegranate
- 600 ml vegetable stock
- Juice of 1 lemon
- 5 prunes, chopped roughly
- 200g quinoa
- 1 tsp ras-el-hanout or Middle Eastern spice mix

Directions:
1. Preheat oven to 350oF. In baking tray, place squash, drizzle with 1 tbsp oil, season with pepper and salt and bake until soft, around 30 to 35 minutes.
2. While waiting for squash, place a large fry pan on medium high fire and heat oil. Once oil is hot, sauté ginger and garlic until garlic is lightly browned around 2 to 3 minutes. Add onions and sauté for another 4 minutes until soft and translucent.
3. Add quinoa and spices. Cook for 3 minutes. Season with pepper and salt.
4. Add soup stock, lemon juice, and prunes. Cover and bring to a boil. Once boiling, lower fire to a simmer and for 25 minutes cook quinoa.
5. If quinoa mixture is already soft and squash is not yet done, turn off fire.
6. Once squash is soft, transfer into pan of quinoa and turn on fire to medium and cook until heated through.
7. To serve, equally transfer stew into serving bowls, garnish with pomegranate seeds and enjoy.

Nutrition Info:
- Calories per Serving: 318; Carbs: 50.0g; Protein: 11.0g; Fat: 8.2g

Summer Vegetables
Servings: 6 | Cooking Time: 1 Hour And 40 Minutes

Ingredients:
- 1 tsp dried marjoram
- 1/3 cup Parmesan cheese
- 1 small eggplant, sliced into ¼-inch thick circles
- 1 small summer squash, peeled and sliced diagonally into ¼-inch thickness
- 3 large tomatoes, sliced into ¼-inch thick circles
- ½ cup dry white wine
- ½ tsp freshly ground pepper, divided
- ½ tsp salt, divided
- 5 cloves garlic, sliced thinly
- 2 cups leeks, sliced thinly
- 4 tbsp extra virgin olive oil, divided

Directions:
1. On medium fire, place a large nonstick saucepan and heat 2 tbsp oil.
2. Sauté garlic and leeks for 6 minutes or until garlic is starting to brown. Season with pepper and salt, ¼ tsp each.
3. Pour in wine and cook for another minute. Transfer to a 2-quart baking dish.
4. In baking dish, layer in alternating pattern the eggplant, summer squash, and tomatoes. Do this until dish is covered with vegetables. If there are excess vegetables, store for future use.
5. Season with remaining pepper and salt. Drizzle with remaining olive oil and pop in a preheated 425oF oven.
6. Bake for 75 minutes. Remove from oven and top with marjoram and cheese.
7. Return to oven and bake for 15 minutes more or until veggies are soft and edges are browned.
8. Allow to cool for at least 5 minutes before serving.

Nutrition Info:
- Calories per Serving: 150; Carbs: 11.8g; Protein: 3.3g; Fat: 10.8g

Savoy Cabbage With Coconut Cream Sauce
Servings: 6 | Cooking Time: Minutes

Ingredients:
- 3 tablespoons olive oil
- 1 onion, chopped
- 4 cloves of garlic, minced
- 1 head savoy cabbage, chopped finely
- 2 cups bone broth
- 1 cup coconut milk, freshly squeezed
- 1 bay leaf
- Salt and pepper to taste
- 2 tablespoons chopped parsley

Directions:
1. Heat oil in a pot for 2 minutes.
2. Stir in the onions, bay leaf, and garlic until fragrant, around 3 minutes.
3. Add the rest of the ingredients, except for the parsley and mix well.
4. Cover pot, bring to a boil, and let it simmer for 5 minutes

or until cabbage is tender to taste.
5. Stir in parsley and serve.

Nutrition Info:
- Calories per serving: 195; Carbs: 12.3g; Protein: 2.7g; Fat: 19.7g

Stir Fried Eggplant
Servings: 2 | Cooking Time: 30 Minutes

Ingredients:
- 1 tsp cornstarch + 2 tbsp water, mixed
- 1 tsp brown sugar
- 2 tbsp oyster sauce
- 1 tbsp fish sauce
- 2 tbsp soy sauce
- ½ cup fresh basil
- 2 tbsp oil
- ¼ cup water
- 2 cups Chinese eggplant, spiral
- 1 red chili
- 6 cloves garlic, minced
- ½ purple onion, sliced thinly
- 1 3-oz package medium firm tofu, cut into slivers

Directions:
1. Prepare sauce by mixing cornstarch and water in a small bowl. In another bowl mix brown sugar, oyster sauce and fish sauce and set aside.
2. On medium high fire, place a large nonstick saucepan and heat 2 tbsp oil. Sauté chili, garlic and onion for 4 minutes. Add tofu, stir fry for 4 minutes.
3. Add eggplant noodles and stir fry for 10 minutes. If pan dries up, add water in small amounts to moisten pan and cook noodles.
4. Pour in sauce and mix well. Once simmering, slowly add cornstarch mixer while continuing to mix vigorously. Once sauce thickens add fresh basil and cook for a minute.
5. Remove from fire, transfer to a serving plate and enjoy.

Nutrition Info:
- Calories per Serving: 369; Carbs: 28.4g; Protein: 11.4g; Fat: 25.3g

Zucchini Fritters
Serves: 1 Fritter | Cooking Time:10 Minutes

Ingredients:
- 2 large zucchini, grated
- 3 whole green onions, finely chopped
- 1/4 cup fresh Italian parsley, finely chopped
- 1 tsp. dried mint
- 1/2 tsp. cayenne
- 1 tsp. salt
- 1/2 tsp. ground black pepper
- 2 large eggs
- 1/2 cup all-purpose flour
- 3 TB. water
- 1 cup extra-virgin olive oil

Directions:
1. In a large bowl, combine zucchini, green onions, Italian parsley, mint, cayenne, salt, black pepper, eggs, all-purpose flour, and water.
2. In a 3-quart pot or fryer over high heat, heat extra-virgin olive oil to 325ºF.
3. Drop batter into the fryer with a large tablespoon, and fry for 3 minutes per side or until golden brown. Do not overcrowd the pot. Remove fritters from the pot, and place on a plate lined with paper towels. Serve immediately.

Roasted Brussels Sprouts And Pecans
Servings: 7 | Cooking Time: Minutes

Ingredients:
- 1 ½ pounds fresh Brussels sprouts
- 4 tablespoons olive oil
- 4 cloves of garlic, minced
- 3 tablespoons water
- Salt and pepper to taste
- ½ cup chopped pecans

Directions:
1. Place all ingredients in the Instant Pot.
2. Combine all ingredients until well combined.
3. Close the lid and make sure that the steam release vent is set to "Venting."
4. Press the "Slow Cook" button and adjust the cooking time to 3 hours.
5. Sprinkle with a dash of lemon juice if desired.

Nutrition Info:
- Calories per serving: 161; Carbs:10.2g; Protein: 4.1g; Fat: 13.1g

Creamy Eggplants
Servings:4 | Cooking Time: 50 Minutes

Ingredients:
- 2 aubergines, sliced
- 1 cup Cheddar cheese, shredded
- ½ cup cream
- 1 teaspoon salt
- 1 teaspoon paprika
- 1 teaspoon ground turmeric
- 1 teaspoon dried dill
- 1 teaspoon olive oil
- ½ teaspoon minced garlic
- 2 eggs, beaten

Directions:
1. Mix up together cream, salt, paprika, ground turmeric, dried dill, and minced garlic. Add eggs and whisk until smooth.
2. Brush the gratin mold with olive oil and arrange the sliced aubergines inside.
3. Top the vegetables with shredded Cheddar cheese and cream mixture.
4. Cover the mold with foil and secure the edges.
5. Bake the gratin for 50 minutes at 365F.

Nutrition Info:
- Per Servingcalories 248, fat 15, fiber 10, carbs 18.5, protein 12.9

Creamy Kale And Mushrooms
Servings: 3 | Cooking Time: 15 Minutes

Ingredients:
- 3 tablespoons coconut oil
- 3 cloves of garlic, minced
- 1 onion, chopped
- 1 bunch kale, stems removed and leaves chopped
- 5 white button mushrooms, chopped
- 1 cup coconut milk
- Salt and pepper to taste

Directions:
1. Heat oil in a pot.
2. Sauté the garlic and onion until fragrant for 2 minutes.
3. Stir in mushrooms. Season with pepper and salt. Cook for 8 minutes.
4. Stir in kale and coconut milk. Simmer for 5 minutes.
5. Adjust seasoning to taste.

Nutrition Info:
- Calories per serving: 365; Carbs: 17.9g; Protein: 6g; Fat: 33.5g

Mediterranean Diet Styled Stuffed Peppers
Servings: 4 | Cooking Time: 30 Minutes

Ingredients:
- A handful of parsley, chopped roughly
- 0.40 lb. of feta cheese, crumbled finely
- 1 lb. of ready to eat quinoa
- 1 courgette, thinly sliced and quartered lengthwise
- 4 red peppers

Directions:
1. Preheat oven to 400oF.
2. Cut the peppers one by one lengthways and place on baking pan with the hollow side up. Remove and discard the seeds, season and drizzle with a tbsp. of olive oil. For fifteen minutes, roast the pepper.
3. In a fry pan, heat a tsp of olive oil and sauté the courgette. Before adding the parsley, feta and quinoa, remove fry pan from fire, season with pepper and mix well.
4. Then equally put the quinoa mixture into the hollow of the pepper and bake again in the oven for five more minutes.
5. Serve and enjoy while hot.

Nutrition Info:
- Calories per Serving: 294; Carbs: 34.2g; Protein: 13.4g; Fat: 12.2g

Paprika 'n Cajun Seasoned Onion Rings
Servings: 6 | Cooking Time: 24 Minutes

Ingredients:
- ¼ cup coconut milk
- ½ teaspoon Cajun seasoning
- ¾ cup almond flour
- 1 ½ teaspoon paprika
- 1 large white onion
- 1 teaspoon garlic powder
- 2 large eggs, beaten
- Salt and pepper to taste

Directions:
1. Preheat a pot with oil for 8 minutes.
2. Peel the onion, cut off the top and slice into circles.
3. In a mixing bowl, combine the coconut milk and the eggs.
4. Soak the onion in the egg mixture.
5. In another bowl, combine the almond flour, paprika garlic powder, Cajun seasoning, salt and pepper.
6. Dredge the onion in the almond flour mixture.
7. Place in the pot and cook in batches until golden brown, around 8 minutes per batch.

Nutrition Info:
- Calories per serving: 62; Carbs: 3.9g; Protein: 2.8g; Fat: 4.1g

Rosemary Sweet Potato
Servings:4 | Cooking Time: 40 Minutes

Ingredients:
- 4 oz Cheddar cheese, sliced
- 4 sweet potatoes
- 2 tablespoons olive oil
- ½ teaspoon salt
- ½ teaspoon dried rosemary

Directions:
1. Make the cross cuts in the sweet potatoes and sprinkle them with salt and dried rosemary.
2. Then fill every sweet potato cut with sliced Cheddar cheese and sprinkle with olive oil.
3. Wrap every sweet potato in the foil and bake at 375F for 40 minutes.
4. Discard the foil and transfer the cooked sweet potatoes in the plates.

Nutrition Info:
- Per Servingcalories 305, fat 16.4, fiber 4.1, carbs 33.5, protein 9.1

Vegetarian Cabbage Rolls
Serves: 2 Rolls | Cooking Time:1½ Hours

Ingredients:
- 1 large head green cabbage
- 1 cup long-grain rice, rinsed
- 2 medium zucchini, finely diced
- 4 TB. minced garlic
- 2 tsp. salt
- 1 tsp. ground black pepper
- 4 cups plain tomato sauce
- 2 cups water
- 1 tsp. dried mint

Directions:
1. Cut around core of cabbage with a knife, and remove core. Place cabbage, core side down, in a large, 3-quart pot. Cover cabbage with water, set over high heat, and cook for 30 minutes. Drain cabbage, set aside to cool, and separate leaves. (You need 24 leaves.)
2. In a large bowl, combine long-grain rice, zucchini, 1 tablespoon garlic, 1 teaspoon salt, and 1/2 teaspoon black pepper.
3. In a 2-quart pot, combine tomato sauce, water, remaining

Mediterranean Diet Cookbook

3 tablespoons garlic, mint, remaining 1 teaspoon salt, and remaining 1/2 teaspoon black pepper.
4. Lay each cabbage leaf flat on your work surface, spoon 2 tablespoons filling on each leaf, and roll leaf. Layer rolls in a large pot, pour sauce into the pot, cover, and cook over medium-low heat for 1 hour.
5. Let rolls rest for 20 minutes before serving warm with Greek yogurt.

Braised Kale And Carrots
Servings: 2 | Cooking Time: 6 Minutes

Ingredients:
- 1 tablespoon coconut oil
- 1 onion, sliced thinly
- 5 cloves of garlic, minced
- 3 medium carrots, sliced thinly
- 10 ounces of kale, chopped
- ½ cup water
- Salt and pepper to taste
- A dash of red pepper flakes

Directions:
1. Heat oil in a skillet over medium flame and sauté the onion and garlic until fragrant.
2. Toss in the carrots and stir for 1 minute. Add the kale and water. Season with salt and pepper to taste.
3. Close the lid and allow to simmer for 5 minutes.
4. Sprinkle with red pepper flakes.
5. Place in individual containers.
6. Put a label and store in the fridge.
7. Allow to warm at room temperature before heating in the microwave oven.

Nutrition Info:
- Calories per serving: 161; Carbs: 19.9g; Protein: 7.5g; Fat: 8.2g; Fiber: 5.9g

Instant Pot Artichoke Hearts
Servings: 6 | Cooking Time: 30 Minutes

Ingredients:
- 4 artichokes, rinsed and trimmed
- Juice from 2 small lemons, freshly squeezed
- 2 cups bone broth
- 1 tablespoon tarragon leaves
- 1 stalk, celery
- ½ cup extra virgin olive oil
- Salt and pepper to taste

Directions:
1. Place all ingredients in a pressure cooker.
2. Give a good stir.
3. Close the lid and seal the valve.
4. Pressure cook for 4 minutes.
5. Allow pressure cooker to release steam naturally.
6. Then serve and enjoy.

Nutrition Info:
- Calories per serving: 133; Carbs: 14.3g; Protein: 4.4g; Fat: 11.7g

Instant Pot Fried Veggies
Servings: 3 | Cooking Time: 6 Minutes

Ingredients:
- 1 tablespoon olive oil
- 1 onion, chopped
- 4 cloves of garlic, minced
- 2 carrots, peeled and julienned
- 1 zucchini, julienned
- 1 large potato, peeled and julienned
- ½ cup chopped tomatoes
- 1 teaspoon rosemary sprig
- Salt and pepper to taste
- Instructions
- Press the Sauté button and heat the oil.
- Sauté the onion and garlic until fragrant.
- Stir in the rest of the ingredients.
- Close the lid and make sure that the vents are sealed.
- Press the Manual button and adjust the cooking time to 1 minute.
- Do quick pressure release.
- Once the lid is open, press the Sauté button and continue stirring until the liquid has reduced.
- Once cooled, evenly divide into serving size, keep in your preferred container, and refrigerate until ready to eat.

Nutrition Info:
- Calories per serving: 97; Carbs: 10.4g; Protein: 0.5g; Fat: 4.2g

Flavors Basil Lemon Ratatouille
Servings: 8 | Cooking Time: 10 Minutes

Ingredients:
- 1 small eggplant, cut into cubes
- 1 cup fresh basil
- 2 cups grape tomatoes
- 1 onion, chopped
- 2 summer squash, sliced
- 2 zucchini, sliced
- 2 tbsp vinegar
- 2 tbsp tomato paste
- 1 tbsp garlic, minced
- 1 fresh lemon juice
- 1/4 cup olive oil
- Salt

Directions:
1. Add basil, vinegar, tomato paste, garlic, lemon juice, oil, and salt into the blender and blend until smooth.
2. Add eggplant, tomatoes, onion, squash, and zucchini into the instant pot.
3. Pour blended basil mixture over vegetables and stir well.
4. Seal pot with lid and cook on high for 10 minutes.
5. Once done, allow to release pressure naturally. Remove lid.
6. Stir well and serve.

Nutrition Info:
- Calories 103 Fat 6.8 g Carbohydrates 10.6 g Sugar 6.1 g Protein 2.4 g Cholesterol 0 mg

Eggplant With Olives
Servings: 4 | Cooking Time: 12 Minutes

Ingredients:
- 4 cups eggplants, cut into cubes
- 1/2 cup vegetable stock
- 1 tsp chili powder
- 1 cup olives, pitted and sliced
- 1 onion, chopped
- 1 tbsp olive oil
- 1/4 cup grape tomatoes
- Pepper
- Salt

Directions:
1. Add oil into the inner pot of instant pot and set the pot on sauté mode.
2. Add onion and sauté for 2 minutes.
3. Add remaining ingredients and stir everything well.
4. Seal pot with lid and cook on high for 12 minutes.
5. Once done, allow to release pressure naturally for 10 minutes then release remaining using quick release. Remove lid.
6. Stir and serve.

Nutrition Info:
- Calories 105 Fat 7.4 g Carbohydrates 10.4 g Sugar 4.1 g Protein 1.6 g Cholesterol 0 mg

Ratatouille Pasta Style
Servings: 4 | Cooking Time: 25 Minutes

Ingredients:
- freshly ground black pepper
- ½ cup shredded fresh basil leaves
- 1 tsp salt
- 4 plum tomatoes, coarsely chopped
- 1 red bell pepper, julienned
- 1 small zucchini, spiralized
- 1 small eggplant, spiralized
- 1 small bay leaf
- 4 garlic cloves, peeled and minced
- 1 onion, sliced thinly
- 3 tbsp olive oil

Directions:
1. Place a large nonstick saucepan on medium slow fire and heat oil.
2. Add bay leaf, garlic and onion. Sauté until onions are translucent and soft.
3. Add eggplant and cook for 7 minutes while occasionally stirring.
4. Add salt, tomatoes, red bell pepper and zucchini then increase fire to medium high. Continue cooking until veggies are tender around 5 to 7 minutes.
5. Turn off fire and add pepper and basil. Stir to mix.
6. Serve and enjoy.

Nutrition Info:
- Calories per Serving: 175; Carbs: 21.1g; Protein: 2.0g; Fat: 10.5g

Garlic Parmesan Artichokes
Servings: 4 | Cooking Time: 10 Minutes

Ingredients:
- 4 artichokes, wash, trim, and cut top
- 1/2 cup vegetable broth
- 1/4 cup parmesan cheese, grated
- 1 tbsp olive oil
- 2 tsp garlic, minced
- Salt

Directions:
1. Pour broth into the instant pot then place steamer rack in the pot.
2. Place artichoke steam side down on steamer rack into the pot.
3. Sprinkle garlic and grated cheese on top of artichokes and season with salt. Drizzle oil over artichokes.
4. Seal pot with lid and cook on high for 10 minutes.
5. Once done, release pressure using quick release. Remove lid.
6. Serve and enjoy.

Nutrition Info:
- Calories 132 Fat 5.2 g Carbohydrates 17.8 g Sugar 1.7 g Protein 7.9 g Cholesterol 4 mg

Refreshing Greek Salad
Servings: 8 | Cooking Time: 0 Minutes

Ingredients:
- ½ red onion, sliced
- 1/3 cup diced oil packed dried tomatoes, oil drained and reserved
- 3 cups diced roma tomatoes
- 1 cup black olives, pitted and sliced
- 1 ½ cups crumbled feta cheese
- 3 cucumbers, seeded and ribbon cut

Directions:
1. Mix thoroughly the red onion, 2 tbsp of reserved sun-dried tomato oil, sundried tomatoes, roma tomatoes, olives, feta cheese and cucumbers in a large salad bowl.
2. Serve and enjoy.

Nutrition Info:
- Calories per Serving: 123; Carbs: 7.1g; Protein: 5.3g; Fat: 8.6g

Vegetarian Bowtie Veggie Pasta
Serves: 1 Cup | Cooking Time: 20 Minutes

Ingredients:
- 2 tsp. salt
- 1 lb. bowtie pasta
- 2 TB. extra-virgin olive oil
- 2 cups crimini mushrooms, cleaned and sliced
- 2 TB. minced garlic
- 1 cup broccoli florets
- 1/2 cup sun-dried tomatoes
- 2 TB. unsalted butter
- 2 cups fresh arugula
- 1 tsp. black pepper

Mediterranean Diet Cookbook

- 1 tsp. crushed red pepper flakes

Directions:
1. Bring a large pot of water to a boil over high heat. Add 1 teaspoon salt and bowtie pasta, stir, and cook for 8 minutes.
2. In a large skillet over medium heat, heat extra-virgin olive oil. Add crimini mushrooms, and cook for 4 minutes.
3. Add garlic, broccoli, and sun-dried tomatoes, and cook for 3 minutes.
4. Add remaining 1 teaspoon salt, unsalted butter, arugula, black pepper, and crushed red pepper flakes. Toss, and cook for 2 minutes.
5. Using a slotted spoon, transfer pasta to the skillet, toss pasta with vegetables, and serve warm.

Sweet And Savory Couscous
Serves: 1 Cup | Cooking Time:23 Minutes

Ingredients:
- 3 TB. extra-virgin olive oil
- 1 large white onion, finely chopped
- 1/2 cup pine nuts
- 2 large carrots, chopped
- 1 cup green peas
- 1 cup golden raisins
- 5 cups vegetable broth
- 1 tsp. salt
- 1/2 tsp. ground cloves
- 1/2 tsp. ground cinnamon
- 1/2 tsp. ground allspice
- 1/2 tsp. ground ginger
- 1 tsp. seven spices
- 1 tsp. ground coriander seeds
- 1/4 cup fresh parsley, finely chopped
- 2 cups instant couscous

Directions:
1. In a large pot over medium heat, heat extra-virgin olive oil. Add white onion, and cook, stirring with a wooden spoon, for 5 minutes.
2. Add pine nuts, and cook for 3 more minutes.
3. Add carrots, green peas, and golden raisins, and cook for 3 minutes.
4. Add vegetable broth, salt, cloves, cinnamon, allspice, ginger, seven spices, and coriander, and cook for 10 minutes.
5. Add parsley and couscous, and cook for 2 minutes. Remove from heat, cover, and set aside for 10 minutes. Fluff couscous with a fork, cover, and set aside for 5 more minutes. Serve warm.

Mushroom And Potato Mix
Servings:4 | Cooking Time: 30 Minutes

Ingredients:
- 2 cups cremini mushrooms, sliced
- 2 potatoes, chopped
- 1 red onion, sliced
- 1 cup of water
- 1 tablespoon sunflower oil
- 1 teaspoon chili powder
- 1 teaspoon paprika
- 1 teaspoon salt
- 1 tablespoon sour cream
- 1/3 cup white beans, cooked

Directions:
1. Heat up olive oil in the skillet and add cremini mushrooms.
2. Sprinkle them with chili powder, paprika, and salt.
3. Add onion and roast the vegetables for 5 minutes.
4. After this, transfer the mushroom mixture in the pot.
5. Add potatoes, white beans, and water.
6. Then add sour cream and close the lid.
7. Bake the pot with stew for 25 minutes at 365F.

Nutrition Info:
- Per Servingcalories 187, fat 4.7, fiber 6.1, carbs 31, protein 6.7

Indian Bell Peppers And Potato Stir Fry
Servings: 2 | Cooking Time: 15 Minutes

Ingredients:
- 1 tablespoon oil
- ½ teaspoon cumin seeds
- 4 cloves of garlic, minced
- 4 potatoes, scrubbed and halved
- Salt and pepper to taste
- 5 tablespoons water
- 2 bell peppers, seeded and julienned
- Chopped cilantro for garnish

Directions:
1. Heat oil in a skillet over medium flame and toast the cumin seeds until fragrant.
2. Add the garlic until fragrant.
3. Stir in the potatoes, salt, pepper, water, and bell peppers.
4. Close the lid and allow to simmer for at least 10 minutes.
5. Garnish with cilantro before cooking time ends.
6. Place in individual containers.
7. Put a label and store in the fridge.
8. Allow to thaw at room temperature before heating in the microwave oven.

Nutrition Info:
- Calories per serving: 83; Carbs: 7.3g; Protein: 2.8g; Fat: 6.4g; Fiber:1.7 g

Cheesy Asparagus
Servings:6 | Cooking Time: 25 Minutes

Ingredients:
- 3 tablespoons olive oil
- 1 teaspoon Italian seasonings
- 2 oz Feta, crumbled
- ½ teaspoon salt
- 1 teaspoon lemon juice
- 1-pound asparagus

Directions:
1. Line the baking tray with baking paper.
2. Chop the asparagus roughly and transfer it in the baking tray.
3. Sprinkle the vegetables with olive oil and Italian seasonings.

4. Mix up well with the help of the fingertips.
5. Bake the asparagus for 25 minutes at 365F or until they are tender.
6. Transfer the cooked asparagus in the serving plates and sprinkle with lemon juice and crumbled Feta cheese.

Nutrition Info:
- Per Servingcalories 103, fat 9.3, fiber 1.6, carbs 3.4, protein 3

Sweet Potatoes Oven Fried
Servings: 7 | Cooking Time: 30 Minutes

Ingredients:
- 1 small garlic clove, minced
- 1 tsp grated orange rind
- 1 tbsp fresh parsley, chopped finely
- ¼ tsp pepper
- ¼ tsp salt
- 1 tbsp olive oil
- 4 medium sweet potatoes, peeled and sliced to ¼-inch thickness

Directions:
1. In a large bowl mix well pepper, salt, olive oil and sweet potatoes.
2. In a greased baking sheet, in a single layer arrange sweet potatoes.
3. Pop in a preheated 400oF oven and bake for 15 minutes, turnover potato slices and return to oven. Bake for another 15 minutes or until tender.
4. Meanwhile, mix well in a small bowl garlic, orange rind and parsley, sprinkle over cooked potato slices and serve.
5. You can store baked sweet potatoes in a lidded container and just microwave whenever you want to eat it. Do consume within 3 days.

Nutrition Info:
- Calories per Serving: 176; Carbs: 36.6g; Protein: 2.5g; Fat: 2.5g

Cheese Onion Spread
Servings:6 | Cooking Time: 10 Minutes

Ingredients:
- 3 onions, chopped
- 1 cup cream
- ½ cup Swiss cheese, shredded
- 1 teaspoon scallions, chopped
- ½ teaspoon chili flakes
- ¾ teaspoon cayenne pepper
- 1 tablespoon butter

Directions:
1. Melt the butter and add onions.
2. Cook the onions until they are translucent.
3. Then pour cream in the saucepan and bring to boil.
4. Add scallions, Swiss cheese, chili flakes, cayenne pepper, and bring the mixture to boil.
5. After this, add onions.
6. With the help of the hand blender blend the dip until homogenous.
7. Transfer it in the bowl and leave in the fridge for 10 minutes.

Nutrition Info:
- Per Servingcalories 100, fat 6.7, fiber 1.3, carbs 7, protein 3.4

Thyme Mushrooms
Servings:3 | Cooking Time: 20 Minutes

Ingredients:
- 3 Portobello mushroom caps
- ½ teaspoon thyme
- ¼ teaspoon salt
- 4 teaspoons butter

Directions:
1. Place the mushroom caps in the tray and sprinkle them with salt and thyme.
2. Then fill the mushrooms with butter.
3. Bake Portobello caps for 20 minutes at 355F.

Nutrition Info:
- Per Servingcalories 65, fat 5.1, fiber 1.1, carbs 3.1, protein 3.1

Mushroom And Zucchini Pie
Servings:6 | Cooking Time: 60 Minutes

Ingredients:
- ½ onion, chopped
- 1 zucchini, chopped
- 1 green bell pepper, chopped
- ¼ cup mushrooms, chopped
- 3 eggs, beaten
- 1 tablespoon sour cream
- 2 oz Feta, crumbled
- 5 oz yeast roll dough
- 1 tablespoon olive oil
- 1 teaspoon salt

Directions:
1. Place the onion, zucchini, bell peppers, and mushrooms in the tray and sprinkle with salt and olive oil.
2. Bake the vegetables for 25 minutes at 365F. Stir them from time to time.
3. Meanwhile, roll up the dough and place it in the springform pan.
4. Flatten it well and spread with sour cream and Feta cheese.
5. Then combine the baked vegetables and eggs.
6. Put the egg mixture over the cheese and flatten well.
7. Bake the strata for 35 minutes at 375F.

Nutrition Info:
- Per Servingcalories 178, fat 9.8, fiber 1.8, carbs 16, protein 6.8

Cold Cucumber Soup

Servings: 4 | Cooking Time: Minutes

Ingredients:
- Chopped fresh dill
- Pepper and salt to taste
- 1 cup fat free plain yogurt
- 1 ½ cups fat free half and half
- 1 ½ cups low-sodium chicken broth
- Juice of 1 lemon
- ½ cup chopped fresh parsley
- 6 medium cucumbers, peeled, halved lengthwise, seeds scraped out and chopped

Directions:
1. In a blender, puree lemon juice, parsley and cucumbers.
2. Pour half of puree in a bowl and put aside.
3. In blender, add yogurt plus half and half on remaining pureed cucumber. Mix with a spoon before pureeing to mix well.
4. Pour back into blender the cucumber puree in a bowl, puree again to mix.
5. Season with pepper and salt.
6. Puree to mix.
7. Refrigerate for at least two hours before serving cold.

Nutrition Info:
- Calories per Serving: 140; Carbs: 21.3g; Protein: 8.0g; Fat: 3.0g

Ginger Vegetable Stir Fry

Servings: 4 | Cooking Time: 5 Minutes

Ingredients:
- 1 tablespoon oil
- 3 cloves of garlic, minced
- 1 onion, chopped
- 1 thumb-size ginger, sliced
- 1 tablespoon water
- 1 large carrots, peeled and julienned
- 1 large green bell pepper, seeded and julienned
- 1 large yellow bell pepper, seeded and julienned
- 1 large red bell pepper, seeded and julienned
- 1 zucchini, julienned
- Salt and pepper to taste

Directions:
1. Heat oil in a skillet over medium flame and sauté the garlic, onion, and ginger until fragrant.
2. Stir in the rest of the ingredients and adjust the flame to high.
3. Keep on stirring for at least 5 minutes until vegetables are half-cooked.
4. Place in individual containers.
5. Put a label and store in the fridge.
6. Allow to thaw at room temperature before heating in the microwave oven.

Nutrition Info:
- Calories per serving: 102; Carbs: 13.6g; Protein:0 g; Fat: 2g; Fiber: 7.6g

Tomato And Palm Salad

Servings:2 | Cooking Time: 0 Minutes

Ingredients:
- ½ cup heart of palm, canned, chopped
- ½ cup cherry tomatoes, halved
- 1 teaspoon balsamic vinegar
- 4 oz Feta cheese, chopped
- ½ teaspoon basil leaves
- ½ teaspoon ground black pepper
- 1 tablespoon olive oil

Directions:
1. Put the chopped heart of palm, cherry tomatoes, Feta cheese, and basil leaves in the salad bowl. Shake the ingredients gently.
2. Then sprinkle the salad with balsamic vinegar, ground black pepper, and olive oil.
3. Mix up the salad with the help of two spoons gently.

Nutrition Info:
- Per Servingcalories 230, fat 19.4, fiber 1.6, carbs 6.1, protein 9.5

Chilli Broccoli

Servings:3 | Cooking Time: 10 Minutes

Ingredients:
- 1 cup broccoli florets
- 1 chili pepper, chopped
- 1 tablespoon soy sauce
- 1 tablespoon olive oil
- 1 garlic clove, chopped
- ½ teaspoon lemon juice
- ½ teaspoon chili flakes

Directions:
1. Heat up olive oil in the wok and add broccoli florets.
2. Sprinkle them with chili flakes and roast for 5 minutes. Stir the vegetables from time to time.
3. Then drizzle the broccoli with lemon juice and soy sauce.
4. Add chili pepper, garlic, and lemon juice. Mix up well.
5. Cook the broccoli for 5 minutes more over the medium heat.

Nutrition Info:
- Per Servingcalories 55, fat 4.8, fiber 0.9, carbs 2.9, protein 1.3

Orange Lettuce Salad

Servings:4 | Cooking Time: 5 Minutes

Ingredients:
- 1-pound Romaine lettuce
- 2 tablespoons orange juice
- 1 teaspoon olive oil
- 1 tablespoon Parmesan, grated
- ½ teaspoon balsamic vinegar
- 1 teaspoon sesame oil

Directions:
1. Preheat the grill to medium heat.
2. Cut the Romaine lettuce lengthwise.

3. Then brush the grill with olive oil.
4. Place the lettuce in the grill and cook it for 2 minutes from each side.
5. Meanwhile, make the dressing: whisk together olive oil, orange juice, balsamic vinegar, and sesame oil.
6. Place the grilled lettuce in the salad plates and sprinkle with Parmesan.
7. Then sprinkle it with dressing.

Nutrition Info:
- Per Servingcalories 50, fat 3.3, fiber 0.7, carbs 4.4, protein 1.7

Cold Watermelon Gazpacho
Servings: 2 | Cooking Time: 0 Minutes

Ingredients:
- 2 basil leaves
- ¼ cup coconut sugar
- 1 tsp kosher salt
- ¼ cup vinegar
- 1 Thai Chili
- ¼ cup green bell pepper, chopped
- ¼ cup red onion, chopped
- ¼ cup cucumber, chopped
- 2 cups ripe tomatoes, chopped
- 2 cups watermelon, chopped

Directions:
1. Combine the tomato, watermelon, onion, cucumber, bell pepper, vinegar, chili, salt and pepper to taste. Blend to a coarse texture.
2. Chill for an hour. Serve cold.

Nutrition Info:
-
- Calories per Serving 133; Carbs: 32.2g; Protein: 1.6g; Fat: 0.3g

Cheese And Broccoli Balls
Servings: 4 | Cooking Time: 5 Minutes

Ingredients:
- ¾ cup almond flour
- 2 large eggs
- 2 teaspoons baking powder
- 4 ounces fresh broccoli
- 4 ounces mozzarella cheese
- 7 tablespoons flaxseed meal
- Salt and Pepper to taste
- ¼ cup fresh chopped dill
- ¼ cup mayonnaise
- ½ tablespoon lemon juice
- Salt and pepper to taste

Directions:
1. To make the cheese and broccoli balls: Place broccoli in food processor and pulse into small pieces. Transfer to a bowl.
2. Add baking powder, ¼ cup flaxseed meal, almond flour, and cheese. Season with pepper and salt if the desired. Mix well. Place remaining flaxseed meal in a small bowl.
3. Add eggs and combine thoroughly. Roll the batter into 1-inch balls. And then roll in flaxseed meal to coat the balls.
4. Cook balls in a 375oF deep fryer until golden brown, about 5 minutes. Transfer cooked balls on to a paper towel lined plate.
5. Meanwhile, make the sauce by combining all ingredients in a medium bowl.
6. Serve cheese and broccoli balls with the dipping sauce on the side.

Nutrition Info:
- Calories per serving: 312; Protein: 18.4g; Carbs: 9.6g; Fat: 23.2g

Mushroom-cauliflower Risotto
Servings: 6 | Cooking Time: 30 Minutes

Ingredients:
- 1 cup heavy cream
- 1 large shallot, minced
- 1 small onion, diced
- 1/2 cup grated Parmesan cheese
- 2 cup chicken stock, divided
- 2 tablespoons chopped fresh flat-leaf parsley
- 2 tablespoons olive oil
- 4 cups riced cauliflower
- 6 cloves garlic, minced
- 8 ounces cremini mushrooms, thinly sliced
- Sea salt and black pepper, to taste

Directions:
1. On medium the fire, place a large nonstick pan and heat olive oil.
2. Sauté garlic for a minute. Add onions and sauté for 5 minutes.
3. Stir in mushrooms and sauté until soft, about 8 minutes.
4. Add chicken stock and bring to a boil.
5. Stir in cauliflower and cook for ten minutes or until tender but not mushy.
6. Stir in heavy cream and lower the fire to low. Mix well.
7. Season with pepper, salt, parsley and Parmesan cheese.
8. Cook until heated through, about 5 minutes.
9. Serve and enjoy.

Nutrition Info:
- Calories per serving: 297; Protein: 7.0g; Carbs: 9.7g; Fat: 26.0g

Poultry Recipes

Poultry Recipes

Curry Chicken, Artichokes And Olives
Servings: 6 | Cooking Time: 7 Hours

Ingredients:
- 2 pounds chicken breasts, boneless, skinless and cubed
- 12 ounces canned artichoke hearts, drained
- 1 cup chicken stock
- 1 red onion, chopped
- 1 tablespoon white wine vinegar
- 1 cup kalamata olives, pitted and chopped
- 1 tablespoon curry powder
- 2 teaspoons basil, dried
- Salt and black pepper to the taste
- ¼ cup rosemary, chopped

Directions:
1. In your slow cooker, combine the chicken with the artichokes, olives and the rest of the ingredients, put the lid on and cook on Low for 7 hours.
2. Divide the mix between plates and serve hot.

Nutrition Info:
- calories 275, fat 11.9, fiber 7.6, carbs 19.7, protein 18.7

Greek Chicken Bites
Servings: 6 | Cooking Time: 20 Minutes

Ingredients:
- 1-pound chicken fillet
- 1 tablespoon Greek seasoning
- 1 teaspoon sesame oil
- ½ teaspoon salt
- 1 teaspoon balsamic vinegar

Directions:
1. Cut the chicken fingers on small tenders (fingers) and sprinkle them with Greek seasoning, salt, and balsamic vinegar. Mix up well with the help of the fingertips.
2. Then sprinkle chicken with sesame oil and shake gently.
3. Line the baking tray with parchment.
4. Place the marinated chicken fingers in the tray in one layer.
5. Bake the chicken fingers for 20 minutes at 355F. Flip them on another side after 10 minutes of cooking.

Nutrition Info:
- Per Servingcalories 154, fat 6.4, fiber 0, carbs 0.8, protein 22

Grilled Chicken On The Bone
Serves: 1 Drumstick And 1 Thigh | Cooking Time: 40 Minutes

Ingredients:
- 4 TB. minced garlic
- 1/2 cup fresh lemon juice
- 1/2 cup extra-virgin olive oil
- 1 TB. dried oregano
- 2 tsp. salt
- 1 tsp. ground black pepper
- 1 tsp. cayenne
- 1 tsp. paprika
- 4 chicken drumsticks
- 4 chicken thighs

Directions:
1. In a small bowl, whisk together garlic, lemon juice, extra-virgin olive oil, oregano, salt, black pepper, cayenne, and paprika.
2. Place chicken drumsticks and chicken thighs in a large bowl, pour 1/2 of dressing over chicken, mix to coat evenly, and set in the refrigerator to marinate for 1 hour.
3. Preheat the grill to medium-high heat.
4. Place chicken evenly on the grill, and cook for 5 minutes per side.
5. Reduce heat to medium-low, cover the grill, and cook chicken for 15 minutes per side or until juices run clear and internal temperature of chicken reads 175ºF.
6. Remove chicken from the grill, and let rest for 5 minutes before serving warm.

Creamy Coriander Chicken
Servings: 4 | Cooking Time: 55 Minutes

Ingredients:
- 2 chicken breasts, boneless, skinless and halved
- 2 tablespoons avocado oil
- ½ teaspoon hot paprika
- 1 cup chicken stock
- 1 tablespoon almonds, chopped
- 2 spring onions, chopped
- 2 garlic cloves, minced
- ¼ cup heavy cream
- A handful coriander, chopped
- Salt and black pepper to the taste

Directions:
1. Grease a roasting pan with the oil, add the chicken, paprika and the rest of the ingredients except the coriander and the heavy cream, toss, introduce in the oven and bake at 360 degrees F for 40 minutes.
2. Add the cream and the coriander, toss, bake for 15 minutes more, divide between plates and serve.

Nutrition Info:
- calories 225, fat 8.9, fiber 10.2, carbs 20.8, protein 17.5

Mediterranean Diet Cookbook

Chipotle Turkey And Tomatoes

Servings: 4 | Cooking Time: 1 Hour

Ingredients:
- 2 pounds cherry tomatoes, halved
- 3 tablespoons olive oil
- 1 red onion, roughly chopped
- 1 big turkey breast, skinless, boneless and sliced
- 3 garlic cloves, chopped
- 3 red chili peppers, chopped
- 4 tablespoons chipotle paste
- Zest of ½ lemon, grated
- Juice of 1 lemon
- Salt and black pepper to the taste
- A handful coriander, chopped

Directions:
1. Heat up a pan with the oil over medium-high heat, add the turkey slices, cook for 4 minutes on each side and transfer to a roasting pan.
2. Heat up the pan again over medium-high heat, add the onion, garlic and chili peppers and sauté for 2 minutes.
3. Add chipotle paste, sauté for 3 minutes more and pour over the turkey slices.
4. Toss the turkey slices with the chipotle mix, also add the rest of the ingredients except the coriander, introduce in the oven and bake at 400 degrees F for 45 minutes.
5. Divide everything between plates, sprinkle the coriander on top and serve.

Nutrition Info:
- calories 264, fat 13.2, fiber 8.7, carbs 23.9, protein 33.2

Sage And Nutmeg Chicken

Servings:6 | Cooking Time: 20 Minutes

Ingredients:
- 2-pound chicken breast, skinless, boneless
- 2 tablespoons lemon juice
- 1 teaspoon sage
- ½ teaspoon ground nutmeg
- ½ teaspoon dried oregano
- 1 teaspoon paprika
- 1 teaspoon onion powder
- 2 tablespoons olive oil
- 1 teaspoon chili flakes
- 1 teaspoon salt
- 1 teaspoon apple cider vinegar

Directions:
1. Make the marinade: whisk together apple cider vinegar, salt, chili flakes, olive oil, onion powder, paprika, dried oregano, ground nutmeg, sage, and lemon juice.
2. Then rub the chicken with marinade carefully and leave for 25 minutes to marinate.
3. Meanwhile, preheat grill to 385F.
4. Place the marinated chicken breast in the grill and cook it for 10 minutes from each side.
5. Cut the cooked chicken on the servings.

Nutrition Info:
- Per Servingcalories 218, fat 8.6, fiber 0.3, carbs 0.9, protein 32.2

Herbed Almond Turkey

Servings: 4 | Cooking Time: 40 Minutes

Ingredients:
- 1 big turkey breast, skinless, boneless and cubed
- 1 tablespoon olive oil
- ½ cup chicken stock
- 1 tablespoon basil, chopped
- 1 tablespoon rosemary, chopped
- 1 tablespoon oregano, chopped
- 1 tablespoon parsley, chopped
- 3 garlic cloves, minced
- ½ cup almonds, toasted and chopped
- 3 cups tomatoes, chopped

Directions:
1. Heat up a pan with the oil over medium-high heat, add the turkey and the garlic and brown for 5 minutes.
2. Add the stock and the rest of the ingredients, bring to a simmer over medium heat and cook for 35 minutes.
3. Divide the mix between plates and serve.

Nutrition Info:
- calories 297, fat 11.2, fiber 9.2, carbs 19.4, protein 23.6

Balsamic Chicken Tortillas

Servings:2 | Cooking Time: 15 Minutes

Ingredients:
- 1 bell pepper
- ½ red onion, peeled
- 5 oz chicken fillets
- 1 garlic clove, sliced
- 1 tablespoon olive oil
- 1 teaspoon balsamic vinegar
- 1 teaspoon chili pepper
- ½ teaspoon salt
- 1 teaspoon lemon juice
- 2 flour tortillas

Directions:
1. Cut the bell pepper and chicken fillet on the wedges.
2. Then slice the onion.
3. Pour olive oil in the skillet and heat it up.
4. Add chicken wedges and sprinkle them with chili pepper and salt.
5. Roast the chicken for 4 minutes. Stir it from time to time.
6. After this, add lemon juice and balsamic vinegar. Mix up well.
7. Add bell pepper, onion, and garlic clove.
8. Roast fajitas for 10 minutes over the medium-high heat. Stir it from time to time.
9. Put the cooked fajitas on the tortillas and transfer in the serving plates.

Nutrition Info:
- Per Servingcalories 363, fat 14.1, fiber 2.5, carbs 33.9, protein 25.2

Chicken And Lemongrass Sauce
Servings:4 | Cooking Time: 20 Minutes

Ingredients:
- 1 tablespoon dried dill
- 1 teaspoon butter, melted
- ½ teaspoon lemongrass
- ½ teaspoon cayenne pepper
- 1 teaspoon tomato sauce
- 3 tablespoons sour cream
- 1 teaspoon salt
- 10 oz chicken fillet, cubed

Directions:
1. Make the sauce: in the saucepan whisk together lemongrass, tomato sauce, sour cream, salt, and dried dill.
2. Bring the sauce to boil.
3. Meanwhile, pour melted butter in the skillet.
4. Add cubed chicken fillet and roast it for 5 minutes. Stir it from time to time.
5. Then place the chicken cubes in the hot sauce.
6. Close the lid and cook the meal for 10 minutes over the low heat.

Nutrition Info:
- Per Servingcalories 166, fat 8.2, fiber 0.2, carbs 1.1, protein 21

Chicken And Parsley Sauce
Servings:4 | Cooking Time: 25 Minutes

Ingredients:
- 1 cup ground chicken
- 2 oz Parmesan, grated
- 1 tablespoon olive oil
- 2 tablespoons fresh parsley, chopped
- 1 teaspoon chili pepper
- 1 teaspoon paprika
- ½ teaspoon dried oregano
- ¼ teaspoon garlic, minced
- ½ teaspoon dried thyme
- 1/3 cup crushed tomatoes

Directions:
1. Heat up olive oil in the skillet.
2. Add ground chicken and sprinkle it with chili pepper, paprika, dried oregano, dried thyme, and parsley. Mix up well.
3. Cook the chicken for 5 minutes and add crushed tomatoes. Mix up well.
4. Close the lid and simmer the chicken mixture for 10 minutes over the low heat.
5. Then add grated Parmesan and mix up.
6. Cook chicken bolognese for 5 minutes more over the medium heat.

Nutrition Info:
- Per Servingcalories 154, fat 9.3, fiber 1.1, carbs 3, protein 15.4

Slow Cooked Chicken And Capers Mix
Servings: 4 | Cooking Time: 7 Hours

Ingredients:
- 2 chicken breasts, skinless, boneless and halved
- 2 cups canned tomatoes, crushed
- 2 garlic cloves, minced
- 1 yellow onion, chopped
- 2 cups chicken stock
- 2 tablespoons capers, drained
- ¼ cup rosemary, chopped
- Salt and black pepper to the taste

Directions:
1. In your slow cooker, combine the chicken with the tomatoes, capers and the rest of the ingredients, put the lid on and cook on Low for 7 hours.
2. Divide the mix between plates and serve.

Nutrition Info:
- calories 292, fat 9.4, fiber 11.8, carbs 25.1, protein 36.4

Chicken And Olives
Servings: 4 | Cooking Time: 15 Minutes

Ingredients:
- 4 chicken breasts, skinless and boneless
- 2 tablespoons garlic, minced
- 1 tablespoon oregano, dried
- Salt and black pepper to the taste
- 2 tablespoons olive oil
- ½ cup chicken stock
- Juice of 1 lemon
- 1 cup red onion, chopped
- 1 and ½ cups tomatoes, cubed
- ¼ cup green olives, pitted and sliced
- A handful parsley, chopped

Directions:
1. Heat up a pan with the oil over medium-high heat, add the chicken, garlic, salt and pepper and brown for 2 minutes on each side.
2. Add the rest of the ingredients, toss, bring the mix to a simmer and cook over medium heat for 13 minutes.
3. Divide the mix between plates and serve.

Nutrition Info:
- calories 135, fat 5.8, fiber 3.4, carbs 12.1, protein 9.6

Chicken And Sweet Potatoes
Servings: 6 | Cooking Time: 40 Minutes

Ingredients:
- 2 pounds chicken breasts, skinless, boneless and sliced
- 2 tablespoons harissa seasoning
- Juice of 1 lemon
- Zest of 1 lemon, grated
- ¼ cup olive oil
- Salt and black pepper to the taste
- 2 sweet potatoes, peeled and roughly cubed
- 1 sweet onion, chopped
- ½ cup feta cheese, crumbled
- ½ cup green olives, pitted and smashed

Mediterranean Diet Cookbook

Directions:
1. In a roasting pan, combine the chicken with the seasoning and the rest of the ingredients except the cheese and the olives, toss and bake at 425 degrees F for 40 minutes.
2. In a bowl, combine the cheese with the smashed olives and stir well.
3. Divide the chicken and sweet potatoes between plates, top each serving with the cheese and olives mix and serve right away.

Nutrition Info:
- calories 303, fat 9.5, fiber 9.2, carbs 21.5, protein 13.6

Chicken And Olives Bowls
Servings:4 | Cooking Time: 10 Minutes

Ingredients:
- 4 oz chicken fillet, chopped
- ¼ cup black olives, chopped
- 2 cups lettuce, chopped
- 1 tablespoon mayo sauce
- 1 teaspoon lemon juice
- ½ oz Parmesan cheese, shaved
- 1 teaspoon olive oil
- ½ teaspoon ground black pepper
- ½ teaspoon coconut oil

Directions:
1. Sprinkle the chicken fillet with ground black pepper.
2. Heat up coconut oil and add chopped chicken fillet.
3. Roast it got 10 minutes or until it is cooked. Stir it from time to time.
4. Meanwhile, mix up together black olives, lettuce, Parmesan in the bowl.
5. Make mayo dressing: whisk together mayo sauce, olive oil, and lemon juice.
6. Add the cooked chicken in the salad and shake well.
7. Pour the mayo sauce dressing over the salad.

Nutrition Info:
- Per Servingcalories 167, fat 13.6, fiber 0.5, carbs 2.2, protein 9.6

Chili Chicken Fillets
Servings:8 | Cooking Time: 7.5 Hours

Ingredients:
- 4 chicken fillets (5 oz each fillet)
- 8 bacon slices
- 1 teaspoon chili pepper
- 1 tablespoon olive oil
- ½ teaspoon salt
- 1 garlic clove, minced

Directions:
1. Cut every chicken fillet lengthwise.
2. In the shallow bowl mix up together chili pepper, olive oil, minced garlic, and salt.
3. Rub every chicken fillet with oil mixture and wrap in the sliced bacon.
4. Transfer the prepared chicken fillets in the baking dish and cover with foil.
5. Bake the chicken fillets for 35 minutes at 365F.

Nutrition Info:
- Per Servingcalories 234, fat 15.2, fiber 0.5, carbs 8, protein 16.6

Duck And Tomato Sauce
Servings: 4 | Cooking Time: 2 Hours

Ingredients:
- 4 duck legs
- 2 yellow onions, sliced
- 4 garlic cloves, minced
- ¼ cup parsley, chopped
- A pinch of salt and black pepper
- 1 teaspoon herbs de Provence
- 1 cup tomato sauce
- 2 cups black olives, pitted and sliced

Directions:
1. In a baking dish, combine the duck legs with the onions, garlic and the rest of the ingredients, introduce in the oven and bake at 370 degrees F for 2 hours.
2. Divide the mix between plates and serve.

Nutrition Info:
- calories 300, fat 13.5, fiber 9.2, carbs 16.7, protein 15.2

Turkey And Chickpeas
Servings: 4 | Cooking Time: 5 Hours

Ingredients:
- 2 tablespoons avocado oil
- 1 big turkey breast, skinless, boneless and roughly cubed
- Salt and black pepper to the taste
- 1 red onion, chopped
- 15 ounces canned chickpeas, drained and rinsed
- 15 ounces canned tomatoes, chopped
- 1 cup kalamata olives, pitted and halved
- 2 tablespoons lime juice
- 1 teaspoon oregano, dried

Directions:
1. Heat up a pan with the oil over medium-high heat, add the meat and the onion, brown for 5 minutes and transfer to a slow cooker.
2. Add the rest of the ingredients, put the lid on and cook on High for 5 hours.
3. Divide between plates and serve right away!

Nutrition Info:
- calories 352, fat 14.4, fiber 11.8, carbs 25.1, protein 26.4

Chicken With Artichokes And Beans
Servings: 4 | Cooking Time: 40 Minutes

Ingredients:
- 2 tablespoons olive oil
- 2 chicken breasts, skinless, boneless and halved
- Zest of 1 lemon, grated
- 3 garlic cloves, crushed
- Juice of 1 lemon
- Salt and black pepper to the taste
- 1 tablespoon thyme, chopped

- 6 ounces canned artichokes hearts, drained
- 1 cup canned fava beans, drained and rinsed
- 1 cup chicken stock
- A pinch of cayenne pepper
- Salt and black pepper to the taste

Directions:
1. Heat up a pan with the oil over medium-high heat, add chicken and brown for 5 minutes.
2. Add lemon juice, lemon zest, salt, pepper and the rest of the ingredients, bring to a simmer and cook over medium heat for 35 minutes.
3. Divide the mix between plates and serve right away.

Nutrition Info:
- calories 291, fat 14.9, fiber 10.5, carbs 23.8, protein 24.2

Turkey And Cranberry Sauce
Servings: 4 | Cooking Time: 50 Minutes

Ingredients:
- 1 cup chicken stock
- 2 tablespoons avocado oil
- ½ cup cranberry sauce
- 1 big turkey breast, skinless, boneless and sliced
- 1 yellow onion, roughly chopped
- Salt and black pepper to the taste

Directions:
1. Heat up a pan with the avocado oil over medium-high heat, add the onion and sauté for 5 minutes.
2. Add the turkey and brown for 5 minutes more.
3. Add the rest of the ingredients, toss, introduce in the oven at 350 degrees F and cook for 40 minutes

Nutrition Info:
- calories 382, fat 12.6, fiber 9.6, carbs 26.6, protein 17.6

Paprika Chicken And Pineapple Mix
Servings: 4 | Cooking Time: 15 Minutes

Ingredients:
- 2 cups pineapple, peeled and cubed
- 2 tablespoons olive oil
- 1 tablespoon smoked paprika
- 2 pounds chicken breasts, skinless, boneless and cubed
- A pinch of salt and black pepper
- 1 tablespoon chives, chopped

Directions:
1. Heat up a pan with the oil over medium-high heat, add the chicken, salt and pepper and brown for 4 minutes on each side.
2. Add the rest of the ingredients, toss, cook for 7 minutes more, divide everything between plates and serve with a side salad.

Nutrition Info:
- calories 264, fat 13.2, fiber 8.3, carbs 25.1, protein 15.4

Turmeric Baked Chicken Breast
Servings: 2 | Cooking Time: 40 Minutes

Ingredients:
- 8 oz chicken breast, skinless, boneless
- 2 tablespoons capers
- 1 teaspoon olive oil
- ½ teaspoon paprika
- ½ teaspoon ground turmeric
- ½ teaspoon salt
- ½ teaspoon minced garlic

Directions:
1. Make the lengthwise cut in the chicken breast.
2. Rub the chicken with olive oil, paprika, capers, ground turmeric, salt, and minced garlic.
3. Then fill the chicken cut with capers and secure it with the toothpicks.
4. Bake the chicken breast for 40 minutes at 350F.
5. Remove the toothpicks from the chicken breast and slice it.

Nutrition Info:
- Per Servingcalories 156, fat 5.4, fiber 0.6, carbs 1.3, protein 24.4

Chicken With Peas
Servings: 4 | Cooking Time: 30 Minutes

Ingredients:
- 4 chicken fillets
- 1 teaspoon cayenne pepper
- 1 teaspoon salt
- 1 tablespoon mayonnaise
- 1 cup green peas
- ¼ cup of water
- 1 carrot, peeled, chopped

Directions:
1. Sprinkle the chicken fillet with cayenne pepper and salt.
2. Line the baking tray with foil and place chicken fillets in it.
3. Then brush the chicken with mayonnaise.
4. Add carrot and green peas.
5. Then add water and cover the ingredients with foil.
6. Bake the chicken for 30 minutes at 355F.

Nutrition Info:
- Per Servingcalories 329 fat 12.3, fiber 2.3, carbs 7.9, protein 44.4

Garlic Chicken And Endives
Servings: 4 | Cooking Time: 15 Minutes

Ingredients:
- 1 pound chicken breasts, skinless, boneless and cubed
- 2 endives, sliced
- 2 tablespoons olive oil
- 4 garlic cloves, minced
- ½ cup chicken stock
- 2 tablespoons parmesan, grated
- 1 tablespoon parsley, chopped
- Salt and black pepper to the taste

Directions:
1. Heat up a pan with the oil over medium-high heat, add the chicken and cook for 5 minutes.
2. Add the endives, garlic, the stock, salt and pepper, stir, bring to a simmer and cook over medium-high heat for 10 minutes.
3. Add the parmesan and the parsley, toss gently, divide ev-

Mediterranean Diet Cookbook

erything between plates and serve.
Nutrition Info:
- calories 280, fat 9.2, fiber 10.8, carbs 21.6, protein 33.8

Chicken Pilaf
Servings: 4 | Cooking Time: 30 Minutes

Ingredients:
- 4 tablespoons avocado oil
- 2 pounds chicken breasts, skinless, boneless and cubed
- ½ cup yellow onion, chopped
- 4 garlic cloves, minced
- 8 ounces brown rice
- 4 cups chicken stock
- ½ cup kalamata olives, pitted
- ½ cup tomatoes, cubed
- 6 ounces baby spinach
- ½ cup feta cheese, crumbled
- A pinch of salt and black pepper
- 1 tablespoon marjoram, chopped
- 1 tablespoon basil, chopped
- Juice of ½ lemon
- ¼ cup pine nuts, toasted

Directions:
1. Heat up a pot with 1 tablespoon avocado oil over medium-high heat, add the chicken, some salt and pepper, brown for 5 minutes on each side and transfer to a bowl.
2. Heat up the pot again with the rest of the avocado oil over medium heat, add the onion and garlic and sauté for 3 minutes.
3. Add the rice, the rest of the ingredients except the pine nuts, also return the chicken, toss, bring to a simmer and cook over medium heat for 20 minutes.
4. Divide the mix between plates, top each serving with some pine nuts and serve.

Nutrition Info:
- calories 283, fat 12.5, fiber 8.2, carbs 21.5, protein 13.4

Turkey And Salsa Verde
Servings: 4 | Cooking Time: 50 Minutes

Ingredients:
- 1 big turkey breast, skinless, boneless and cubed
- 1 and ½ cups Salsa Verde
- Salt and black pepper to the taste
- 1 tablespoon olive oil
- 1 and ½ cups feta cheese, crumbled
- ¼ cup cilantro, chopped

Directions:
1. In a roasting pan greased with the oil combine the turkey with the salsa, salt and pepper and bake 400 degrees F for 50 minutes.
2. Add the cheese and the cilantro, toss gently, divide everything between plates and serve.

Nutrition Info:
- calories 332, fat 15.4, fiber 10.5, carbs 22.1, protein 34.5

Chicken And Rice
Servings: 8 | Cooking Time: 35 Minutes

Ingredients:
- 1 ½ cup basmati rice
- 3 cups chicken stock
- 1-pound chicken fillet, chopped
- 1 carrot, grated
- 1 oz dried grape, chopped
- 1 teaspoon white pepper
- 1 teaspoon salt
- 1 teaspoon curry powder
- 1 teaspoon paprika
- ½ teaspoon cayenne pepper
- 1 onion, diced
- 1 teaspoon coconut oil

Directions:
1. Toss coconut oil in the saucepan and melt it.
2. Add chicken fillet, diced onion, and grated carrot.
3. Mix up the ingredients and start to cook them.
4. Sprinkle the chicken with curry powder, white pepper, salt, paprika, cayenne pepper, and mix up well.
5. Cook the chicken mixture for 3 minutes.
6. Then add rice basmati and chicken stock.
7. Add dried grape and mix up the pilaf.
8. Close the lid and simmer the pilaf for 25 minutes over the low heat.
9. The cooked pilaf with soak all liquid.

Nutrition Info:
- Per Servingcalories 256, fat 5.3, fiber 1.2, carbs 31.2, 19.5

Chicken Roulade
Serves: 1 Slice | Cooking Time: 50 Minutes

Ingredients:
- 4 TB. extra-virgin olive oil
- 6 cups fresh spinach, chopped
- 1 large red bell pepper, roasted, ribs and seeds removed, and chopped
- 2 lb. ground chicken
- 2 tsp. salt
- 1 tsp. ground black pepper
- 1 tsp. garlic powder
- 1 tsp. paprika
- 1/2 tsp. onion powder
- 1/2 cup plain breadcrumbs
- 1 lb. ricotta cheese
- 1 cup shredded Parmesan cheese
- 1/2 cup fresh Italian parsley, chopped

Directions:
1. Preheat the oven to 425°F. Evenly spray a 9×5-inch bread loaf pan with olive oil spray.
2. In a large skillet over medium heat, heat 2 tablespoons extra-virgin olive oil. Add spinach, and cook for 3 minutes.
3. Add roasted red bell pepper, and cook for 2 minutes. Set aside.
4. In a large bowl, combine chicken, salt, black pepper, garlic powder, paprika, onion powder, and breadcrumbs.

Mediterranean Diet Cookbook

5. Lay out a long, 30×10-inch piece of parchment or waxed paper on your counter, and spray with olive oil spray.
6. Spread chicken mixture onto the paper and shape into a rectangle slightly smaller than the size of the paper.
7. Evenly distribute spinach and red bell pepper over chicken, followed by ricotta cheese, Parmesan cheese, and Italian parsley.
8. Gently pull one end of the paper up and forward, causing end of chicken to fold over, and continue to pull the paper forward, allowing chicken to roll up into a loaf.
9. Place chicken loaf in the prepared bread loaf pan, and drizzle with remaining 2 tablespoons extra-virgin olive oil. Cover the pan with aluminum foil, and bake for 35 minutes.
10. Remove the foil, and cook for 5 more minutes.
11. Let loaf rest for 15 minutes. Slice loaf, revealing the pinwheel appearance of chicken, cheese, and vegetables, and serve warm.

Chicken Skewers
Servings:4 | Cooking Time: 10 Minutes

Ingredients:
- 1-pound chicken breast, skinless, boneless
- 2 bell peppers
- 1 tablespoon paprika
- 1 tablespoon avocado oil
- 1 teaspoon salt
- 1 teaspoon mayo sauce
- 1 teaspoon dried dill

Directions:
1. Cut the chicken breast on the medium cubes and place them in the bowl.
2. Sprinkle the chicken with paprika, avocado oil, salt, mayo sauce, and dried dill.
3. Mix up the chicken well and leave for 15 minutes to marinate.
4. Trim the bell peppers and remove the seeds.
5. After this, cut the peppers on the medium squares.
6. Skew the chicken and peppers on the skewers one-by-one and grill in the grill at 390F for 4-5 minutes from each side.

Nutrition Info:
- Per Servingcalories 170, fat 4.9, fiber 1.6, carbs 5.8, protein 25

Tomato Chicken And Lentils
Servings: 8 | Cooking Time: 1 Hour

Ingredients:
- 2 tablespoons olive oil
- 2 celery stalks, chopped
- 1 red onion, chopped
- 2 tablespoons tomato paste
- 2 garlic cloves, chopped
- ½ cup chicken stock
- 2 cups French lentils
- 1 pound chicken thighs, boneless and skinless
- Salt and black pepper to the taste
- 1 tablespoon cilantro, chopped

Directions:
1. Heat up a Dutch oven with the oil over medium-high heat, add the onion and the garlic and sauté for 2 minutes.
2. Add the chicken and brown for 3 minutes on each side.
3. Add the rest of the ingredients except the cilantro, bring to a simmer and cook over medium-low heat for 45 minutes.
4. Add the cilantro, stir, divide the mix into bowls and serve.

Nutrition Info:
- calories 249, fat 9.7, fiber 11.9, carbs 25.3, protein 24.3

Creamy Chicken And Mushrooms
Servings: 4 | Cooking Time: 30 Minutes

Ingredients:
- 1 red onion, chopped
- 1 tablespoon olive oil
- 2 garlic cloves, minced
- 2 carrots chopped
- Salt and black pepper to the taste
- 1 tablespoon thyme, chopped
- 1 and ½ cups chicken stock
- ½ pound Bella mushrooms, sliced
- 1 cup heavy cream
- 2 chicken breasts, skinless, boneless and cubed
- 2 tablespoons chives, chopped
- 1 tablespoon parsley, chopped

Directions:
1. Heat up a Dutch oven with the oil over medium-high heat, add the onion and the garlic and sauté for 5 minutes.
2. Add the chicken and the mushrooms, and sauté for 10 minutes more.
3. Add the rest of the ingredients except the chives and the parsley, bring to a simmer and cook over medium heat for 15 minutes.
4. Add the chives and parsley, divide the mix between plates and serve.

Nutrition Info:
- calories 275, fat 11.9, fiber 10.6, carbs 26.7, protein 23.7

Oregano Chicken And Zucchini Pan
Servings: 4 | Cooking Time: 30 Minutes

Ingredients:
- 2 cups tomatoes, peeled and crushed
- 1 and ½ pounds chicken breast, boneless, skinless and cubed
- 2 tablespoons olive oil
- Salt and black pepper to the taste
- 1 small yellow onion, sliced
- 2 garlic cloves, minced
- 2 zucchinis, sliced
- 2 tablespoons oregano, chopped
- 1 cup chicken stock

Directions:
1. Heat up a pan with the oil over medium-high heat, add the chicken and brown for 3 minute son each side.
2. Add the onion and the garlic and sauté for 4 minutes more.
3. Add the rest of the ingredients except the oregano, bring to a simmer and cook over medium heat and cook for 20 minutes.

4. Divide the mix between plates, sprinkle the oregano on top and serve.
Nutrition Info:
- calories 228, fat 9.5, fiber 9.1, carbs 15.6, protein 18.6

Turkey And Asparagus Mix
Servings: 4 | Cooking Time: 30 Minutes

Ingredients:
- 1 bunch asparagus, trimmed and halved
- 1 big turkey breast, skinless, boneless and cut into strips
- 1 teaspoon basil, dried
- 2 tablespoons olive oil
- A pinch of salt and black pepper
- ½ cup tomato sauce
- 1 tablespoon chives, chopped

Directions:
1. Heat up a pan with the oil over medium-high heat, add the turkey and brown for 4 minutes.
2. Add the asparagus and the rest of the ingredients except the chives, bring to a simmer and cook over medium heat for 25 minutes.
3. Add the chives, divide the mix between plates and serve.

Nutrition Info:
- calories 337, fat 21.2, fiber 10.2, carbs 21.4, protein 17.6

Chicken Wings And Dates Mix
Servings: 6 | Cooking Time: 1 Hour

Ingredients:
- 12 chicken wings, halved
- 2 garlic cloves, minced
- Juice of 1 lime
- Zest of 1 lime
- 2 tablespoons avocado oil
- 1 cup dates, pitted and halved
- 1 teaspoon cumin, ground
- Salt and black pepper to the taste
- ½ cup chicken stock
- 1 tablespoon chives, chopped

Directions:
1. In a roasting pan, combine the chicken wings with the garlic, lime juice and the rest of the ingredients, toss, introduce in the oven and bake at 360 degrees F for 1 hour.
2. Divide everything between plates and serve with a side salad.

Nutrition Info:
- calories 294, fat 19.4, fiber 11.8, carbs 21.4, protein 17.5

Chicken Salad And Mustard Dressing
Servings: 8 | Cooking Time: 0 Minutes

Ingredients:
- 1 cup rotisserie chicken, skinless, boneless and cubed
- ½ cup sun-dried tomatoes, chopped
- ½ cup marinated artichoke hearts, drained and chopped
- 1 cucumber, chopped
- 1/3 cup kalamata olives, pitted and sliced
- 2 cups baby arugula
- ¼ cup parsley, chopped
- 1 avocado, peeled, pitted and cubed
- ½ cup feta cheese, crumbled
- 4 tablespoons red wine vinegar
- 2 tablespoons Dijon mustard
- 1 teaspoon basil, dried
- 1 garlic clove, minced
- 2 teaspoons honey
- ½ cup olive oil
- Salt and black pepper to the taste
- 3 tablespoons lemon juice

Directions:
1. In a salad bowl, mix the chicken with the tomatoes, artichokes, cucumber, olives, arugula, parsley and the avocado and toss.
2. In a different bowl, mix the vinegar with the mustard and the remaining ingredients except the cheese, whisk well, add to the salad, and toss.
3. Sprinkle the cheese on top and serve.

Nutrition Info:
- calories 326, fat 21.7, fiber 1.7, carbs 24.9, protein 8.8

Bbq Chicken Mix
Servings:6 | Cooking Time: 45 Minutes

Ingredients:
- 1.5-pound chicken breast, skinless, boneless
- 2 tablespoons BBQ sauce
- 1 tablespoon butter
- 1 teaspoon Dijon mustard
- 1 tablespoon olive oil
- 1 teaspoon cream cheese
- 1 teaspoon salt
- 1 teaspoon cayenne pepper

Directions:
1. Sprinkle the chicken breast with cayenne pepper, salt, and olive oil.
2. Place it in the baking tray and bake for 35 minutes at 365F. Flip it from time to time to avoid burning.
3. When the chicken breast is cooked, transfer it on the chopping board and shred with the help of the fork.
4. Put the shredded chicken in the saucepan.
5. Add butter, cream cheese, mustard, and BBQ sauce. Mix up gently and heat it up until boiling.
6. Remove the cooked meal from the heat and stir well.

Nutrition Info:
- Per Servingcalories 178, fat 7.4, fiber 0.1, carbs 2.1, protein 24.2

Chicken And Greens Salad
Servings:3 | Cooking Time: 12 Minutes

Ingredients:
- 1 cup lettuce, chopped
- 1 cup arugula, chopped
- 1 mango, peeled, chopped
- 8 oz chicken breast, skinless, boneless
- 1 tablespoon lime juice

- 1 teaspoon sesame oil
- ½ teaspoon salt
- ½ teaspoon ground black pepper
- 1 teaspoon butter

Directions:
1. Sprinkle the chicken breast with salt and ground black pepper.
2. Melt butter in the skillet and add chicken breast.
3. Roast it for 10 minutes over the medium heat. Flip it on another side from time to time.
4. Meanwhile, combine together lettuce, arugula, mango, and sesame oil in the salad bowl.
5. Add lime juice.
6. Chop the cooked chicken breast roughly and chill it to the room temperature.
7. Add it in the mango salad and mix up.

Nutrition Info:
- Per Servingcalories 183, fat 5.2, fiber 2.1, carbs 17.8, protein 17.3

Stuffed Chicken
Servings:2 | Cooking Time: 35 Minutes

Ingredients:
- 10 oz chicken breast, skinless, boneless
- 2 tablespoons fresh cilantro, chopped
- 1 tomato, sliced
- 1 teaspoon fresh parsley, chopped
- 1 teaspoon sour cream
- ½ teaspoon salt
- ½ teaspoon sage
- 1 oz Mozzarella, sliced
- 1 tablespoon pesto sauce

Directions:
1. Make the lengthwise cut in the chicken breast and fill it with fresh parsley, cilantro, sliced Mozzarella, and sliced tomatoes. Secure the chicken breast with toothpicks.
2. After this, sprinkle the chicken with sage, salt, sour cream, and pesto sauce.
3. Wrap the stuffed chicken breast in the foil and bake in the preheated to the 365F oven for 35 minutes.

Nutrition Info:
- Per Servingcalories 246, fat 9.8, fiber 0.6, carbs 2.5, protein 35.2

Lemony Turkey And Pine Nuts
Servings: 4 | Cooking Time: 30 Minutes

Ingredients:
- 2 turkey breasts, boneless, skinless and halved
- A pinch of salt and black pepper
- 2 tablespoons avocado oil
- Juice of 2 lemons
- 1 tablespoon rosemary, chopped
- 3 garlic cloves, minced
- ¼ cup pine nuts, chopped
- 1 cup chicken stock

Directions:
1. Heat up a pan with the oil over medium-high heat, add the garlic and the turkey and brown for 4 minutes on each side.
2. Add the rest of the ingredients, bring to a simmer and cook over medium heat for 20 minutes.
3. Divide the mix between plates and serve with a side salad.

Nutrition Info:
- calories 293, fat 12.4, fiber 9.3, carbs 17.8, protein 24.5

Chicken And Sausage Mix
Servings: 4 | Cooking Time: 50 Minutes

Ingredients:
- 2 zucchinis, cubed
- 1 pound Italian sausage, cubed
- 2 tablespoons olive oil
- 1 red bell pepper, chopped
- 1 red onion, sliced
- 2 tablespoons garlic, minced
- 2 chicken breasts, boneless, skinless and halved
- Salt and black pepper to the taste
- ½ cup chicken stock
- 1 tablespoon balsamic vinegar

Directions:
1. Heat up a pan with half of the oil over medium-high heat, add the sausages, brown for 3 minutes on each side and transfer to a bowl.
2. Heat up the pan again with the rest of the oil over medium-high heat, add the chicken and brown for 4 minutes on each side.
3. Return the sausage, add the rest of the ingredients as well, bring to a simmer, introduce in the oven and bake at 400 degrees F for 30 minutes.
4. Divide everything between plates and serve.

Nutrition Info:
- calories 293, fat 13.1, fiber 8.1, carbs 16.6, protein 26.1

Mediterranean Diet Cookbook

Beans & Grains Recipes

Beans & Grains Recipes

Pecorino Pasta With Sausage And Fresh Tomato
Servings: 4 | Cooking Time: 20 Minutes

Ingredients:
- ¼ cup torn fresh basil leaves
- 1/8 tsp black pepper
- ¼ tsp salt
- 6 tbsp grated fresh pecorino Romano cheese, divided
- 1 ¼ lbs. tomatoes, chopped
- 2 tsp minced garlic
- 1 cup vertically sliced onions
- 2 tsp olive oil
- 8 oz sweet Italian sausage
- 8 oz uncooked penne, cooked and drained

Directions:
1. On medium high fire, place a nonstick fry pan with oil and cook for five minutes onion and sausage. Stir constantly to break sausage into pieces.
2. Stir in garlic and continue cooking for two minutes more.
3. Add tomatoes and cook for another two minutes.
4. Remove pan from fire, season with pepper and salt. Mix well.
5. Stir in 2 tbsp cheese and pasta. Toss well.
6. Transfer to a serving dish, garnish with basil and remaining cheese before serving.

Nutrition Info:
- Calories per Serving: 376; Carbs: 50.8g; Protein: 17.8g; Fat: 11.6g

Feta, Eggplant And Sausage Penne
Servings: 6 | Cooking Time: 30 Minutes

Ingredients:
- ¼ cup chopped fresh parsley
- ½ cup crumbled feta cheese
- 6 cups hot cooked penne
- 1 14.5oz can diced tomatoes
- ¼ tsp ground black pepper
- 1 tsp dried oregano
- 2 tbsp tomato paste
- 4 garlic cloves, minced
- ½ lb. bulk pork breakfast sausage
- 4 ½ cups cubed peeled eggplant

Directions:
1. On medium high fire, place a nonstick, big fry pan and cook for seven minutes garlic, sausage and eggplant or until eggplants are soft and sausage are lightly browned.
2. Stir in diced tomatoes, black pepper, oregano and tomato paste. Cover and simmer for five minutes while occasionally stirring.
3. Remove pan from fire, stir in pasta and mix well.
4. Transfer to a serving dish, garnish with parsley and cheese before serving.

Nutrition Info:
- Calories per Serving: 376; Carbs: 50.8g; Protein: 17.8g; Fat: 11.6g

Ricotta And Spinach Ravioli
Servings: 2 | Cooking Time: 15 Minutes

Ingredients:
- 1 cup chicken stock
- 1 cup frozen spinach, thawed
- 1 batch pasta dough
- 3 tbsp heavy cream
- 1 cup ricotta
- 1 ¾ cups baby spinach
- 1 small onion, finely chopped
- 2 tbsp butter

Directions:
1. Create the filling: In a fry pan, sauté onion and butter around five minutes. Add the baby spinach leaves and continue simmering for another four minutes. Remove from fire, drain liquid and mince the onion and leaves. Then combine with 2 tbsp cream and the ricotta ensuring that it is well combined. Add pepper and salt to taste.
2. With your pasta dough, divide it into four balls. Roll out one ball to ¼ inch thick rectangular spread. Cut a 1 ½ inch by 3-inch rectangles. Place filling on the middle of the rectangles, around 1 tablespoonful and brush filling with cold water. Fold the rectangles in half, ensuring that no air is trapped within and seal using a cookie cutter. Use up all the filling.
3. Create Pasta Sauce: Until smooth, puree chicken stock and spinach. Pour into heated fry pan and for two minutes cook it. Add 1 tbsp cream and season with pepper and salt. Continue cooking for a minute and turn of fire.
4. Cook the raviolis by submerging in a boiling pot of water with salt. Cook until al dente then drain. Then quickly transfer the cooked ravioli into the fry pan of pasta sauce, toss to mix and serve.

Nutrition Info:
- Calories per Serving: 443; Carbs: 12.3g; Protein: 18.8g; Fat: 36.8g

Red Quinoa Peach Porridge
Servings: 1 | Cooking Time: 30 Minutes

Ingredients:
- ¼ cup old fashioned rolled oats
- ¼ cup red quinoa
- ½ cup milk
- 1 ½ cups water
- 2 peaches, peeled and sliced

Directions:
1. On a small saucepan, place the peaches and quinoa. Add water and cook for 30 minutes.
2. Add the oatmeal and milk last and cook until the oats become tender.
3. Stir occasionally to avoid the porridge from sticking on the bottom of the pan.

Nutrition Info:
- Calories per Serving: 456.6; Carbs: 77.3g; Protein: 16.6g; Fat: 9g

Seafood Paella With Couscous
Servings: 4 | Cooking Time: 15 Minutes

Ingredients:
- ½ cup whole wheat couscous
- 4 oz small shrimp, peeled and deveined
- 4 oz bay scallops, tough muscle removed
- ¼ cup vegetable broth
- 1 cup freshly diced tomatoes and juice
- Pinch of crumbled saffron threads
- ¼ tsp freshly ground pepper
- ¼ tsp salt
- ½ tsp fennel seed
- ½ tsp dried thyme
- 1 clove garlic, minced
- 1 medium onion, chopped
- 2 tsp extra virgin olive oil

Directions:
1. Put on medium fire a large saucepan and add oil. Stir in the onion and sauté for three minutes before adding: saffron, pepper, salt, fennel seed, thyme, and garlic. Continue to sauté for another minute.
2. Then add the broth and tomatoes and let boil. Once boiling, reduce the fire, cover and continue to cook for another 2 minutes.
3. Add the scallops and increase fire to medium and stir occasionally and cook for two minutes. Add the shrimp and wait for two minutes more before adding the couscous. Then remove from fire, cover and set aside for five minutes before carefully mixing.

Nutrition Info:
- Calories per Serving: 117; Carbs: 11.7g; Protein: 11.5g; Fat: 3.1g

Belly-filling Cajun Rice & Chicken
Servings: 6 | Cooking Time: 20 Minutes

Ingredients:
- 1 tablespoon oil
- 1 onion, diced
- 3 cloves of garlic, minced
- 1-pound chicken breasts, sliced
- 1 tablespoon Cajun seasoning
- 1 tablespoon tomato paste
- 2 cups chicken broth
- 1 ½ cups white rice, rinsed
- 1 bell pepper, chopped

Directions:
1. Press the Sauté on the Instant Pot and pour the oil.
2. Sauté the onion and garlic until fragrant.
3. Stir in the chicken breasts and season with Cajun seasoning.
4. Continue cooking for 3 minutes.
5. Add the tomato paste and chicken broth. Dissolve the tomato paste before adding the rice and bell pepper.
6. Close the lid and press the rice button.
7. Once done cooking, do a natural release for 10 minutes.
8. Then, do a quick release.
9. Once cooled, evenly divide into serving size, keep in your preferred container, and refrigerate until ready to eat.

Nutrition Info:
- Calories per serving: 337; Carbohydrates: 44.3g; Protein: 26.1g; Fat: 5.0g

Garbanzo And Kidney Bean Salad
Servings: 4 | Cooking Time: 0 Minutes

Ingredients:
- 1 (15 ounce) can kidney beans, drained
- 1 (15.5 ounce) can garbanzo beans, drained
- 1 lemon, zested and juiced
- 1 medium tomato, chopped
- 1 teaspoon capers, rinsed and drained
- 1/2 cup chopped fresh parsley
- 1/2 teaspoon salt, or to taste
- 1/4 cup chopped red onion
- 3 tablespoons extra virgin olive oil

Directions:
1. In a salad bowl, whisk well lemon juice, olive oil and salt until dissolved.
2. Stir in garbanzo, kidney beans, tomato, red onion, parsley, and capers. Toss well to coat.
3. Allow flavors to mix for 30 minutes by setting in the fridge.
4. Mix again before serving.

Nutrition Info:
- Calories per serving: 329; Protein: 12.1g; Carbs: 46.6g; Fat: 12.0g

Sun-dried Tomatoes And Chickpeas
Servings: 6 | Cooking Time: 22 Minutes

Ingredients:
- 1 red bell pepper
- 1/2 cup parsley, chopped
- 1/4 cup red wine vinegar
- 2 14.5-ounce cans chickpeas, drained and rinsed
- 2 cloves garlic, chopped
- 2 cups water
- 2 tablespoons extra-virgin olive oil
- 4 sun-dried tomatoes
- Salt to taste

Directions:
1. Lengthwise, slice bell pepper in half. Place on baking sheet with skin side up. Broil on top rack for 5 minutes until skin is blistered.
2. In a brown paper bag, place the charred bell pepper halves. Fold bag and leave in there for 10 minutes. Remove pepper and peel off skin. Slice into thin strips.
3. Meanwhile, microwave 2 cups of water to boiling. Add the sun-dried tomatoes and leave in to reconstitute for 10 minutes. Drain and slice into thin strips.
4. Whisk well olive oil, garlic, and red wine vinegar.
5. Mix in parsley, sun-dried tomato, bell pepper, and chickpeas.
6. Season with salt to taste and serve.

Nutrition Info:
- Calories per serving: 195; Protein: 8.0g; Carbs: 26.0g; Fat: 7.0g

Leek, Bacon And Pea Risotto
Servings: 4 | Cooking Time: 60 Minutes

Ingredients:
- Salt and pepper to taste
- 2 tbsp fresh lemon juice
- ½ cup grated parmesan cheese
- ¾ cup frozen peas
- 1 cup dry white wine
- 2 ½ cups Arborio rice
- 4 slices bacon (cut into strips)
- 12 cups low sodium chicken broth
- 2 leeks cut lengthwise

Directions:
1. In a saucepan, bring the broth to a simmer over medium flame.
2. On another skillet, cook bacon and stir continuously to avoid the bacon from burning. Cook more for five minutes and add the leeks and cook for two more minutes.
3. Increase the heat to medium high and add the rice until the grains become translucent.
4. Add the wine and stir until it evaporates.
5. Add 1 cup of broth to the mixture and reduce the heat to medium low. Stir constantly for two minutes.
6. Gradually add the remaining broth until the rice becomes al dente and it becomes creamy.
7. Add the peas and the rest of the broth.
8. Remove the skillet or turn off the heat and add the Parmesan cheese.
9. Cover the skillet and let the cheese melt. Season the risotto with lemon juice, salt and pepper.
10. Serve the risotto with more parmesan cheese.

Nutrition Info:
- Calories per Serving: 742; Carbs: 57.6g; Protein: 38.67g; Fat: 39.6g

Mediterranean Diet Pasta With Mussels
Servings: 4 | Cooking Time: 20 Minutes

Ingredients:
- 1 tbsp finely grated lemon zest
- ¼ cup chopped fresh parsley
- Freshly ground pepper to taste
- ¼ tsp salt
- Big pinch of crushed red pepper
- ¾ cup dry white wine
- 2 lbs. mussels, cleaned
- Big pinch of saffron threads soaked in 2 tbsp of water
- 1 can of 15 oz crushed tomatoes with basil
- 2 large cloves garlic, chopped
- ¼ cup extra virgin olive oil
- 8 oz whole wheat linguine or spaghetti

Directions:
1. Cook your pasta following the package label, drain and set aside while covering it to keep it warm.
2. On medium heat, place a large pan and heat oil. Sauté for two to three minutes the garlic and add the saffron plus liquid and the crushed tomatoes. Let it simmer for five minutes.
3. On high heat and in a different pot, boil the wine and mussels for four to six minutes or until it opens. Then transfer the mussels into a clean bowl while disposing of the unopened ones.
4. Then, with a sieve strain the mussel soup into the tomato sauce, add the red pepper and continue for a minute to simmer the sauce. Lastly, season with pepper and salt.
5. Then transfer half of the sauce into the pasta bowl and toss to mix. Then ladle the pasta into 4 medium sized serving bowls, top with mussels, remaining sauce, lemon zest and parsley in that order before serving.

Nutrition Info:
- Calories per Serving: 402; Carbs: 26.0g; Protein: 35.0g; Fat: 17.5g

Kidney Bean And Parsley-lemon Salad
Servings: 6 | Cooking Time: 0 Minutes

Ingredients:
- ¼ cup lemon juice (about 1 ½ lemons)
- ¼ cup olive oil
- ¾ cup chopped fresh parsley
- ¾ teaspoon salt
- 1 can (15 ounces) chickpeas, rinsed and drained, or 1 ½ cups cooked chickpeas
- 1 medium cucumber, peeled, seeded and diced
- 1 small red onion, diced
- 2 cans (15 ounces each) red kidney beans, rinsed and drained, or 3 cups cooked kidney beans
- 2 stalks celery, sliced in half or thirds lengthwise and chopped
- 2 tablespoons chopped fresh dill or mint
- 3 cloves garlic, pressed or minced
- Small pinch red pepper flakes

Directions:
1. Whisk well in a small bowl the pepper flakes, salt, garlic, and lemon juice until emulsified.
2. In a serving bowl, combine the prepared kidney beans, chickpeas, onion, celery, cucumber, parsley and dill (or mint).
3. Drizzle salad with the dressing and toss well to coat.
4. Serve and enjoy.

Nutrition Info:
- Calories per serving: 228; Protein: 8.5g; Carbs: 26.2g; Fat: 11.0g

Lemon Asparagus Risotto
Servings: 5 | Cooking Time: 6 Minutes

Ingredients:
- 1 tablespoons olive oil
- 1 shallot, chopped
- 1 clove of garlic, minced
- 1 ½ cup Arborio rice
- 1/3 cup white wine
- 3 cups vegetable broth
- 1 teaspoon lemon zest
- 2 teaspoon thyme leaves
- Salt and pepper to taste
- 1 bunch asparagus spears, trimmed
- 1 tablespoons butter
- 2 tablespoons parmesan cheese, grated

Directions:
1. Heat olive oil in a pot for 2 minutes.
2. Sauté the shallot and garlic until fragrant, around 2 minutes.
3. Add the Arborio rice and stir for 2 minutes before adding the white wine.
4. Pour in the vegetable broth. Season with salt and pepper to taste.
5. Stir in the lemon zest and thyme leaves.
6. Cover and cook on medium fire for 15 minutes.
7. Stir in the asparagus spears and allow to simmer for 3 minutes.
8. Add the butter and sprinkle with parmesan cheese.
9. Turn off fire and let it sit covered for 10 minutes.

Nutrition Info:
- Calories per serving: 179; Carbohydrates: 21.4g; Protein:5.7g; Fat: 12.9g

Pasta Primavera Without Cream
Servings: 6 | Cooking Time: 30 Minutes

Ingredients:
- ½ cup grated Romano cheese
- 3 tbsp balsamic vinegar
- 1/3 cup chopped fresh parsley
- 1/3 cup chopped fresh basil
- 2 tsp lemon zest
- 2 cloves garlic, sliced thinly
- ¼ large yellow onion, sliced thinly
- 1 tbsp butter
- 1 tbsp Italian seasoning
- ¼ tsp coarsely ground black pepper
- ¼ tsp salt
- ¼ cup olive oil, divided
- 5 spears asparagus, trimmed and cut into 1-inch pieces
- 1 cup fresh green beans, trimmed and cut into 1-inch pieces
- ½ pint grape tomatoes
- ½ red bell pepper, julienned
- 1 carrot, julienned
- 1 zucchini, chopped
- 1 package 12-oz penne pasta

Directions:
1. Cook pasta according to manufacturer's instructions, drain and rinse in running cold water.
2. Line baking sheet with aluminum foil and preheat oven to 450oF.
3. Mix thoroughly together in a bowl Italian seasoning, lemon juice, pepper, salt, 2 tbsp olive oil, asparagus, green beans, tomatoes, red bell pepper, carrot, zucchini and squash.
4. Arrange veggies in baking sheet and bake until tender for 15 minutes. Remove from oven.
5. In a large skillet, heat butter and stir fry garlic and onion until soft.
6. Add balsamic vinegar, parsley, basil, lemon zest and pasta. Continue cooking until heated through while gently tossing around the pasta.
7. Remove from fire and transfer to a large serving bowl and mix in the roasted veggies.
8. Serve and enjoy.

Nutrition Info:
- Calories per Serving: 406; Carbs: 54.4g; Protein: 15.4g; Fat: 13.6g

Italian White Bean Soup
Servings: 4 | Cooking Time: 50 Minutes

Ingredients:
- 1 (14 ounce) can chicken broth
- 1 bunch fresh spinach, rinsed and thinly sliced
- 1 clove garlic, minced
- 1 stalk celery, chopped
- 1 tablespoon lemon juice
- 1 tablespoon vegetable oil
- 1 onion, chopped
- 1/4 teaspoon ground black pepper
- 1/8 teaspoon dried thyme
- 2 (16 ounce) cans white kidney beans, rinsed and drained
- 2 cups water

Directions:
1. Place a pot on medium high fire and heat pot for a minute. Add oil and heat for another minute.
2. Stir in celery and onion. Sauté for 7 minutes.
3. Stir in garlic and cook for another minute.
4. Add water, thyme, pepper, chicken broth, and beans. Cover and simmer for 15 minutes.
5. Remove 2 cups of the bean and celery mixture with a slotted spoon and set aside.
6. With an immersion blender, puree remaining soup in pot until smooth and creamy.
7. Return the 2 cups of bean mixture. Stir in spinach and lemon juice. Cook for 2 minutes until heated through and spinach is wilted.
8. Serve and enjoy.

Nutrition Info:
- Calories per serving: 245; Protein: 12.0g; Carbs: 38.1g; Fat: 4.9g

Fruity Asparagus-quinoa Salad
Servings: 8 | Cooking Time: 25 Minutes

Ingredients:
- ¼ cup chopped pecans, toasted
- ½ cup finely chopped white onion
- ½ jalapeno pepper, diced
- ½ lb. asparagus, sliced to 2-inch lengths, steamed and chilled
- ½ tsp kosher salt
- 1 cup fresh orange sections
- 1 cup uncooked quinoa
- 1 tsp olive oil
- 2 cups water
- 2 tbsp minced red onion
- 5 dates, pitted and chopped
- ¼ tsp ground black pepper
- ¼ tsp kosher salt
- 1 garlic clove, minced
- 1 tbsp olive oil
- 2 tbsp chopped fresh mint
- 2 tbsp fresh lemon juice
- Mint sprigs – optional

Directions:
1. Wash and rub with your hands the quinoa in a bowl at least three times, discarding water each and every time.
2. On medium high fire, place a large nonstick fry pan and heat 1 tsp olive oil. For two minutes, sauté onions before adding quinoa and sautéing for another five minutes.
3. Add ½ tsp salt and 2 cups water and bring to a boil. Lower fire to a simmer, cover and cook for 15 minutes. Turn off fire and let stand until water is absorbed.
4. Add pepper, asparagus, dates, pecans and orange sections into a salad bowl. Add cooked quinoa, toss to mix well.
5. In a small bowl, whisk mint, garlic, black pepper, salt, olive oil and lemon juice to create the dressing.
6. Pour dressing over salad, serve and enjoy.

Nutrition Info:
- Calories per Serving: 172.7; Fat: 6.3g; Protein: 4.3g; Carbohydrates: 24.7g

Spanish Rice Casserole With Cheesy Beef
Servings: 2 | Cooking Time: 32 Minutes

Ingredients:
- 2 tablespoons chopped green bell pepper
- 1/4 teaspoon Worcestershire sauce
- 1/4 teaspoon ground cumin
- 1/4 cup shredded Cheddar cheese
- 1/4 cup finely chopped onion
- 1/4 cup chile sauce
- 1/3 cup uncooked long grain rice
- 1/2-pound lean ground beef
- 1/2 teaspoon salt
- 1/2 teaspoon brown sugar
- 1/2 pinch ground black pepper
- 1/2 cup water
- 1/2 (14.5 ounce) can canned tomatoes
- 1 tablespoon chopped fresh cilantro

Directions:
1. Place a nonstick saucepan on medium fire and brown beef for 10 minutes while crumbling beef. Discard fat.
2. Stir in pepper, Worcestershire sauce, cumin, brown sugar, salt, chile sauce, rice, water, tomatoes, green bell pepper, and onion. Mix well and cook for 10 minutes until blended and a bit tender.
3. Transfer to an ovenproof casserole and press down firmly. Sprinkle cheese on top and cook for 7 minutes at 400oF preheated oven. Broil for 3 minutes until top is lightly browned.
4. Serve and enjoy with chopped cilantro.

Nutrition Info:
- Calories per serving: 460; Carbohydrates: 35.8g; Protein: 37.8g; Fat: 17.9g

Mediterranean Diet Cookbook

Chorizo-kidney Beans Quinoa Pilaf

Servings: 4 | Cooking Time: 35 Minutes

Ingredients:
- ¼ pound dried Spanish chorizo diced (about 2/3 cup)
- ¼ teaspoon red pepper flakes
- ¼ teaspoon smoked paprika
- ½ teaspoon cumin
- ½ teaspoon sea salt
- 1 3/4 cups water
- 1 cup quinoa
- 1 large clove garlic minced
- 1 small red bell pepper finely diced
- 1 small red onion finely diced
- 1 tablespoon tomato paste
- 1 15-ounce can kidney beans rinsed and drained

Directions:
1. Place a nonstick pot on medium high fire and heat for 2 minutes. Add chorizo and sauté for 5 minutes until lightly browned.
2. Stir in peppers and onion. Sauté for 5 minutes.
3. Add tomato paste, red pepper flakes, salt, paprika, cumin, and garlic. Sauté for 2 minutes.
4. Stir in quinoa and mix well. Sauté for 2 minutes.
5. Add water and beans. Mix well. Cover and simmer for 20 minutes or until liquid is fully absorbed.
6. Turn off fire and fluff quinoa. Let it sit for 5 minutes more while uncovered.
7. Serve and enjoy.

Nutrition Info:
- Calories per serving: 260; Protein: 9.6g; Carbs: 40.9g; Fat: 6.8g

Delicious Pasta Primavera

Servings: 4 | Cooking Time: 4 Minutes

Ingredients:
- 8 oz whole wheat penne pasta
- 1 tbsp fresh lemon juice
- 2 tbsp fresh parsley, chopped
- 1/4 cup almonds slivered
- 1/4 cup parmesan cheese, grated
- 14 oz can tomatoes, diced
- 1/2 cup prunes
- 1/2 cup zucchini, chopped
- 1/2 cup asparagus, cut into 1-inch pieces
- 1/2 cup carrots, chopped
- 1/2 cup broccoli, chopped
- 1 3/4 cups vegetable stock
- Pepper
- Salt

Directions:
1. Add stock, pars, tomatoes, prunes, zucchini, asparagus, carrots, and broccoli into the instant pot and stir well.
2. Seal pot with lid and cook on high for 4 minutes.
3. Once done, release pressure using quick release. Remove lid.
4. Add remaining ingredients and stir well and serve.

Nutrition Info:
- Calories 303 Fat 2.6 g Carbohydrates 63.5 g Sugar 13.4 g Protein 12.8 g Cholesterol 1 mg

Nutty And Fruity Amaranth Porridge

Servings: 2 | Cooking Time: 30 Minutes

Ingredients:
- ¼ cup pumpkin seeds
- ½ cup blueberries
- 1 medium pear, chopped
- 1 tbsp raw honey
- 1 tsp cinnamon
- 2 cups filtered water
- 2/3 cups whole-grain amaranth

Directions:
1. In a nonstick pan with cover, boil water and amaranth. Slow fire to a simmer and continue cooking until liquid is absorbed completely, around 25-30 minutes.
2. Turn off fire.
3. Mix in cinnamon, honey and pumpkin seeds. Mix well.
4. Pour equally into two bowls.
5. Garnish with pear and blueberries.
6. Serve and enjoy.

Nutrition Info:
- Calories per Serving: 393.4; Carbs: 68.5g; Protein: 10.5g; Fat: 8.6g

Lime-cilantro Rice Chipotle Style

Servings: 10 | Cooking Time: 17 Minutes

Ingredients:
- 1 can vegetable broth
- ¾ cup water
- 2 tablespoons canola oil
- 3 tablespoons juice of lime juice
- 2 cups long grain white rice, rinsed
- Zest of 1 lime
- ½ cup cilantro, chopped
- ½ teaspoon salt
- Instructions
- Place everything in the pot and give a good stir.
- Give a good stir and close the lid.
- Seal off the vent.
- Press the Rice button and adjust the cooking time to 17 minutes.
- Do natural pressure release.
- Fluff the rice before serving.
- Once cooled, evenly divide into serving size, keep in your preferred container, and refrigerate until ready to eat.

Nutrition Info:
- Calories per serving: 166; Carbohydrates: 31.2g; Protein:2.7 g; Fat: 3.1g

Mediterranean Diet Cookbook

Rice And Chickpea Stew

Servings: 6 | Cooking Time: 60 Minutes

Ingredients:
- ½ cup chopped fresh cilantro
- ¼ tsp freshly ground pepper
- ¼ tsp salt
- 2/3 cup brown basmati rice
- 3 cups peeled and diced sweet potato
- 2 15-oz cans chickpeas, rinsed
- 4 cups reduced-sodium chicken broth
- 1 cup orange juice
- 2 tsp ground coriander
- 2 tsp ground cumin
- 3 medium onions, halved and thinly sliced
- 1 tbsp extra virgin olive oil

Directions:
1. On medium fire, place a large nonstick fry pan and heat oil.
2. Sauté onions for 8 minutes or until soft and translucent.
3. Add coriander and cumin, sauté for half a minute.
4. Add broth and orange juice.
5. Add salt, rice, sweet potato, and chickpeas.
6. Bring to a boil, once boiling lower fire to a simmer, cover and cook.
7. Stir occasionally, cook for 45 minutes or until potatoes and rice are tender.
8. Season with pepper.
9. Stew will be thick, if you want a less thick soup, just add water and adjust salt and pepper to taste.
10. To serve, garnish with cilantro.

Nutrition Info:
- Calories per serving: 332; Protein: 13.01g; Carbs: 55.5g; Fat: 7.5g

Orange, Dates And Asparagus On Quinoa Salad

Servings: 8 | Cooking Time: 25 Minutes

Ingredients:
- ¼ cup chopped pecans, toasted
- ½ cup white onion, finely chopped
- ½ jalapeno pepper, diced
- ½ lb. asparagus, sliced into 2-inch lengths, steamed and chilled
- ½ tsp salt
- 1 cup fresh orange sections
- 1 cup uncooked quinoa
- 1 tsp olive oil
- 2 cups water
- 2 tbsp minced red onion
- 5 dates, pitted and chopped
- ¼ tsp freshly ground black pepper
- ¼ tsp salt
- 1 garlic clove, minced
- 1 tbsp extra virgin olive oil
- 2 tbsp chopped fresh mint
- 2 tbsp fresh lemon juice
- Mint sprigs – optional

Directions:
1. On medium high fire, place a large nonstick pan and heat 1 tsp oil.
2. Add white onion and sauté for two minutes.
3. Add quinoa and for 5 minutes sauté it.
4. Add salt and water. Bring to a boil, once boiling, slow fire to a simmer and cook for 15 minutes while covered.
5. Turn off fire and leave for 15 minutes, to let quinoa absorb the remaining water.
6. Transfer quinoa to a large salad bowl. Add jalapeno pepper, asparagus, dates, red onion, pecans and oranges. Toss to combine.
7. Make the dressing by mixing garlic, pepper, salt, olive oil and lemon juice in a small bowl.
8. Pour dressing into quinoa salad along with chopped mint, mix well.
9. If desired, garnish with mint sprigs before serving.

Nutrition Info:
- Calories per Serving: 265.2; Carbs: 28.3g; Protein: 14.6g; Fat: 10.4g

Raw Tomato Sauce & Brie On Linguine

Servings: 4 | Cooking Time: 12 Minutes

Ingredients:
- ¼ cup grated low-fat Parmesan cheese
- ½ cup loosely packed fresh basil leaves, torn
- 12 oz whole wheat linguine
- 2 cups loosely packed baby arugula
- 2 green onions, green parts only, sliced thinly
- 2 tbsp balsamic vinegar
- 2 tbsp extra virgin olive oil
- 3 large vine-ripened tomatoes
- 3 oz low-fat Brie cheese, cubed, rind removed and discarded
- 3 tbsp toasted pine nuts
- Pepper and salt to taste

Directions:
1. Toss together pepper, salt, vinegar, oil, onions, Parmesan, basil, arugula, Brie and tomatoes in a large bowl and set aside.
2. Cook linguine following package instructions. Reserve 1 cup of pasta cooking water after linguine is cooked. Drain and discard the rest of the pasta. Do not run under cold water, instead immediately add into bowl of salad. Let it stand for a minute without mixing.
3. Add ¼ cup of reserved pasta water into bowl to make a creamy sauce. Add more pasta water if desired. Toss to mix well.
4. Serve and enjoy.

Nutrition Info:
- Calories per Serving: 274.7; Carbs: 30.9g; Protein: 14.6g; Fat: 10.3g

Seafood And Veggie Pasta
Servings: 4 | Cooking Time: 20 Minutes

Ingredients:
- ¼ tsp pepper
- ¼ tsp salt
- 1 lb raw shelled shrimp
- 1 lemon, cut into wedges
- 1 tbsp butter
- 1 tbsp olive oil
- 2 5-oz cans chopped clams, drained (reserve 2 tbsp clam juice)
- 2 tbsp dry white wine
- 4 cloves garlic, minced
- 4 cups zucchini, spiraled (use a veggie spiralizer)
- 4 tbsp Parmesan Cheese
- Chopped fresh parsley to garnish

Directions:
1. Ready the zucchini and spiralize with a veggie spiralizer. Arrange 1 cup of zucchini noodle per bowl. Total of 4 bowls.
2. On medium fire, place a large nonstick saucepan and heat oil and butter.
3. For a minute, sauté garlic. Add shrimp and cook for 3 minutes until opaque or cooked.
4. Add white wine, reserved clam juice and clams. Bring to a simmer and continue simmering for 2 minutes or until half of liquid has evaporated. Stir constantly.
5. Season with pepper and salt. And if needed add more to taste.
6. Remove from fire and evenly distribute seafood sauce to 4 bowls.
7. Top with a tablespoonful of Parmesan cheese per bowl, serve and enjoy.

Nutrition Info:
- Calories per Serving: 324.9; Carbs: 12g; Protein: 43.8g; Fat: 11.3g

Appetizing Mushroom Lasagna
Servings: 8 | Cooking Time: 75 Minutes

Ingredients:
- ½ cup grated Parmigiano-Reggiano cheese
- No boil lasagna noodles
- Cooking spray
- ¼ cup all-purpose flour
- 3 cups reduced fat milk, divided
- 2 tbsp chopped fresh chives, divided
- 1/3 cup less fat cream cheese
- ½ cup white wine
- 6 garlic cloves, minced and divided
- 1 ½ tbsp. Chopped fresh thyme
- ½ tsp freshly ground black pepper, divided
- 1 tsp salt, divided
- 1 package 4 oz pre-sliced exotic mushroom blend
- 1 package 8oz pre-sliced cremini mushrooms
- 1 ¼ cups chopped shallots
- 2 tbsp olive oil, divided
- 1 tbsp butter
- 1 oz dried porcini mushrooms
- 1 cup boiling water

Directions:
1. For 30 minutes, submerge porcini in 1 cup boiling hot water. With a sieve, strain mushroom and reserve liquid.
2. Over medium high fire melt butter on a fry pan. Mix in 2 tbsp oil and for three minutes fry shallots. Add ¼ tsp pepper, ½ tsp salt, exotic mushrooms and cremini, cook for six minutes. Stir in 3 garlic cloves and thyme, cook for a minute. Bring to a boil as you pour wine by increasing fire to high and cook until liquid evaporates around a minute. Turn off fire and stir in porcini mushrooms, 1 tbsp chives and cream cheese. Mix well.
3. On medium high fire, place a separate medium sized pan with 1 tbsp oil. Sauté for half a minute 3 garlic cloves. Then bring to a boil as you pour 2 ¾ cups milk and reserved porcini liquid. Season with remaining pepper and salt. In a separate bowl whisk together flour and ¼ cup milk and pour into pan. Stir constantly and cook until mixture thickens.
4. In a greased rectangular glass dish, pour and spread ½ cup of sauce, top with lasagna, top with half of mushroom mixture and another layer of lasagna. Repeat the layering process and instead of lasagna layer, end with the mushroom mixture and cover with cheese.
5. For 45 minutes, bake the lasagna in a preheated 350oF oven. Garnish with chives before serving.

Nutrition Info:
- Calories per Serving: 268; Carbs: 29.6g; Protein: 10.2g; Fat: 12.6g

Breakfast Salad From Grains And Fruits
Servings: 6 | Cooking Time: 20 Minutes

Ingredients:
- ¼ tsp salt
- ¾ cup bulgur
- ¾ cup quick cooking brown rice
- 1 8-oz low fat vanilla yogurt
- 1 cup raisins
- 1 Granny Smith apple
- 1 orange
- 1 Red delicious apple
- 3 cups water

Directions:
1. On high fire, place a large pot and bring water to a boil.
2. Add bulgur and rice. Lower fire to a simmer and cook for ten minutes while covered.
3. Turn off fire, set aside for 2 minutes while covered.
4. In baking sheet, transfer and evenly spread grains to cool.
5. Meanwhile, peel oranges and cut into sections. Chop and core apples.
6. Once grains are cool, transfer to a large serving bowl along with fruits.
7. Add yogurt and mix well to coat.
8. Serve and enjoy.

Nutrition Info:
- Calories per Serving: 48.6; Carbs: 23.9g; Protein: 3.7g; Fat: 1.1g

Cinnamon Quinoa Bars

Servings: 4 | Cooking Time: 30 Minutes

Ingredients:
- 2 ½ cups cooked quinoa
- 4 large eggs
- 1/3 cup unsweetened almond milk
- 1/3 cup pure maple syrup
- Seeds from ½ whole vanilla bean pod or 1 tbsp vanilla extract
- 1 ½ tbsp cinnamon
- 1/4 tsp salt

Directions:
1. Preheat oven to 375oF.
2. Combine all ingredients into large bowl and mix well.
3. In an 8 x 8 Baking pan, cover with parchment paper.
4. Pour batter evenly into baking dish.
5. Bake for 25-30 minutes or until it has set. It should not wiggle when you lightly shake the pan because the eggs are fully cooked.
6. Remove as quickly as possible from pan and parchment paper onto cooling rack.
7. Cut into 4 pieces.
8. Enjoy on its own, with a small spread of almond or nut butter or wait until it cools to enjoy the next morning.

Nutrition Info:
- Calories per serving: 285; Carbs: 46.2g; Protein: 8.5g; Fat: 7.4g

Filling Macaroni Soup

Servings: 6 | Cooking Time: 45 Minutes

Ingredients:
- 1 cup of minced beef or chicken or a combination of both
- 1 cup carrots, diced
- 1 cup milk
- ½ medium onion, sliced thinly
- 3 garlic cloves, minced
- Salt and pepper to taste
- 2 cups broth (chicken, vegetable or beef)
- ½ tbsp olive oil
- 1 cup uncooked whole wheat pasta like macaroni, shells, even angel hair broken to pieces
- 1 cup water

Directions:
1. In a heavy bottomed pot on medium high fire heat oil.
2. Add garlic and sauté for a minute or two until fragrant but not browned.
3. Add onions and sauté for 3 minutes or until soft and translucent.
4. Add a cup of minced meat. You can also use whatever leftover frozen meat you have.
5. Sauté the meat well until cooked around 8 minutes. While sautéing, season meat with pepper and salt.
6. Add water and broth and bring to a boil.
7. Once boiling, add pasta. I use any leftover pasta that I have in the pantry. If all you have left is spaghetti, lasagna, angel hair or fettuccine, just break them into pieces—around 1-inch in length before adding to the pot.
8. Slow fire to a simmer and cook while covered until pasta is soft.
9. Halfway through cooking the pasta, around 8 minutes I add the carrots.
10. Once the pasta is soft, turn off fire and add milk.
11. Mix well and season to taste again if needed.
12. Serve and enjoy.

Nutrition Info:
- Calories per Serving: 125; Carbs: 11.4g; Protein: 10.1g; Fat: 4.3g

Cilantro-dijon Vinaigrette On Kidney Bean Salad

Servings: 4 | Cooking Time: 0 Minutes

Ingredients:
- 1 15-oz. can kidney beans, drained and rinsed
- 1/2 English cucumbers, chopped
- 1 Medium-sized heirloom tomato, chopped
- 1 bunch fresh cilantro, stems removed, chopped (about 1 1/4 cup)
- 1 red onion, chopped (about 1 cup)
- 1 large lime or lemon, juice of
- 3 tbsp Private Reserve or Early Harvest Greek extra virgin olive oil
- 1 tsp Dijon mustard
- ½ tsp fresh garlic paste, or finely chopped garlic
- 1 tsp sumac
- Salt and pepper, to taste

Directions:
1. In a small bowl, whisk well all vinaigrette ingredients.
2. In a salad bowl, combine cilantro chopped veggies, and kidney beans.
3. Add vinaigrette to salad and toss well to mix.
4. For 30 minutes allow for flavors to mix and set in the fridge.
5. Mix and adjust seasoning if needed before serving.

Nutrition Info:
- Calories per serving: 154; Protein: 5.5g; Carbs: 18.3g; Fat: 7.4g

Goat Cheese 'n Red Beans Salad

Servings: 6 | Cooking Time: 0 Minutes

Ingredients:
- 2 cans of Red Kidney Beans, drained and rinsed well
- Water or vegetable broth to cover beans
- 1 bunch parsley, chopped
- 1 1/2 cups red grape tomatoes, halved
- 3 cloves garlic, minced
- 3 tablespoons olive oil
- 3 tablespoons lemon juice
- 1/2 teaspoon salt
- 1/2 teaspoon white pepper
- 6 ounces goat cheese, crumbled

Directions:
1. In a large bowl, combine beans, parsley, tomatoes and garlic.
2. Add olive oil, lemon juice, salt and pepper.
3. Mix well and refrigerate until ready to serve.
4. Spoon into individual dishes topped with crumbled goat cheese.

Nutrition Info:
- Calories per serving: 385; Protein: 22.5g; Carbs: 44.0g; Fat: 15.0g

Cucumber Olive Rice

Servings: 8 | Cooking Time: 10 Minutes

Ingredients:
- 2 cups rice, rinsed
- 1/2 cup olives, pitted
- 1 cup cucumber, chopped
- 1 tbsp red wine vinegar
- 1 tsp lemon zest, grated
- 1 tbsp fresh lemon juice
- 2 tbsp olive oil
- 2 cups vegetable broth
- 1/2 tsp dried oregano
- 1 red bell pepper, chopped
- 1/2 cup onion, chopped
- 1 tbsp olive oil
- Pepper
- Salt

Directions:
1. Add oil into the inner pot of instant pot and set the pot on sauté mode.
2. Add onion and sauté for 3 minutes.
3. Add bell pepper and oregano and sauté for 1 minute.
4. Add rice and broth and stir well.
5. Seal pot with lid and cook on high for 6 minutes.
6. Once done, allow to release pressure naturally for 10 minutes then release remaining using quick release. Remove lid.
7. Add remaining ingredients and stir everything well to mix.
8. Serve immediately and enjoy it.

Nutrition Info:
- Calories 229 Fat 5.1 g Carbohydrates 40.2 g Sugar 1.6 g Protein 4.9 g Cholesterol 0 mg

Feta On Tomato-black Bean

Servings: 8 | Cooking Time: 0 Minutes

Ingredients:
- 1/2 red onion, sliced
- 1/4 cup crumbled feta cheese
- 1/4 cup fresh dill, chopped
- 2 14.5-ounce cans black beans, drained and rinsed
- 2 tablespoons extra-virgin olive oil
- 4 Roma or plum tomatoes, diced
- Juice of 1 lemon
- Salt to taste

Directions:
1. Except for feta, mix well all ingredients in a salad bowl.
2. Sprinkle with feta.
3. Serve and enjoy.

Nutrition Info:
- Calories per serving: 121; Protein: 6.0g; Carbs: 15.0g; Fat: 5.0g

Baked Parmesan And Eggplant Pasta

Servings: 8 | Cooking Time: 50 Minutes

Ingredients:
- ½ tsp dried basil
- ½ cup grated Parmesan cheese, divided
- 8-oz mozzarella cheese, shredded and divided
- 6 cups spaghetti sauce
- 2 cups Italian seasoned breadcrumbs
- ½ lb. ground beef
- 6 cups eggplant, spiralized
- 1 tbsp olive oil

Directions:
1. Grease a 9x13 baking dish and preheat oven to 350oF.
2. On medium high fire, place a nonstick large saucepan and heat oil. Sauté ground beef until cooked around 8 minutes. Pour in spaghetti sauce and cook until heated through.
3. Scoop out two cups of spaghetti meat sauce and set aside.
4. Add eggplant spirals in saucepan and mix well.
5. Scoop out half of eggplant spaghetti into baking dish, top with half of mozzarella cheese and cover with breadcrumbs. Top again with the remaining spaghetti, mozzarella and Parmesan cheese.
6. Pop into oven and bake until tops are golden brown around 35 minutes.
7. Remove from oven and evenly slice into 8 pieces.
8. Serve and enjoy while warm.

Nutrition Info:
- Calories per Serving: 297; Carbs: 26.6g; Protein: 22.9g; Fat: 11.1g

Chickpea-crouton Kale Caesar Salad

Servings: 4 | Cooking Time: 35 Minutes

Ingredients:
- 1 large bunch Tuscan kale, stem removed & thinly sliced
- ½ cup toasted pepitas
- 1 cup chickpeas, rinsed and drained
- 1 tbsp Dijon mustard
- 1 tbsp nutritional yeast
- 2 tbsp olive oil
- salt and pepper, to taste
- ½ cup silken tofu
- 2 tablespoons olive oil
- 1 lemon, zested and juiced
- 1 clove garlic
- 2 teaspoons capers, drained
- 2 tablespoons nutritional yeast
- 1 teaspoon Dijon mustard
- salt and pepper, to taste

Directions:
1. Heat oven to 350oF. Toss the chickpeas in the garlic, Dijon, nutritional yeast, olive oil, and salt and pepper. Roast for 30-35 minutes, until browned and crispy.
2. In a blender, add all dressing ingredients. Puree until smooth and creamy.
3. In a large salad bowl, toss the kale with dressing to taste, massaging lightly to tenderize the kale.
4. Top with the chickpea croutons, pepitas, and enjoy!

Nutrition Info:
- Calories per serving: 327; Protein: 11.9g; Carbs: 20.3g; Fat: 23.8g

Italian Mac & Cheese

Servings: 4 | Cooking Time: 6 Minutes

Ingredients:
- 1 lb whole grain pasta
- 2 tsp Italian seasoning
- 1 1/2 tsp garlic powder
- 1 1/2 tsp onion powder
- 1 cup sour cream
- 4 cups of water
- 4 oz parmesan cheese, shredded
- 12 oz ricotta cheese
- Pepper
- Salt

Directions:
1. Add all ingredients except ricotta cheese into the inner pot of instant pot and stir well.
2. Seal pot with lid and cook on high for 6 minutes.
3. Once done, allow to release pressure naturally for 5 minutes then release remaining using quick release. Remove lid.
4. Add ricotta cheese and stir well and serve.

Nutrition Info:
- Calories 388 Fat 25.8 g Carbohydrates 18.1 g Sugar 4 g Protein 22.8 g Cholesterol 74 mg

Vegan Olive Pasta

Servings: 4 | Cooking Time: 5 Minutes

Ingredients:
- 4 cups whole grain penne pasta
- 1/2 cup olives, sliced
- 1 tbsp capers
- 1/4 tsp red pepper flakes
- 3 cups of water
- 4 cups pasta sauce, homemade
- 1 tbsp garlic, minced
- Pepper
- Salt

Directions:
1. Add all ingredients into the inner pot of instant pot and stir well.
2. Seal pot with lid and cook on high for 5 minutes.
3. Once done, release pressure using quick release. Remove lid.
4. Stir and serve.

Nutrition Info:
- Calories 441 Fat 10.1 g Carbohydrates 77.3 g Sugar 24.1 g Protein 11.8 g Cholesterol 5 mg

Puttanesca Style Bucatini

Servings: 4 | Cooking Time: 40 Minutes

Ingredients:
- 1 tbsp capers, rinsed
- 1 tsp coarsely chopped fresh oregano
- 1 tsp finely chopped garlic
- 1/8 tsp salt
- 12-oz bucatini pasta
- 2 cups coarsely chopped canned no-salt-added whole peeled tomatoes with their juice
- 3 tbsp extra virgin olive oil, divided
- 4 anchovy fillets, chopped
- 8 black Kalamata olives, pitted and sliced into slivers

Directions:
1. Cook bucatini pasta according to package directions. Drain, keep warm, and set aside.
2. On medium fire, place a large nonstick saucepan and heat 2 tbsp oil.
3. Sauté anchovies until it starts to disintegrate.
4. Add garlic and sauté for 15 seconds.
5. Add tomatoes, sauté for 15 to 20 minutes or until no longer watery. Season with 1/8 tsp salt.
6. Add oregano, capers, and olives.
7. Add pasta, sautéing until heated through.
8. To serve, drizzle pasta with remaining olive oil and enjoy.

Nutrition Info:
- Calories per Serving: 207.4; Carbs: 31g; Protein: 5.1g; Fat: 7g

Mediterranean Diet Cookbook

Escarole And Cannellini Beans On Pasta
Servings: 8 | Cooking Time: 25 Minutes

Ingredients:
- Pepper and salt to taste
- 1 can 14.5-oz diced tomatoes with garlic and onion, drained
- 1 can 15.5-oz cannellini beans, with liquid
- 1 head escarole chopped
- 1 package 16-oz dry penne pasta

Directions:
1. Cook pasta according to package instructions, then drain and rinse under cold running water.
2. On medium high fire, place skillet and cook diced tomatoes, cannellini beans with liquid and escarole.
3. Season with pepper and salt and cook until boiling.
4. Remove from fire and mix pasta.
5. Serve and enjoy.

Nutrition Info:
- Calories per Serving: 310; Carbs: 60.1g; Protein: 13.7g; Fat: 2.0g

Saffron Green Bean-quinoa Soup
Servings: 6 | Cooking Time: 20 Minutes

Ingredients:
- 2 tablespoons extra virgin olive oil
- 1 large leek, white and light green parts only, halved, washed, and sliced
- 2 cloves garlic, minced
- 8 ounces fresh green beans, trimmed and chopped into 1" pieces
- 2 large pinches saffron, or one capsule
- 15 ounces chickpeas and liquid (do not rinse!)
- 1 large tomato, seeded and chopped into 1" pieces
- salt and freshly ground pepper, to taste
- freshly chopped basil, for serving
- 1 large carrot, chopped into 1/2" pieces
- 1 large celery stalk, chopped into 1/2" pieces
- 1 large zucchini, chopped into 1/2" pieces
- 1/2 cup quinoa, rinsed
- 4-5 cups vegetable stock

Directions:
1. Place a large pot on medium fire and heat olive oil for 2 minutes.
2. Stir in celery and carrots. Cook for 6 minutes or until soft.
3. Mix in garlic and leek. Sauté for 3 minutes.
4. Add the zucchini and green beans, and sauté 1 minute more.
5. Pour in broth and saffron. Bring to a boil. Stir in chickpeas and quinoa. Cook until quinoa is soft, around 11 minutes while covered.
6. Stir in the diced tomato and salt and pepper, to taste, and remove from heat.
7. Serve the soup with the freshly chopped basil and enjoy!

Nutrition Info:
- Calories per serving: 196; Protein: 7.9g; Carbs: 26.6g; Fat: 7.5g

Bean And Toasted Pita Salad
Servings: 4 | Cooking Time: 10 Minutes

Ingredients:
- 3 tbsp chopped fresh mint
- 3 tbsp chopped fresh parsley
- 1 cup crumbled feta cheese
- 1 cup sliced romaine lettuce
- ½ cucumber, peeled and sliced
- 1 cup diced plum tomatoes
- 2 cups cooked pinto beans, well drained and slightly warmed
- Pepper to taste
- 3 tbsp extra virgin olive oil
- 2 tbsp ground toasted cumin seeds
- 2 tbsp fresh lemon juice
- 1/8 tsp salt
- 2 cloves garlic, peeled
- 2 6-inch whole wheat pita bread, cut or torn into bite-sized pieces

Directions:
1. In large baking sheet, spread torn pita bread and bake in a preheated 400oF oven for 6 minutes.
2. With the back of a knife, mash garlic and salt until paste like. Add into a medium bowl.
3. Whisk in ground cumin and lemon juice. In a steady and slow stream, pour oil as you whisk continuously. Season with pepper.
4. In a large salad bowl, mix cucumber, tomatoes and beans. Pour in dressing, toss to coat well.
5. Add mint, parsley, feta, lettuce and toasted pita, toss to mix once again and serve.

Nutrition Info:
- Calories per serving: 427; Protein: 17.7g; Carbs: 47.3g; Fat: 20.4g

Cucumber And Tomato Salad
Servings: 4 | Cooking Time: 0 Minutes

Ingredients:
- Ground pepper to taste
- Salt to taste
- 1 tbsp fresh lemon juice
- 1 onion, chopped
- 1 cucumber, peeled and diced
- 2 tomatoes, chopped
- 4 cups spinach

Directions:
1. In a salad bowl, mix onions, cucumbers and tomatoes.
2. Season with pepper and salt to taste.
3. Add lemon juice and mix well.
4. Add spinach, toss to coat, serve and enjoy.

Nutrition Info:
- Calories per Serving: 70.3; Fat: 0.3g; Protein: 1.3g; Carbohydrates: 7.1g

Lunch & Dinner Recipes

Lunch & Dinner Recipes

Honey Roasted Chicken With Rosemary Potatoes
Servings: 8 | Cooking Time: 1 ¾ Hours

Ingredients:
- 1 whole chicken
- 2 tablespoons honey
- 2 tablespoons olive oil
- 1 teaspoon cumin powder
- 1 teaspoon chili powder
- 1 teaspoon dried thyme
- 1 teaspoon dried sage
- 1 teaspoon smoked paprika
- Salt and pepper
- 2 pounds potatoes, peeled and cubed
- 2 rosemary sprigs
- ¼ cup white wine
- ¼ cup vegetable stock

Directions:
1. Mix the honey, oil, spices, herbs, salt and pepper in a bowl.
2. Spread this mixture over the chicken and rub it well into the skin.
3. Place the chicken in a deep dish baking pan.
4. Place the potatoes around the chicken and add the rosemary, wine and stock.
5. Cover with aluminum foil and cook in the preheated oven at 350F for 1 hour then remove the foil and continue cooking for 20 more minutes.
6. Serve the chicken and potatoes warm and fresh.

Nutrition Info:
- Per Serving: Calories: 167 Fat: 5.1g Protein: 7.1g Carbohydrates: 22.9g

Fettuccine With Spinach And Shrimp
Servings: 4-6

Cooking Time: 10 Minutes

Ingredients:
- 8 ounces whole-wheat fettuccine pasta, uncooked
- 3 garlic cloves, peeled, chopped
- 2 teaspoons dried basil, crushed
- 12 ounces medium raw shrimp, peeled, deveined
- 1/4 teaspoon crushed red pepper flakes
- 1/2 cup crumbled feta cheese
- 1 teaspoon salt
- 1 package (10 ounce) frozen spinach, thawed
- 1 cup sour cream

Directions:
1. In a large-sized mixing bowl, combine sour cream, the feta, basil, garlic, salt, and red pepper.
2. According to the package instructions, cook the fettucine. After the first 8 minutes of cooking, add the spinach and the shrimp to the boiling water with pasta; boil for 2 minutes more and then drain thoroughly.
3. Add the hot pasta, spinach, and shrimp mixture into the bowl with the sour cream mix; lightly toss and serve immediately.

Nutrition Info:
- Per Serving: 417.9 Cal, 18 g total fat (9.8 g sat. fat), 197.6 mg chol., 1395.6 mg sodium, 39.7 g carb., 2.5 g fiber, 3.3 g sugar, and 25.2 g protein.

Caramelized Onion Pasta
Servings: 4 | Cooking Time: 35 Minutes

Ingredients:
- 8 oz. whole wheat spaghetti
- 4 red onions, sliced
- 3 tablespoons olive oil
- ¼ cup white wine
- 1 thyme sprig
- Salt and pepper to taste
- 4 oz. feta cheese, crumbled

Directions:
1. Heat the oil in a skillet and stir in the onions.
2. Cook on low to medium heat for 15 minutes, stirring often, until the onions are caramelized and slightly golden.
3. Add the wine, thyme, salt and pepper and cook for 5 more minutes.
4. In the meantime, cook the spaghetti in a large pot of water until al dente, not more than 8 minutes.
5. Drain well and mix the pasta with the onions.
6. Place in serving bowls and top with cheese.
7. Serve the pasta fresh and warm.

Nutrition Info:
- Per Serving: Calories: 291 Fat: 16.9g Protein: 8.3g Carbohydrates: 26.9g

Beets Salad
Servings: 4 | Cooking Time: 20 Minutes

Ingredients:
- 2 beets, trimmed
- 2 oz Parmesan
- 2 cups Romaine lettuce, chopped
- 2 cup arugula, chopped
- 1 teaspoon honey
- 1 teaspoon olive oil
- 1 tablespoon lemon juice
- 3 tablespoons almonds, sliced

Directions:
1. Line the baking tray with parchment.
2. Place the beets in the tray and bake them at 365F for 20 minutes or until the beets are tender.
3. When the beets are cooked, chill them and peel.

4. Chop the peeled beets roughly and put in the salad bowl.
5. Add lettuce, arugula, and almonds.
6. The dressing: mix up together lemon juice, olive oil, and honey.
7. Pour the dressing over the salad and mix up it gently.
8. Then shave Parmesan over the salad. Don't stir it anymore.

Nutrition Info:
- Per Servingcalories 151, fat 10.3, fiber 2.2, carbs 9.7, protein 7.3

Yogurt Marinated Pork Chops
Servings: 6 | Cooking Time:2 Hours

Ingredients:
- 6 pork chops
- 1 cup plain yogurt
- 1 mandarin, sliced
- 2 garlic cloves, chopped
- 1 red pepper, chopped
- Salt and pepper to taste

Directions:
1. Season the pork with salt and pepper and mix it with the remaining ingredients in a zip lock bag.
2. Marinate for 1 ½ hours in the fridge.
3. Heat a grill pan over medium flame and cook the pork chops on each side until browned.
4. Serve the pork chops fresh and warm.

Nutrition Info:
- Per Serving:Calories:293 Fat:20.4g Protein:20.6g Carbohydrates:4.4g

Shrimp Pancakes
Servings: 4 | Cooking Time: 10 Minutes

Ingredients:
- 4 eggs, beaten
- 4 teaspoons sour cream
- 1 cup shrimps, peeled, boiled
- 1 teaspoon butter
- 1 teaspoon olive oil
- 1/3 cup Mozzarella, shredded
- ½ teaspoon salt
- 1 teaspoon dried oregano

Directions:
1. In the mixing bowl, combine together sour cream, eggs, salt, and dried oregano.
2. Place butter and olive oil in the crepe skillet and heat the ingredients up.
3. Separate the egg liquid into 4 parts.
4. Ladle the first part of the egg liquid in the skillet and flatten it in the shape of crepe.
5. Sprinkle the egg crepe with ¼ part of shrimps and a small amount of Mozzarella.
6. Roast the crepe for 2 minutes from one side and then flip it onto another.
7. Cook the crepe for 30 seconds more.
8. Repeat the same steps with all remaining ingredients.

Nutrition Info:
- Per Servingcalories 148, fat 8.5, fiber 0.2, carbs 1.5, protein 16.1

Ratatouille Spaghetti
Servings: 4 | Cooking Time:1 1/4 Hours

Ingredients:
- 8 oz. whole wheat spaghetti
- 2 tablespoons olive oil
- 1 sweet onion, sliced
- 2 garlic cloves, chopped
- 2 red bell peppers, cored and sliced
- 2 tomatoes, peeled and sliced
- 1 zucchini, sliced
- 1 eggplant, sliced
- 1 teaspoon dried basil
- 1 teaspoon dried oregano
- ½ cup vegetable stock
- Salt and pepper to taste
- ½ cup grated Parmesan cheese

Directions:
1. Combine the oil, onion, garlic, bell peppers, tomatoes, zucchini, eggplant, dried herbs and stock, as well as salt and pepper in a deep dish baking pan.
2. Cook in the preheated oven at 350F for 25 minutes.
3. In the meantime, cook the spaghetti in a large pot of salty water until al dente, not more than 8 minutes.
4. Drain well and mix with the ratatouille.
5. Top with grated cheese before serving.

Nutrition Info:
- Per Serving:Calories:211 Fat:8.0g Protein:6.3g Carbohydrates:32.7g

Parsley Beef Stew
Servings: 4 | Cooking Time: 7 Hours

Ingredients:
- 2 pounds beef stew meat, cubed
- Salt and black pepper to the taste
- 2 cups beef stock
- 2 tablespoons olive oil
- 1 yellow onion, chopped
- 2 tablespoons thyme, chopped
- 4 garlic cloves, minced
- 3 carrots, chopped
- 3 celery stalks, chopped
- 28 ounces canned tomatoes, crushed
- ½ cup parsley, chopped

Directions:
1. In your slow cooker, combine the beef with the stock and all the other ingredients, put the lid on and cook on Low for 7 hours.
2. Divide the stew into bowls and serve.

Nutrition Info:
- calories 364, fat 16.5, fiber 4.5, carbs 27.6, protein 33.3

Stuffed Eggplants
Servings: 4 | Cooking Time: 35 Minutes

Ingredients:
- 2 eggplants, halved lengthwise and 2/3 of the flesh scooped out
- 3 tablespoons olive oil
- 1 red onion, chopped
- 2 garlic cloves, minced
- 1 pint white mushrooms, sliced
- 2 cups kale, torn
- 2 cups quinoa, cooked
- 1 tablespoon thyme, chopped
- Zest and juice of 1 lemon
- Salt and black pepper to the taste
- ½ cup Greek yogurt
- 3 tablespoons parsley, chopped

Directions:
1. Rub the inside of each eggplant half with half of the oil and arrange them on a baking sheet lined with parchment paper.
2. Heat up a pan with the rest of the oil over medium heat, add the onion and the garlic and sauté for 5 minutes.
3. Add the mushrooms and cook for 5 minutes more.
4. Add the kale, salt, pepper, thyme, lemon zest and juice, stir, cook for 5 minutes more and take off the heat.
5. Stuff the eggplant halves with the mushroom mix, introduce them in the oven and bake 400 degrees F for 20 minutes.
6. Divide the eggplants between plates, sprinkle the parsley and the yogurt on top and serve for lunch.

Nutrition Info:
- calories 512, fat 16.4, fiber 17.5, carbs 78, protein 17.2

Lentil Tabbouleh And Haloumi
Servings:4 | Cooking Time:5 Minutes

Ingredients:
- 1 bunch flat-leaf parsley, leaves picked
- 1 teaspoon ground cinnamon
- 1 teaspoon ground cumin
- 180 g haloumi
- 2 tablespoons extra-virgin olive oil
- 2 tablespoons lemon juice
- 3 tomatoes, roughly chopped
- 400 g can lentils, rinsed, and drained
- 8 black olives
- Finely grated zest of 1 piece lemon
- Handful of mint leaves
- Lemon wedges, to serve

Directions:
1. Roughly chop the mint leaves and the parsley, reserving a few pieces of whole leaves for garnishing. Toss the chopped herbs with the tomatoes, olive oil, lemon juice, cumin, and cinnamon; season with black pepper.
2. Slice the haloumi into thick pieces, and then fry in a non-stick dry pan for about 1 to 2 minutes over medium-high heat until golden. Flip and then fry for 1 to minutes more until the other side is golden.
3. Place the lentils into a serving plate. Top with the tomato mix and then with the haloumi. Scatter the olives over, then the lemon zest and the reserve whole leave herbs. Serve with the lemon wedges.

Nutrition Info:
- Per Serving:280.3 cal., 22.10 g fat (8.20 g sat fat), 18.10 g carb., 2.7 g sugar, 7.4 g fiber, 26 mg chol., 1043 mg sodium, and 56 g protein.

Cherry Braised Lamb Shanks
Servings: 4 | Cooking Time:2 Hours

Ingredients:
- 4 lamb shanks
- 3 tablespoons olive oil
- 3 red onions, chopped
- 4 garlic cloves, minced
- 1 pound cherry tomatoes, pitted
- 1 cup red wine
- ½ cup vegetable stock
- 1 bay leaf
- 1 thyme sprig
- 1 rosemary sprig
- 1 mint sprig
- Salt and pepper to taste

Directions:
1. Heat the oil in a deep skillet and add the lamb shanks. Cook on each side for 4-5 minutes until golden brown.
2. Add the rest of the ingredients and season with salt and pepper.
3. Cook in the preheated oven at 300F for 1 ½ hours then continue cooking for another 20 minutes at 350F.
4. Serve the lamb shanks warm and fresh.

Nutrition Info:
- Per Serving:Calories:336 Fat:16.3g Protein:23.2g Carbohydrates:14.7g

Chicken Breasts Mediterranean-style With Avocado Tapenade
Servings: 4 | Cooking Time:10 Minutes

Ingredients:
- 4 chicken breast halves, boneless skinless
- For the marinade:
- 1 tablespoon grated lemon peel
- 2 tablespoons freshly-squeezed lemon juice
- 1/2 teaspoon salt
- 1/4 teaspoon ground black pepper
- 1 garlic clove, finely chopped
- 2 tablespoons olive oil
- 3 tablespoons freshly-squeezed lemon juice
- 2 garlic cloves, roasted, mashed
- 1/2 teaspoon sea salt
- 1/4 teaspoon fresh ground pepper
- 1 medium tomatoes, seeded and finely chopped
- 1/4 cup small green pimento stuffed olive, thinly sliced
- 1/2 teaspoon olive oil
- 3 tablespoons capers, rinsed
- 2 tablespoons fresh basil leaves, finely sliced

- 1 large Hass avocado, ripe, finely chopped

Directions:

1. In a sealable plastic bag, combine the chicken and the marinade ingredients, seal the bag and refrigerate for about 30 minutes.
2. In a bowl, whisk the lemon juice, olive oil, roasted garlic, salt, and pepper. Add the green olives, tomato, basil, capers, and avocado; mix to combine and set aside.
3. Remove the chicken from the marinade; discard the marinade. Grill over medium-hot coals for about 4 to 5 minutes each side or to desired doneness. Serve with the tapenade.

Nutrition Info:

- Per Serving:147 Cal, 16.4 g total fat (2.5 g sat. fat), 75.5 mg chol., 914.6 mg sodium, 6.9 g carb., 3.2 g fiber, 1.5 g sugar, and 26.4 g protein.

Pistachio Crusted Lamb Chops
Servings: 6 | Cooking Time:45 Minutes

Ingredients:

- 6 lamb chops
- 3 tablespoons olive oil
- 1 teaspoon chili powder
- 1 cup ground pistachios
- Salt and pepper to taste

Directions:

1. Season the lamb chops with salt, pepper and chili powder then drizzle with oil and rub it well into the meat.
2. Roll the meat chops into the ground pistachios and place them in a baking tray.
3. Cook in the preheated oven at 350F for 20 minutes.
4. Serve the lamb chops warm and fresh.

Nutrition Info:

- Per Serving:Calories:185 Fat:12.0g Protein:18.8g Carbohydrates:0.2g

Tomato Topped Eggplant Pie
Servings: 4 | Cooking Time:30 Minutes

Ingredients:

- 1 egg, beaten
- 1 eggplant
- 1 onion, sautéed
- 1 tablespoon pesto
- 1 tablespoon olive oil
- 2 cloves garlic
- 2 tomatoes
- Fresh basil
- Parmesan cheese, grated
- Whole-wheat breadcrumbs

Directions:

1. Peel and then cube the eggplant; cook in boiling water until soft, drain, and then mash.
2. Sauté the onion; add into the mashed eggplant. Ad d the breadcrumbs, garlic, olive oil, eggs, and pesto; mix well.
3. Grease a pie pan. Slice 1 tomato and layer into the bottom of the greased pan. Pour the eggplant mixture over the tomato layer. Slice the remaining 1 tomato; layer on top of the eggplant mixture. Sprinkle the parmesan cheese all over the top, then sprinkle with the fresh basil; bake for about 30 minutes or up to golden brown at 350F.

Nutrition Info:

- Per Serving:130 cal., 4.5 g total fat (2.5 g sat fat), 60 mg chol., 120 mg sodium, 540 mg potassium, 19 g carb., 6 g fiber, 6 g sugar, and 5 g protein.

Crispy Pollock And Gazpacho
Servings: 4 | Cooking Time:15 Minutes

Ingredients:

- 85 g whole-wheat bread, torn into chunks
- 4 tablespoons olive oil
- 4 pieces Pollock fillets, skinless
- 4 large tomatoes, cut into chunks
- 3/4 cucumber, cut into chunks
- 2 tablespoons sherry vinegar
- 2 garlic cloves, crushed
- 1/2 red onion, thinly sliced
- 1 yellow pepper, deseeded, cut into chunks

Directions:

1. Preheat the oven to 200C, gas to 6, or fan to 180C.
2. Over a baking tray, scatter the chunks of bread. Toss with 1 tablespoon of the olive oil and bake for about 10 minutes, or until golden and crispy.
3. Meanwhile, mix the cucumber, tomatoes, onion, pepper, crushed garlic, sherry vinegar, and 2 tablespoons of the olive oil; season well.
4. Heat a non-stick large frying pan. Add the remaining 1 tablespoon of the olive oil and heat. When the oil is hot, add the fish; cook for about 4 minutes or until golden. Flip the fillet; cook for additional 1 to 2 minutes or until the fish cooked through.
5. In a mixing bowl, quickly toss the salad and the croutons; divide among 4 plates and then serve with the fish.

Nutrition Info:

- Per Serving:296 Cal, 13 g total fat (2 g sat. fat), 19 g carb., 9 g sugar, 3 g fiber, 27 g protein, and 0.67 g sodium.

Herbed Beef And Tomato Soup
Servings: 8 | Cooking Time: 1 Hour

Ingredients:

- 1 pound beef stew meat, cubed
- 2 tablespoons olive oil
- 2 celery stalks, chopped
- 2 carrots, chopped
- 1 yellow onion, chopped
- Salt and black pepper to the taste
- 3 garlic cloves, chopped
- 1 quart chicken stock
- 1 and ½ teaspoons cilantro, dried
- 1 teaspoon oregano, dried
- 28 ounces canned tomatoes, chopped
- ¼ cup parsley, chopped

Directions:

1. Heat up a pot with the oil over medium high heat, add the

meat, onion and the garlic and brown for 10 minutes.
2. Add the rest of the ingredients except the parsley, bring the soup to a boil and simmer for 50 minutes.
3. Add the parsley, divide the soup into bowls and serve.

Nutrition Info:
- calories 347, fat 15.2, fiber 4.2, carbs 15.5, protein 37.7

Pork Fennel Meatballs
Servings: 4 | Cooking Time:1 Hour

Ingredients:
- 1 pound ground pork
- 4 garlic cloves, minced
- 1 shallot, chopped
- 1 tablespoon chopped dill
- 2 tablespoons chopped parsley
- 1 pinch chili flakes
- 2 tablespoons olive oil
- 1 fennel bulb, sliced
- 2 garlic cloves, chopped
- 1 can diced tomatoes
- ½ cup dry red wine
- ½ cup vegetable stock
- 1 bay leaf
- 1 teaspoon sherry vinegar
- Salt and pepper to taste

Directions:
1. Mix the ground pork, minced garlic, shallot, dill, parsley and chili in a bowl. Add salt and pepper and mix well.
2. Form small meatballs and place them on a chopping board.
3. Heat the oil in a skillet and add the garlic and fennel.
4. Cook for 5 minutes until fragrant and softened then stir in the tomatoes, red wine, stock, bay leaf and vinegar.
5. Add salt and pepper to taste and cook for 5 minutes.
6. Place the meatballs in the sauce and cook on low heat for 30 minutes.
7. Serve the meatballs and the sauce warm and fresh.

Nutrition Info:
- Per Serving:Calories:280 Fat:11.2g Protein:31.2g Carbohydrates:8.4g

Sesame Turkey Fillets With Fresh Greens
Servings: 4 | Cooking Time:45 Minutes

Ingredients:
- 4 turkey filets
- Salt and pepper to taste
- 1 teaspoon chili powder
- 3 tablespoons olive oil
- ¼ cup sesame seeds
- 4 cups mixed greens
- 1 orange, cut into segments
- 2 tablespoons pine nuts
- 1 lemon, juiced

Directions:
1. Season the turkey with salt, pepper and chili powder.
2. Drizzle with oil and place the fillets in a deep dish baking pan.
3. Cook in the preheated oven at 350F for 30 minutes.
4. For the side dish, mix the greens, segments, pine nuts and lemon juice, as well as salt and pepper.
5. Serve the turkey with the greens.

Nutrition Info:
- Per Serving:Calories:313 Fat:18.3g Protein:7.9g Carbohydrates:32.3g

Turkey Fritters And Sauce
Servings: 4 | Cooking Time: 30 Minutes

Ingredients:
- 2 garlic cloves, minced
- 1 egg
- 1 red onion, chopped
- 1 tablespoon olive oil
- ¼ teaspoon red pepper flakes
- 1 pound turkey meat, ground
- ½ teaspoon oregano, dried
- Cooking spray
- For the sauce:
- 1 cup Greek yogurt
- 1 cucumber, chopped
- 1 tablespoon olive oil
- ¼ teaspoon garlic powder
- 2 tablespoons lemon juice
- ¼ cup parsley, chopped

Directions:
1. Heat up a pan with 1 tablespoon oil over medium heat, add the onion and the garlic, sauté for 5 minutes, cool down and transfer to a bowl.
2. Add the meat, turkey, oregano and pepper flakes, stir and shape medium fritters out of this mix.
3. Heat up another pan greased with cooking spray over medium-high heat, add the turkey fritters and brown for 5 minutes on each side.
4. Introduce the pan in the oven and bake the fritters at 375 degrees F for 15 minutes more.
5. Meanwhile, in a bowl, mix the yogurt with the cucumber, oil, garlic powder, lemon juice and parsley and whisk really well.
6. Divide the fritters between plates, spread the sauce all over and serve for lunch.

Nutrition Info:
- calories 364, fat 16.8, fiber 5.5, carbs 26.8, protein 23.4

Chorizo Broiled Mussels
Servings: 6 | Cooking Time:35 Minutes

Ingredients:
- 3 tablespoons olive oil
- 2 chorizo links, sliced
- 1 shallot, sliced
- 2 garlic cloves, minced
- 1 jalapeno, chopped
- 2 pounds fresh mussels, cleaned and rinsed
- ½ cup dry white wine
- Salt and pepper to taste

Mediterranean Diet Cookbook

Directions:
1. Heat the oil in a saucepan. Add the chorizo, shallot, garlic and jalapeno and cook for 5 minutes.
2. Add the wine and mussels and cook for 10 minutes until they're all opened up.
3. Serve right away.

Nutrition Info:
- Per Serving:Calories:300 Fat:18.1g Protein:22.9g Carbohydrates:7.1g

Fig And Prosciutto Pita Bread Pizza
Servings: 6 | Cooking Time:20 Minutes

Ingredients:
- 4 pita breads
- 8 figs, quartered
- 8 slices prosciutto
- 8 oz. mozzarella, crumbled

Directions:
1. Place the pita breads on a baking tray.
2. Top with crumbled cheese then figs and prosciutto.
3. Bake in the preheated oven at 350F for 8 minutes.
4. Serve the pizza right away.

Nutrition Info:
- Per Serving:Calories:445 Fat:13.7 Protein:39.0g Carbohydrates:41.5g

Mediterranean-style Salmon Fillet
Servings: 6 | Cooking Time:20 Minutes

Ingredients:
- 1 whole (about 800 g or 28.2 oz.) salmon fillet, skin-on, well-trimmed (organic is preferred)
- 18 pieces black olives (preferably Niçoise), pitted
- 9 marinated sundried tomato, halved
- 3 tablespoons olive oil
- 18 pieces basil leaves

Directions:
1. Preheat the oven to 200C, gas to 6, or fan to 180C.
2. Place the salmon fillet on a clean cutting board. With an apple corer, create 3 rows of 6 holes in the length of the fillet, making 18 holes in all and going just down until it reaches the skin, but not holing all the way through.
3. With a basil leaf, wrap together 1 piece of sundried tomato and 1 piece of olive together, rolling the leaf to make a tight parcel that is big enough to fit the holes.
4. Stuff the parcels into each holes in the fillet.
5. Put the salmon into foiled and then greased baking tray; season with salt, pepper, and then drizzle with the 3 tablespoons olive oil.
6. Place the tray in the oven; roast for about 20 minutes or until the salmon is just cooked.
7. Remove the tray from the oven, let cool until the fillet is just warm. Carefully transfer the fillet onto a serving dish; serve. Alternatively, you can let the fillet cool completely.

Nutrition Info:
- Per Serving:322 Cal, 23 g total fat (4 g sat. fat), 2 g carb., 2 g sugar, 1 g fiber, 27 g protein, and 0.51 g sodium.

Mint Chicken Soup
Servings: 4 | Cooking Time: 30 Minutes

Ingredients:
- Salt and black pepper to the taste
- 6 cups chicken stock
- ¼ cup lemon juice
- 1 chicken breast, boneless, skinless and cubed
- ½ cup white rice
- 6 tablespoons mint, chopped

Directions:
1. Put the stock in a pot, add salt and pepper, bring to a simmer over medium heat, add the rice and cook for 15 minutes.
2. Add the rest of the ingredients, stir, cook for 15 minutes more, divide into bowls and serve.

Nutrition Info:
- calories 232, fat 11, fiber 2.4, carbs 14.3, protein 12.4

Basil Rice Soup
Servings: 4 | Cooking Time: 25 Minutes

Ingredients:
- 1 cup of rice
- 5 cups chicken stock
- 4 eggs
- 1 cup lemon juice, freshly squeezed
- ½ teaspoon salt
- ¼ teaspoon dried basil

Directions:
1. Wash rice carefully and place it in the pan.
2. Add chicken stock and stir gently.
3. Close the lid and cook rice for 15 minutes over the medium heat.
4. Meanwhile, separate egg yolks and egg whites and place them into the separated bowls.
5. Whisk the egg whites until you get the soft peaks.
6. Then add egg yolks and whisk until homogenous.
7. Add lemon juice and stir it for 30 seconds.
8. After this. Add a ½ cup of hot chicken stock from the pan. Add it gradually and whisk all the time.
9. When the rice is cooked, reduce the heat to low and gradually add the egg-lemon mixture.
10. Whisk it carefully until you get homogenous soup texture.
11. Bring the soup to boil and simmer it for 3 minutes.

Nutrition Info:
- Per Servingcalories 257, fat 5.6, fiber 0.8, carbs 42.2, protein 10

Tomato Roasted Feta
Servings: 4 | Cooking Time:45 Minutes

Ingredients:
- 8 oz. feta cheese
- 2 tomatoes, peeled and diced
- 2 garlic cloves, chopped
- 1 cup tomato juice
- 1 thyme sprig
- 1 oregano sprig

Directions:
1. Mix the tomatoes, garlic, tomato juice, thyme and oregano in a small deep dish baking pan.
2. Place the feta in the pan as well and cover with aluminum foil.
3. Cook in the preheated oven at 350F for 10 minutes.
4. Serve the feta and the sauce fresh.

Nutrition Info:
- Per Serving:Calories:173 Fat:12.2g Protein:9.2g Carbohydrates:7.8g

Quinoa Chicken Casserole
Servings: 8 | Cooking Time:1 ¼ Hours

Ingredients:
- ¾ cup quinoa, rinsed
- 1 carrot, diced
- 1 celery stalk, diced
- 1 shallot, chopped
- 1 red bell pepper, cored and diced
- 1 yellow bell pepper, cored and diced
- 2 garlic cloves, chopped
- 2 tomatoes, peeled and diced
- 4 chicken breasts, halved
- 1 rosemary sprig
- 2 cups chicken stock

Directions:
1. Combine the quinoa, carrot, celery, shallot, bell peppers, garlic and tomatoes in a deep dish baking pan.
2. Pour in the stock then place the chicken and rosemary on top.
3. Cover the pan with aluminum foil and cook in the preheated oven at 330F for 45 minutes.
4. Serve the casserole warm and fresh.

Nutrition Info:
- Per Serving:Calories:215 Fat:6.5g Protein:23.4g Carbohydrates:14.8g

Bean And Beef Chili
Servings: 4 | Cooking Time: 25 Minutes

Ingredients:
- 1 teaspoon Greek seasoning
- 1 cup red kidney beans, canned, drained
- 1 cup ground beef
- 1 yellow onion, diced
- 1 bell pepper, chopped
- 1 teaspoon tomato paste
- 1 cup corn kernels
- 1 tablespoon olive oil
- ½ teaspoon salt
- 1 ½ cup chicken stock
- 4 oz Cheddar cheese, shredded

Directions:
1. Pour olive oil in the saucepan and heat it up.
2. Add ground beef and Greek seasonings. Stir well.
3. After this, add tomato paste and diced onion.
4. Cook the ingredients for 10 minutes over the medium heat.
5. Then add corn kernels, salt, bell pepper, and red kidney beans.
6. Add chicken stock and mix up chili well with the help of the spatula.
7. Close the lid and cook chili for 10 minutes.
8. Then top the chili with Cheddar cheese and transfer in the serving bowls.

Nutrition Info:
- Per Servingcalories 423, fat 18.3, fiber 9.1, carbs 41.3, protein 26.1

Parmesan Penne
Servings: 4 | Cooking Time: 25 Minutes

Ingredients:
- ½ cup penne, dried
- 9 oz chicken fillet
- 1 teaspoon Italian seasoning
- 1 tablespoon olive oil
- 1 tomato, chopped
- 1 cup heavy cream
- 1 tablespoon fresh basil, chopped
- ½ teaspoon salt
- 2 oz Parmesan, grated
- 1 cup water, for cooking

Directions:
1. Pour water in the pan, add penne, and boil it for 15 minutes. Then drain water.
2. Pour olive oil in the skillet and heat it up.
3. Slice the chicken fillet and put it in the hot oil.
4. Sprinkle chicken with Italian seasoning and roast for 2 minutes from each side.
5. Then add fresh basil, salt, tomato, and grated cheese.
6. Stir well.
7. Add heavy cream and cooked penne.
8. Cook the meal for 5 minutes more over the medium heat. Stir it from time to time.

Nutrition Info:
- Per Servingcalories 388, fat 23.4, fiber 0.2, carbs 17.6, protein 17.6

Garlicky Roasted Chicken
Servings: 8 | Cooking Time:2 ½ Hours

Ingredients:
- 1 whole chicken
- 8 garlic cloves, minced
- 2 tablespoons chopped rosemary
- 1 teaspoon dried basil
- ¼ cup butter, softened
- Salt and pepper to taste

Directions:
1. Mix the garlic, rosemary, basil, butter, salt and pepper in a bowl.
2. Spread the mixture over the chicken and place it in a deep dish baking pan.
3. Cover the chicken with aluminum foil and cook in the preheated oven at 330F for 2 hours.

4. Serve the chicken warm and fresh.

Nutrition Info:
- Per Serving:Calories:183 Fat:14.4g Protein:10.7g Carbohydrates:3.1g

Kalamata Olives Penne
Servings: 4 | Cooking Time:50 Minutes

Ingredients:
- 2 tablespoons olive oil
- 1 shallot, chopped
- 2 garlic cloves, minced
- 1 carrot, grated
- 2 tomatoes, peeled and diced
- ½ cup tomato juice
- ½ cup vegetable stock
- 1 cup kalamata olives
- 2 cups baby spinach
- Salt and pepper to taste
- 8 oz. penne pasta

Directions:
1. Heat the oil in a skillet and stir in the shallot, garlic and carrot. Cook for 5 minutes then add the tomatoes, tomato juice and olives, as well as salt and pepper. Continue cooking for 10 minutes on low heat.
2. Add the kalamata olives and spinach and cook for another 5 minutes.
3. Cook the pasta in a large pot of salty water until al dente, not more than 8 minutes. Drain well.
4. Mix the cooked pasta with the sauce and serve right away.

Nutrition Info:
- Per Serving:Calories:292 Fat:12.1g Protein:8.2g Carbohydrates:39.8g

Fish Parcels
Servings: 2 | Cooking Time:40 Minutes

Ingredients:
- 250 g (9 oz.) baby new potato, scrubbed
- 1 small lemon, finely grated zest
- 2 teaspoon tomato paste (sun-dried) or tomato purée
- 2 teaspoon lemon juice
- 2 sprigs fresh rosemary or thyme
- 2 pieces (175 g or 6 oz. each) fish fillets, firm white, such as haddock or whiting
- 1 teaspoon olive oil
- 1 tablespoon capers, rinsed
- 10 pieces black or green olives

Directions:
1. Preheat the oven to 190C, gas to 5, or fan to 170C.
2. In lightly salted boiling water, cook the potatoes for 12 minutes or until they are tender; drain well.
3. Brush the middle of 2 large pieces, about 30-cm or 12-inch square, foil sheets with olive oil. Place the fish on top of the oiled part. Top the fish with the tomato paste. Sprinkle with the lemon zest and the juice, the cooked potatoes, the capers, and the olives; season with the pepper and put a sprig of thyme on top.
4. Loosely wrap the foil over around the ingredients and tightly secure each parcel.
5. Place the parcels into a baking sheet; bae for about 20-25 minutes or until the fish flakes easily when shredded with a fork.
6. Serve immediately with steamed green beans.

Nutrition Info:
- Per Serving:275 Cal, 6.4 g total fat (0.7 g sat. fat), 21 g carb., 0 g sugar, 1.9 g fiber, 34.6 g protein, and 1.33 g sodium.

Sage Pork And Beans Stew
Servings: 4 | Cooking Time: 4 Hours And 10 Minutes

Ingredients:
- 2 pounds pork stew meat, cubed
- 2 tablespoons olive oil
- 1 sweet onion, chopped
- 1 red bell pepper, chopped
- 3 garlic cloves, minced
- 2 teaspoons sage, dried
- 4 ounces canned white beans, drained
- 1 cup beef stock
- 2 zucchinis, chopped
- 2 tablespoons tomato paste
- 1 tablespoon cilantro, chopped

Directions:
1. Heat up a pan with the oil over medium-high heat, add the meat, brown for 10 minutes and transfer to your slow cooker.
2. Add the rest of the ingredients except the cilantro, put the lid on and cook on High for 4 hours.
3. Divide the stew into bowls, sprinkle the cilantro on top and serve.

Nutrition Info:
- calories 423, fat 15.4, fiber 9.6, carbs 27.4, protein 43

Layered Potato Chicken Casserole
Servings: 8 | Cooking Time:1 ¼ Hours

Ingredients:
- 3 tablespoons olive oil
- 2 garlic cloves, minced
- 1 shallot, chopped
- 2 pounds ground chicken
- 1 can diced tomatoes
- 1 teaspoon dried oregano
- 1 teaspoon dried basil
- 1 ½ pounds potatoes, peeled and sliced
- ½ cup vegetable stock
- Salt and pepper to taste
- ½ cup grated Parmesan

Directions:
1. Heat the oil in a skillet and add the garlic, shallot and chicken. Cook for 5 minutes then stir in the tomatoes, oregano and basil, as well as salt and pepper.
2. Cook for another 10 minutes then remove from heat.
3. Layer the potatoes and the chicken sauce in a deep dish baking pan.
4. Pour in the stock then top with the grated Parmesan.

Mediterranean Diet Cookbook

5. Cook in the preheated oven at 350F for 45 minutes.
6. Serve the casserole warm and fresh.

Nutrition Info:
- Per Serving:Calories:324 Fat:13.8g Protein:34.4g Carbohydrates:14.4g

Veggie And Pasta Soup
Servings: 4 | Cooking Time: 25 Minutes

Ingredients:
- 2 oz celery stalk, chopped
- 1 russet potato, chopped
- ½ cup butternut squash, chopped
- 1 teaspoon fresh rosemary
- ½ teaspoon salt
- ½ teaspoon ground black pepper
- 2 oz Parmesan, grated
- 1 tablespoon butter
- ½ zucchini, chopped
- ¼ cup green beans, chopped
- 2 oz whole wheat pasta
- 4 cups chicken stock
- ½ teaspoon tomato paste
- ¾ cup red kidney beans, canned, drained

Directions:
1. In the saucepan combine together celery stalk, potato, butternut squash, rosemary, salt, ground black pepper, butter, and stir well.
2. Cook the vegetables for 5 minutes over the medium-low heat.
3. After this, add zucchini, green beans, whole wheat pasta, chicken stock, and tomato paste.
4. Add red kidney beans and chicken stock.
5. Stir the soup well and cook it for 15 minutes over the medium-high heat.
6. Then add Parmesan and stir minestrone.
7. Cook it for 2 minutes more.
8. Ladle minestrone in the serving bowls immediately.

Nutrition Info:
- Per Servingcalories 340, fat 7.5, fiber 9.5, carbs 53.1, protein 17.5

Garlic Butter Seafood
Servings:6 | Cooking Time:10 Minutes

Ingredients:
- 1.5 kg black mussels, scrubbed, and debearded
- 750 g prawns, peeled leaving tails intact, deveined
- 530 g whole-wheat loaf sourdough bread, rye and seeds
- 250 ml (1 cup) white wine or fish stock
- 2 tablespoons olive oil spread or butter, divided (I Can't Believe It's Not Butter! ®)
- 2 cloves garlic, diced
- 1 tablespoon Gourmet Garden Mediterranean Herb and Spice Blend

Directions:
1. In a deep, large saucepan, melt the spread over high heat. Add the garlic; cook until fragrant. Add the prawns, mussels, and the wine or the stock; cover and cook, for about 8 to 10 minutes, shaking the pan, until the pawns are tender and the mussels are open. Discard unopened mussels.
2. With a tong, transfer the prawns and the mussels into a deep serving dish. Stir the herb blend into the pan; season with the pepper then pour over the seafood. Cut the bread into thick slices; serve with the seafood.

Nutrition Info:
- Per Serving:502 cal., 15 g fat (2.5 g sat fat), 29 g carb., 0 g sugar, 9 g fiber, and 51 g protein.

Beef Stuffed Bell Peppers
Servings: 6 | Cooking Time:1 Hour

Ingredients:
- 6 red bell peppers
- 1 pound ground beef
- 2 sweet onions, chopped
- 1 garlic cloves, minced
- 1 carrot, grated
- 1 celery stalk, finely chopped
- 1 tablespoon pesto sauce
- 2 tablespoons tomato paste
- ½ cup white rice
- Salt and pepper to taste
- 1 cup tomato juice
- 1 ½ cups beef stock
- 1 thyme sprig

Directions:
1. Place the thyme sprig at the bottom of a pot.
2. Mix the beef, onions, garlic, carrot, celery, pesto sauce and tomato paste, as well as rice, salt and pepper in a bowl.
3. Cut the top of each bell pepper and remove the vines.
4. Stuff the bell peppers with the beef mixture and place them in the pot.
5. Pour in the tomato juice and stock and cover with a lid.
6. Cook on low heat for 45 minutes.
7. Serve the bell peppers warm and fresh.

Nutrition Info:
- Per Serving:Calories:280 Fat:6.5g Protein:27.2g Carbohydrates:27.1g

Mediterranean Flounder
Servings: 4 | Cooking Time:30 Minutes

Ingredients:
- 6 leaves fresh basil, chopped
- 5 roma tomatoes, chopped or 1 (15 ounce) can chopped tomatoes
- 4 tablespoons capers
- 3 tablespoons parmesan cheese
- 24 Kalamata olives, pitted, chopped
- 2 tablespoons olive oil
- 2 garlic cloves, chopped
- 1/4 cup white wine
- 1/2 onion, chopped
- 1 teaspoon lemon juice, freshly squeezed
- 1 pound flounder (or sole, halibut, mahi-mahi or tilapia fillet

- 1 pinch Italian seasoning

Directions:
1. Preheat the oven to 425F.
2. Bring water to a boil and place a bowl of ice water near the oven. Plunge the tomatoes into the boiling water, immediately remove them and plunge into the ice water; peel the skins. Alternatively, you can chop them with the skins on or you can use canned if you prefer.
3. In a medium-sized skillet, heat the olive oil over medium flame or heat. Add the onion; sauté until tender. Add the garlic and the Italian seasoning, stirring to combine. Add the tomatoes; cook until tender. Mix in the wine, capers, olives, 1/2 of the basil, and lemon juice. Alternatively, you can use a couple teaspoons of dried basil. However, fresh is preferred.
4. Reduce the heat, add the parmesan cheese; cook until the mixture is bubbly and hot. If you want a thicker sauce, cook for about 15 minutes or up to thick.
5. Place the fish in a shallow baking dish, pour the sauce over the fish, and bake for about 15 to 20 minutes until it easily flakes with a fork. Take note, the mah-mahi will not easily flake even when it is done.

Nutrition Info:
- Per Serving:221.9 Cal, 13.1 g total fat (2.5 g sat. fat), 54.4 mg chol., 848.1 mg sodium, 7.5 g carb., 2.3 g fiber, 2.9 g sugar, and 16.9 g protein.

Mussels And Shrimp In Wine Sauce And Garlic Crostini

Servings: 4 | Cooking Time:20 Minutes

Ingredients:
- 1 loaf whole-wheat French bread (about 12-inch long), cut into 1/2-inch slices
- 1 medium shallot or onion, chopped
- 1 pound raw large shrimp, peeled, deveined
- 1 teaspoon fresh thyme, chopped (or 1/4 teaspoon dried thyme, crushed)
- 1/2 cup dry white wine or chicken broth
- 2 1/2 pounds mussels, well-scrubbed
- 2 cloves garlic, divided
- 2 tablespoons fresh parsley, finely chopped
- 6 tablespoons olive oil spread or butter, divided (I Can't Believe It's Not Butter! ®)

Directions:
1. Preheat the oven to 400F.
2. Brush both sides of the bread slices with 3 tablespoons of the Olive Oil spread. Arrange the slices of bread on a baking sheet; bake for 5 minutes or until toasted lightly. Cut 1 garlic clove in half; rub on the toasted bread and set aside.
3. Meanwhile, chop the remaining garlic cloves finely.
4. In a 12-inch wide, deep skillet, melt 1 tablespoon of the olive oil spread over medium flame or heat. Add the shallot; cook for about 4 minutes, stirring occasionally, until tender. Stir in the garlic and the thyme; cook for 1 minute, stirring occasionally. Add the wine; bring to boil over high heat. Add the mussels and the shrimps; bring to boil again. When boiling, reduce the heat to low; simmer covered for 3 minutes or till the mussels open and the shrimp are pink. Discard any unopened shells.
5. Stir in the remaining 2tablespoons olive oil spread and the parsley. Serve with the Garlic Crostini. Serve over hot cooked whole-wheat pasta, if desired.

Nutrition Info:
- Per Serving:440 cal., 14 g total fat (3 g sat fat), 0 mg chol., 790 mg sodium, 260 mg potassium, 62 g carb., 2 g fiber, 3 g sugar, and 13 g protein.

Raisin Stuffed Lamb

Servings: 10 | Cooking Time:2 ½ Hours

Ingredients:
- 4 pounds lamb shoulder
- 1 teaspoon garlic powder
- 1 teaspoon onion powder
- 1 teaspoon chili powder
- Salt and pepper to taste
- 1 cup golden raisins
- 2 red apples, cored and diced
- 1 teaspoon mustard powder
- 1 teaspoon cumin powder
- 2 tablespoons pine nuts
- 1 cup dry white wine

Directions:
1. Season the lamb with garlic powder, onion powder, chili, salt and pepper.
2. Cut a pocket into the lamb.
3. Mix the raisins, red apples, mustard, cumin and pine nuts and stuff the mixture into the lamb.
4. Place the lamb in a deep dish baking pan and cover with aluminum foil.
5. Cook in the preheated oven at 330F for 2 hours.
6. Serve the lamb warm and fresh.

Nutrition Info:
- Per Serving:Calories:436 Fat:14.8g Protein:52.0g Carbohydrates:18.1g

Mediterranean Diet Cookbook

Fish And Seafood Recipes

Fish And Seafood Recipes

Honey Halibut
Servings:5 | Cooking Time: 15 Minutes

Ingredients:
- 1-pound halibut
- 1 teaspoon lime zest
- ½ teaspoon honey
- 1 teaspoon olive oil
- ½ teaspoon lime juice
- ¼ teaspoon salt
- ¼ teaspoon chili flakes

Directions:
1. Cut the fish on the sticks and sprinkle with salt and chili flakes.
2. Whisk together lime zest, honey, olive oil, and lime juice.
3. Brush the halibut sticks with the honey mixture from each side.
4. Line the baking tray with baking paper and place the fish inside.
5. Bake the halibut for 15 minutes at 375F. Flip the fish on another side after 7 minutes of cooking.

Nutrition Info:
- Per Servingcalories 254, fat 19, fiber 0, carbs 0.7, protein 18.8

Orange Herbed Sauced White Bass
Servings: 6 | Cooking Time: 33 Minutes

Ingredients:
- ¼ cup thinly sliced green onions
- ½ cup orange juice
- 1 ½ tbsp fresh lemon juice
- 1 ½ tbsp olive oil
- 1 large onion, halved, thinly sliced
- 1 large orange, unpeeled, sliced
- 3 tbsp chopped fresh dill
- 6 3-oz skinless white bass fillets
- Additional unpeeled orange slices

Directions:
1. Grease a 13 x 9-inch glass baking dish and preheat oven to 400oF.
2. Arrange orange slices in single layer on baking dish, top with onion slices, seasoned with pepper and salt plus drizzled with oil.
3. Pop in the oven and roast for 25 minutes or until onions are tender and browned.
4. Remove from oven and increased oven temperature to 450oF.
5. Push onion and orange slices on sides of dish and place bass fillets in middle of dish. Season with 1 ½ tbsp dill, pepper and salt. Arrange onions and orange slices on top of fish and pop into the oven.
6. Roast for 8 minutes or until salmon is opaque and flaky.
7. In a small bowl, mix 1 ½ tbsp dill, lemon juice, green onions and orange juice.
8. Transfer salmon to a serving plate, discard roasted onions, drizzle with the newly made orange sauce and garnish with fresh orange slices.
9. Serve and enjoy.

Nutrition Info:
- Calories per serving: 312.42; Protein: 84.22; Fat: 23.14; Carbs: 33.91g

Shrimp And Yogurt Sauce
Servings:2 | Cooking Time: 15 Minutes

Ingredients:
- 1 cinnamon stick
- 1/3 cup Plain yogurt
- 1 teaspoon minced ginger
- ½ teaspoon ground coriander
- ½ teaspoon salt
- 1 teaspoon olive oil
- 1 tablespoon tomato paste
- 1 teaspoon jalapeno pepper
- 1 cup shrimps, peeled
- ¼ cup of water
- 1 teaspoon turmeric
- ½ teaspoon paprika
- ½ teaspoon sage

Directions:
1. In the saucepan mix up together Plain yogurt, minced ginger, ground coriander, salt, tomato paste, and water.
2. Then pour olive oil in the skillet and preheat it.
3. Add jalapeno pepper and roast it for 2 minutes.
4. After this, transfer the roasted jalapeno in the saucepan.
5. Add turmeric, paprika, and sage.
6. Bring the liquid to boil and add shrimps.
7. Close the lid and cook korma for 10 minutes over the medium heat.

Nutrition Info:
- Per Servingcalories 148, fat 4.1, fiber 1.6, carbs 7.1, protein 21

Baked Tilapia
Servings:3 | Cooking Time: 20 Minutes

Ingredients:
- 3 tilapia fillets (4 oz each fish fillet)
- ½ teaspoon cayenne pepper
- ½ teaspoon salt
- 3 teaspoons olive oil
- 1 red onion, sliced
- 3 lemon slices
- 1 zucchini, chopped

Directions:
1. Make the medium packets from the foil and brush them with olive oil from inside.
2. Then sprinkle tilapia fillets with salt and cayenne pepper from each side and arrange in the foil packets.
3. Add sliced lemon on the top of the fish.
4. Then add sliced onion and zucchini.
5. Bake the fish packets for 20 minutes at 360F or until vegetables are tender.

Nutrition Info:
- Per Servingcalories 161, fat 5.9, fiber 1.8, carbs 6.4, protein 22.3

Kale, Beets And Cod Mix
Servings: 4 | Cooking Time: 20 Minutes

Ingredients:
- 2 tablespoons apple cider vinegar
- ½ cup chicken stock
- 1 red onion, sliced
- 4 golden beets, trimmed, peeled and cubed
- 2 tablespoons olive oil
- Salt and black pepper to the taste
- 4 cups kale, torn
- 2 tablespoons walnuts, chopped
- 1 pound cod fillets, boneless, skinless and cubed

Directions:
1. Heat up a pan with the oil over medium-high heat, add the onion and the beets and cook for 3-4 minutes.
2. Add the rest of the ingredients except the fish and the walnuts, stir, bring to a simmer and cook for 5 minutes more.
3. Add the fish, cook for 10 minutes, divide between plates and serve.

Nutrition Info:
- calories 285, fat 7.6, fiber 6.5, carbs 16.7, protein 12.5

Salmon And Zucchini Rolls
Servings: 8 | Cooking Time: 0 Minutes

Ingredients:
- 8 slices smoked salmon, boneless
- 2 zucchinis, sliced lengthwise in 8 pieces
- 1 cup ricotta cheese, soft
- 2 teaspoons lemon zest, grated
- 1 tablespoon dill, chopped
- 1 small red onion, sliced
- Salt and pepper to the taste

Directions:
1. In a bowl, mix the ricotta cheese with the rest of the ingredients except the salmon and the zucchini and whisk well.
2. Arrange the zucchini slices on a working surface, and divide the salmon on top.
3. Spread the cheese mix all over, roll and secure with toothpicks and serve right away.

Nutrition Info:
- calories 297, fat 24.3, fiber 11.6, carbs 15.4, protein 11.6

Fried Salmon
Servings: 2 | Cooking Time: 8 Minutes

Ingredients:
- 5 oz salmon fillet
- ¼ teaspoon salt
- ½ teaspoon ground black pepper
- 1 tablespoon sunflower oil
- ¼ teaspoon lime juice

Directions:
1. Cut the salmon fillet on 2 lengthwise pieces.
2. Sprinkle every fish piece with salt, ground black pepper, and lime juice.
3. Pour sunflower oil in the skillet and preheat it until shimmering.
4. Then place fish fillets in the hot oil and cook them for 3 minutes from each side.

Nutrition Info:
- Per Servingcalories 157, fat 11.4, fiber 0.1, carbs 0.3, protein 13.8

Baked Sea Bass
Servings: 4 | Cooking Time: 12 Minutes

Ingredients:
- 4 sea bass fillets, boneless
- Sal and black pepper to the taste
- 2 cups potato chips, crushed
- 1 tablespoon mayonnaise

Directions:
1. Season the fish fillets with salt and pepper, brush with the mayonnaise and dredge each in the potato chips.
2. Arrange the fillets on a baking sheet lined with parchment paper and bake at 400 degrees F for 12 minutes.
3. Divide the fish between plates and serve with a side salad.

Nutrition Info:
- calories 228, fat 8.6, fiber 0.6, carbs 9.3, protein 25

Dijon Mustard And Lime Marinated Shrimp
Servings: 8 | Cooking Time: 10 Minutes

Ingredients:
- ½ cup fresh lime juice, plus lime zest as garnish
- ½ cup rice vinegar
- ½ tsp hot sauce
- 1 bay leaf
- 1 cup water
- 1 lb. uncooked shrimp, peeled and deveined
- 1 medium red onion, chopped
- 2 tbsp capers
- 2 tbsp Dijon mustard
- 3 whole cloves

Directions:
1. Mix hot sauce, mustard, capers, lime juice and onion in a shallow baking dish and set aside.
2. Bring to a boil in a large saucepan bay leaf, cloves, vinegar and water.

3. Once boiling, add shrimps and cook for a minute while stirring continuously.
4. Drain shrimps and pour shrimps into onion mixture.
5. For an hour, refrigerate while covered the shrimps.
6. Then serve shrimps cold and garnished with lime zest.

Nutrition Info:
- Calories per serving: 232.2; Protein: 17.8g; Fat: 3g; Carbs: 15g

Shrimp And Calamari Mix
Servings: 4 | Cooking Time: 12 Minutes

Ingredients:
- 1 pound shrimp, peeled and deveined
- Salt and black pepper to the taste
- 3 garlic cloves, minced
- 1 tablespoon avocado oil
- ½ pound calamari rings
- ½ teaspoon basil, dried
- 1 teaspoon rosemary, dried
- 1 red onion, chopped
- 1 cup chicken stock
- Juice of 1 lemon
- 1 tablespoon parsley, chopped

Directions:
1. Heat up a pan with the oil over medium-high heat, add the onion and the garlic and sauté for 4 minutes.
2. Add the shrimp, the calamari and the rest of the ingredients except the parsley, stir, bring to a simmer and cook for 8 minutes.
3. Add the parsley, divide everything into bowls and serve.

Nutrition Info:
- calories 288, fat 12.8, fiber 10.2, carbs 22.2, protein 6.8

Lemon-garlic Baked Halibut
Servings: 2 | Cooking Time: 15 Minutes

Ingredients:
- 1 large garlic clove, minced
- 1 tbsp chopped flat leaf parsley
- 1 tsp olive oil
- 2 5-oz boneless, skin-on halibut fillets
- 2 tsp lemon zest
- Juice of ½ lemon, divided
- Salt and pepper to taste

Directions:
1. Grease a baking dish with cooking spray and preheat oven to 400oF.
2. Place halibut with skin touching the dish and drizzle with olive oil.
3. Season with pepper and salt.
4. Pop into the oven and bake until flaky around 12-15 minutes.
5. Remove from oven and drizzle with remaining lemon juice, serve and enjoy with a side of salad greens.

Nutrition Info:
- Calories per serving: 315.3; Protein: 14.1g; Fat: 10.5g; Carbs: 36.6g

Tuna Risotto
Servings: 6 | Cooking Time: 23 Minutes

Ingredients:
- 1 cup of rice
- 1/3 cup parmesan cheese, grated
- 1 1/2 cups fish broth
- 1 lemon juice
- 1 tbsp garlic, minced
- 1 onion, chopped
- 2 tbsp olive oil
- 2 cups can tuna, cut into chunks
- Pepper
- Salt

Directions:
1. Add oil into the inner pot of instant pot and set the pot on sauté mode.
2. Add garlic, onion, and tuna and cook for 3 minutes.
3. Add remaining ingredients except for parmesan cheese and stir well.
4. Seal pot with lid and cook on high for 20 minutes.
5. Once done, release pressure using quick release. Remove lid.
6. Stir in parmesan cheese and serve.

Nutrition Info:
- Calories 228 Fat 7 g Carbohydrates 27.7 g Sugar 1.2 g Protein 12.6 g Cholesterol 21 mg

Fish And Orzo
Servings: 4 | Cooking Time: 35 Minutes

Ingredients:
- 1 teaspoon garlic, minced
- 1 teaspoon red pepper, crushed
- 2 shallots, chopped
- 1 tablespoon olive oil
- 1 teaspoon anchovy paste
- 1 tablespoon oregano, chopped
- 2 tablespoons black olives, pitted and chopped
- 2 tablespoons capers, drained
- 15 ounces canned tomatoes, crushed
- A pinch of salt and black pepper
- 4 cod fillets, boneless
- 1 ounce feta cheese, crumbled
- 1 tablespoons parsley, chopped
- 3 cups chicken stock
- 1 cup orzo pasta
- Zest of 1 lemon, grated

Directions:
1. Heat up a pan with the oil over medium heat, add the garlic, red pepper and the shallots and sauté for 5 minutes.
2. Add the anchovy paste, oregano, black olives, capers, tomatoes, salt and pepper, stir and cook for 5 minutes more.
3. Add the cod fillets, sprinkle the cheese and the parsley on top, introduce in the oven and bake at 375 degrees F for 15 minutes more.
4. Meanwhile, put the stock in a pot, bring to a boil over medium heat, add the orzo and the lemon zest, bring to a simmer,

cook for 10 minutes, fluff with a fork, and divide between plates.
5. Top each serving with the fish mix and serve.

Nutrition Info:
- calories 402, fat 21, fiber 8, carbs 21, protein 31

Smoked Trout Tartine
Servings: 4 | Cooking Time: 0 Minutes

Ingredients:
- ½ 15-oz can cannellini beans
- ½ cup diced roasted red peppers
- ¾ lb. smoked trout, flaked into bite-sized pieces
- 1 stalk celery, finely chopped
- 1 tbsp extra virgin olive oil
- 1 tsp chopped fresh dill
- 1 tsp Dijon mustard
- 2 tbsp capers, rinsed and drained
- 2 tbsp freshly squeezed lemon juice
- 2 tsp minced onion
- 4 large whole grain bread, toasted
- Dill sprigs – for garnish
- Pinch of sugar

Directions:
1. Mix sugar, mustard, olive oil and lemon juice in a big bowl.
2. Add the rest of the ingredients except for toasted bread.
3. Toss to mix well.
4. Evenly divide fish mixture on top of bread slices and garnish with dill sprigs.
5. Serve and enjoy.

Nutrition Info:
- Calories per serving: 348.1; Protein: 28.2 g; Fat: 10.1g; Carbs: 36.1g

Leeks And Calamari Mix
Servings: 6 | Cooking Time: 15 Minutes

Ingredients:
- 2 tablespoon avocado oil
- 2 leeks, chopped
- 1 red onion, chopped
- Salt and black to the taste
- 1 pound calamari rings
- 1 tablespoon parsley, chopped
- 1 tablespoon chives, chopped
- 2 tablespoons tomato paste

Directions:
1. Heat up a pan with the avocado oil over medium heat, add the leeks and the onion, stir and sauté for 5 minutes.
2. Add the rest of the ingredients, toss, simmer over medium heat for 10 minutes, divide into bowls and serve.

Nutrition Info:
- calories 238, fat 9, fiber 5.6, carbs 14.4, protein 8.4

Italian Tuna Pasta
Servings: 6 | Cooking Time: 5 Minutes

Ingredients:
- 15 oz whole wheat pasta
- 2 tbsp capers
- 3 oz tuna
- 2 cups can tomatoes, crushed
- 2 anchovies
- 1 tsp garlic, minced
- 1 tbsp olive oil
- Salt

Directions:
1. Add oil into the inner pot of instant pot and set the pot on sauté mode.
2. Add anchovies and garlic and sauté for 1 minute.
3. Add remaining ingredients and stir well. Pour enough water into the pot to cover the pasta.
4. Seal pot with a lid and select manual and cook on low for 4 minutes.
5. Once done, release pressure using quick release. Remove lid.
6. Stir and serve.

Nutrition Info:
- Calories 339 Fat 6 g Carbohydrates 56.5 g Sugar 5.2 g Protein 15.2 g Cholesterol 10 mg

Parmesan Salmon Balls
Servings:5 | Cooking Time: 15 Minutes

Ingredients:
- 1-pound salmon fillet
- 2 teaspoons cream cheese
- 3 tablespoons panko breadcrumbs
- ½ teaspoon salt
- 1 oz Parmesan, grated
- ½ teaspoon ground black pepper
- 1 teaspoon dried oregano
- 1 tablespoon sunflower oil

Directions:
1. Grind the salmon fillet and combine it together with cream cheese, panko breadcrumbs, salt, Parmesan, ground black pepper, and dried oregano.
2. Then make the small balls from the mixture and place them in the non-sticky tray.
3. Sprinkle the balls with sunflower oil and bake in the preheated to the 365F oven for 15 minutes. Flip the balls on another side after 10 minutes of cooking.

Nutrition Info:
- Per Servingcalories 180, fat 10.2, fiber 0.5, carbs 2.8, protein 19.9

Crazy Saganaki Shrimp
Servings: 4 | Cooking Time: 10 Minutes

Ingredients:
- ¼ tsp salt
- ½ cup Chardonnay
- ½ cup crumbled Greek feta cheese
- 1 medium bulb. fennel, cored and finely chopped
- 1 small Chile pepper, seeded and minced
- 1 tbsp extra virgin olive oil
- 12 jumbo shrimps, peeled and deveined with tails left on
- 2 tbsp lemon juice, divided
- 5 scallions sliced thinly
- Pepper to taste

Directions:
1. In medium bowl, mix salt, lemon juice and shrimp.
2. On medium fire, place a saganaki pan (or large nonstick saucepan) and heat oil.
3. Sauté Chile pepper, scallions, and fennel for 4 minutes or until starting to brown and is already soft.
4. Add wine and sauté for another minute.
5. Place shrimps on top of fennel, cover and cook for 4 minutes or until shrimps are pink.
6. Remove just the shrimp and transfer to a plate.
7. Add pepper, feta and 1 tbsp lemon juice to pan and cook for a minute or until cheese begins to melt.
8. To serve, place cheese and fennel mixture on a serving plate and top with shrimps.

Nutrition Info:
- Calories per serving: 310; Protein: 49.7g; Fat: 6.8g; Carbs: 8.4g

Creamy Bacon-fish Chowder
Servings: 8 | Cooking Time: 30 Minutes

Ingredients:
- 1 1/2 lbs. cod
- 1 1/2 tsp dried thyme
- 1 large onion, chopped
- 1 medium carrot, coarsely chopped
- 1 tbsp butter, cut into small pieces
- 1 tsp salt, divided
- 3 1/2 cups baking potato, peeled and cubed
- 3 slices uncooked bacon
- 3/4 tsp freshly ground black pepper, divided
- 4 1/2 cups water
- 4 bay leaves
- 4 cups 2% reduced-fat milk

Directions:
1. In a large skillet, add the water and bay leaves and let it simmer. Add the fish. Cover and let it simmer some more until the flesh flakes easily with fork. Remove the fish from the skillet and cut into large pieces. Set aside the cooking liquid.
2. Place Dutch oven in medium heat and cook the bacon until crisp. Remove the bacon and reserve the bacon drippings. Crush the bacon and set aside.
3. Stir potato, onion and carrot in the pan with the bacon drippings, cook over medium heat for 10 minutes. Add the cooking liquid, bay leaves, 1/2 tsp salt, 1/4 tsp pepper and thyme, let it boil. Lower the heat and let simmer for 10 minutes. Add the milk and butter, simmer until the potatoes becomes tender, but do not boil. Add the fish, 1/2 tsp salt, 1/2 tsp pepper. Remove the bay leaves.
4. Serve sprinkled with the crushed bacon.

Nutrition Info:
- Calories per serving: 400; Carbs: 34.5g; Protein: 20.8g; Fat: 19.7g

Avocado Peach Salsa On Grilled Swordfish
Servings: 2 | Cooking Time: 10 Minutes

Ingredients:
- 1 garlic clove, minced
- 1 lemon juice
- 1 tbsp apple cider vinegar
- 1 tbsp coconut oil
- 1 tsp honey
- 2 swordfish fillets (around 4oz each)
- pinch cayenne pepper
- pinch of pepper and salt
- ¼ red onion, finely chopped
- ½ cup cilantro, finely chopped
- 1 avocado, halved and diced
- 1 garlic clove, minced
- 2 peaches, seeded and diced
- juice of 1 lime
- salt to taste

Directions:
1. In a shallow dish, mix all swordfish marinade ingredients except fillet. Mix well then add fillets to marinate. Place in refrigerator for at least an hour.
2. Meanwhile create salsa by mixing all salsa ingredients in a medium bowl. Put in the refrigerator to cool.
3. Preheat grill and grill fish on medium fire after marinating until cooked around 4 minutes per side.
4. Place each cooked fillet on one serving plate, top with half of salsa, serve and enjoy.

Nutrition Info:
- Calories per serving: 416; Carbohydrates: 21g; Protein: 30g; Fat: 23.5g

Salmon And Peach Pan
Servings: 4 | Cooking Time: 11 Minutes

Ingredients:
- 1 tablespoon balsamic vinegar
- 1 teaspoon thyme, chopped
- 1 tablespoon ginger, grated
- 2 tablespoons olive oil
- Sea salt and black pepper to the taste
- 3 peaches, cut into medium wedges
- 4 salmon fillets, boneless

Directions:
1. Heat up a pan with the oil over medium-high heat, add the salmon and cook for 3 minutes on each side.
2. Add the vinegar, the peaches and the rest of the ingredients,

cook for 5 minutes more, divide everything between plates and serve.

Nutrition Info:
- calories 293, fat 17.1, fiber 4.1, carbs 26.4, protein 24.5

Mahi Mahi And Pomegranate Sauce
Servings: 4 | Cooking Time: 10 Minutes

Ingredients:
- 1 and ½ cups chicken stock
- 1 tablespoon olive oil
- 4 mahi mahi fillets, boneless
- 4 tablespoons tahini paste
- Juice of 1 lime
- Seeds from 1 pomegranate
- 1 tablespoon parsley, chopped

Directions:
1. Heat up a pan with the oil over medium-high heat, add the fish and cook for 3 minutes on each side.
2. Add the rest of the ingredients, flip the fish again, cook for 4 minutes more, divide everything between plates and serve.

Nutrition Info:
- calories 224, fat 11.1, fiber 5.5, carbs 16.7, protein 11.4

Greek Trout Spread
Servings: 8 | Cooking Time: 0 Minutes

Ingredients:
- 4 ounces smoked trout, skinless, boneless and flaked
- 1 tablespoon lemon juice
- 1 cup Greek yogurt
- tablespoon dill, chopped
- Salt and black pepper to the taste
- A drizzle of olive oil

Directions:
1. In a bowl, combine the trout with the lemon juice and the rest of the ingredients and whisk really well.
2. Divide the spread into bowls and serve.

Nutrition Info:
- calories 258, fat 4,5, fiber 2, carbs 5.5, protein 7.6

Salmon And Green Beans
Servings: 4 | Cooking Time: 15 Minutes

Ingredients:
- 3 tablespoons balsamic vinegar
- 2 tablespoons olive oil
- 1 garlic clove, minced
- ½ teaspoons red pepper flakes, crushed
- ½ teaspoon lime zest, grated
- 1 and ½ pounds green beans, chopped
- Salt and black pepper to the taste
- 1 red onion, sliced
- 4 salmon fillets, boneless

Directions:
1. Heat up a pan with half of the oil, add the vinegar, onion, garlic and the other ingredients except the salmon, toss, cook for 6 minutes and divide between plates.
2. Heat up the same pan with the rest of the oil over medium-high heat, add the salmon, salt and pepper, cook for 4 minutes on each side, add next to the green beans and serve.

Nutrition Info:
- calories 224, fat 15.5, fiber 8.2, carbs 22.7, protein 16.3

Salsa Fish Fillets
Servings: 4 | Cooking Time: 2 Minutes

Ingredients:
- 1 lb tilapia fillets
- 1/2 cup salsa
- 1 cup of water
- Pepper
- Salt

Directions:
1. Place fish fillets on aluminum foil and top with salsa and season with pepper and salt.
2. Fold foil around the fish fillets.
3. Pour water into the instant pot and place trivet in the pot.
4. Place foil fish packet on the trivet.
5. Seal pot with lid and cook on high for 2 minutes.
6. Once done, release pressure using quick release. Remove lid.
7. Serve and enjoy.

Nutrition Info:
- Calories 342 Fat 10.5 g Carbohydrates 41.5 g Sugar 1.9 g Protein 18.9 g Cholesterol 31 mg

Stewed Mussels & Scallops
Servings: 4 | Cooking Time: 11 Minutes

Ingredients:
- 2 cups mussels
- 1 cup scallops
- 2 cups fish stock
- 2 bell peppers, diced
- 2 cups cauliflower rice
- 1 onion, chopped
- 1 tbsp olive oil
- Pepper
- Salt

Directions:
1. Add oil into the inner pot of instant pot and set the pot on sauté mode.
2. Add onion and peppers and sauté for 3 minutes.
3. Add scallops and cook for 2 minutes.
4. Add remaining ingredients and stir well.
5. Seal pot with lid and cook on high for 6 minutes.
6. Once done, allow to release pressure naturally. Remove lid.
7. Stir and serve.

Nutrition Info:
- Calories 191 Fat 7.4 g Carbohydrates 13.7 g Sugar 6.2 g Protein 18 g
- Cholesterol 29 mg

Leftover Salmon Salad Power Bowls
Servings: 1 | Cooking Time: 10 Minutes

Ingredients:
- ½ cup raspberries
- ½ cup zucchini, sliced
- 1 lemon, juice squeezed
- 1 tablespoon balsamic glaze
- 2 sprigs of thyme, chopped
- 2 tablespoon olive oil
- 4 cups seasonal greens
- 4 ounces leftover grilled salmon
- Salt and pepper to taste

Directions:
1. Heat oil in a skillet over medium flame and sauté the zucchini. Season with salt and pepper to taste.
2. In a mixing bowl, mix all ingredients together.
3. Toss to combine everything.
4. Sprinkle with nut cheese.

Nutrition Info:
- Calories per Serving: 450.3; Fat: 35.5 g; Protein: 23.4g; Carbs: 9.3 g

Easy Fish Curry
Servings: 4 | Cooking Time: 20 Minutes

Ingredients:
- Juice of half a lime
- A handful of coriander leaves
- ½ pound white fish cut into large strips
- Salt and pepper to taste
- 2 tomatoes, chopped
- ½ cup coconut milk
- 15 curry leaves
- 1 teaspoon turmeric, ground
- 2 teaspoon curry powder
- 2 tablespoon ginger, grated
- 3 cloves garlic, sliced
- 1 onion, chopped
- 2 tablespoon coconut oil

Directions:
1. Heat oil in a medium saucepan. Sauté the onion over medium heat until translucent.
2. Add the ginger and garlic and cook for a minute before adding the curry powder, curry leaves and turmeric. Continue cooking for a minute before adding the coconut milk.
3. Add the chopped tomatoes and simmer for 5 minutes or until the tomatoes are soft.
4. Add the fish and season with salt and pepper to taste. Cook for 8 minutes before adding the lime juice and coriander leaves.
5. Serve warm.

Nutrition Info:
- Calories per Serving: 213; Fat: 14.7g; Protein: 12.3g; Carbs: 10.5g

Minty Sardines Salad
Servings: 4 | Cooking Time: 0 Minutes

Ingredients:
- 4 ounces canned sardines in olive oil, skinless, boneless and flaked
- 2 teaspoons avocado oil
- 2 tablespoons mint, chopped
- A pinch of salt and black pepper
- 1 avocado, peeled, pitted and cubed
- 1 cucumber, cubed
- 2 tomatoes, cubed
- 2 spring onions, chopped

Directions:
1. In a bowl, combine the sardines with the oil and the rest of the ingredients, toss, divide into small cups and keep in the fridge for 10 minutes before serving.

Nutrition Info:
- calories 261, fat 7.6, fiber 2.2, carbs 22.8, protein 12.5

Dill Calamari
Servings:4 | Cooking Time: 5 Minutes

Ingredients:
- 1-pound calamari
- 3 tablespoons lime juice
- 1 tablespoon fresh dill, chopped
- 1/3 teaspoon minced garlic
- 1 tablespoon butter
- 1/3 teaspoon salt
- ¼ teaspoon chili pepper

Directions:
1. Slice cleaned and washed calamari into the rings and after this, place them in the mixing bowl.
2. Sprinkle the calamari rings with salt and chili pepper. Mix up well.
3. After this, toss the butter in the skillet and melt it.
4. Add minced garlic, dill, and lime juice.
5. Bring the liquid to boil and add calamari rings.
6. Cook the seafood for 3 minutes over the medium-high heat. Stir them once during the cooking time.
7. Remove the cooked calamari rings from the heat and transfer in the serving plates.

Nutrition Info:
- Per Servingcalories 137, fat 6.9, fiber 0.7, carbs 9.6, protein 8.2

Shrimp And Lemon Sauce
Servings: 4 | Cooking Time: 15 Minutes

Ingredients:
- 1 pound shrimp, peeled and deveined
- 1/3 cup lemon juice
- 4 egg yolks
- 2 tablespoons olive oil
- 1 cup chicken stock
- Salt and black pepper to the taste
- 1 cup black olives, pitted and halved
- 1 tablespoon thyme, chopped

Mediterranean Diet Cookbook

Directions:
1. In a bowl, mix the lemon juice with the egg yolks and whisk well.
2. Heat up a pan with the oil over medium heat, add the shrimp and cook for 2 minutes on each side and transfer to a plate.
3. Heat up a pan with the stock over medium heat, add some of this over the egg yolks and lemon juice mix and whisk well.
4. Add this over the rest of the stock, also add salt and pepper, whisk well and simmer for 2 minutes.
5. Add the shrimp and the rest of the ingredients, toss and serve right away.

Nutrition Info:
- calories 237, fat 15.3, fiber 4.6, carbs 15.4, protein 7.6

Walnut Salmon Mix
Servings:4 | Cooking Time: 25 Minutes

Ingredients:
- 12 oz salmon fillet
- 1/3 cup walnuts
- 1 tablespoon panko breadcrumbs
- 1 tablespoon dried oregano
- 1 tablespoon sunflower oil
- ½ teaspoon salt
- ½ teaspoon ground black pepper
- 1 tablespoon mustard

Directions:
1. Put the walnuts, panko bread crumbs, dried oregano, sunflower oil, salt, and ground black pepper in the blender.
2. Blend the ingredients until you get smooth and sticky mass.
3. After this, line the baking tray with baking paper.
4. Brush the salmon fillet with mustard from all sides and coat in the blended walnut mixture generously.
5. Bake the salmon for 25 minutes at 365F. Flip the salmon fillet on another side after 15 minutes of cooking.

Nutrition Info:
- Per Servingcalories 233, fat 15.9, fiber 1.9, carbs 4.7, protein 20.1

Lemon Swordfish
Servings:2 | Cooking Time: 6 Minutes

Ingredients:
- 12 oz swordfish steaks (6 oz every fish steak)
- 1 teaspoon ground cumin
- 1 tablespoon lemon juice
- ¼ teaspoon salt
- 1 teaspoon olive oil

Directions:
1. Sprinkle the fish steaks with ground cumin and salt from each side.
2. Then drizzle the lemon juice over the steaks and massage them gently with the help of the fingertips.
3. Preheat the grill to 395F.
4. Bruhs every fish steak with olive oil and place in the grill.
5. Cook the swordfish for 3 minutes from each side.

Nutrition Info:
- Per Servingcalories 289, fat 1.4, fiber 0.1, carbs 0.6, protein 43.4

Warm Caper Tapenade On Cod
Servings: 4 | Cooking Time: 30 Minutes

Ingredients:
- ¼ cup chopped cured olives
- ¼ tsp freshly ground pepper
- 1 ½ tsp chopped fresh oregano
- 1 cup halved cherry tomatoes
- 1 lb. cod fillet
- 1 tbsp capers, rinsed and chopped
- 1 tbsp minced shallot
- 1 tsp balsamic vinegar
- 3 tsp extra virgin olive oil, divided

Directions:
1. Grease baking sheet with cooking spray and preheat oven to 450oF.
2. Place cod on prepared baking sheet. Rub with 2 tsp oil and season with pepper.
3. Roast in oven for 15 to 20 minutes or until cod is flaky.
4. While waiting for cod to cook, on medium fire, place a small fry pan and heat 1 tsp oil.
5. Sauté shallots for a minute.
6. Add tomatoes and cook for two minutes or until soft.
7. Add capers and olives. Sauté for another minute.
8. Add vinegar and oregano. Turn off fire and stir to mix well.
9. Evenly divide cod into 4 servings and place on a plate.
10. To serve, top cod with Caper-Olive-Tomato Tapenade and enjoy.

Nutrition Info:
- Calories per Serving: 107; Fat: 2.9g; Protein: 17.6g; Carbs: 2.0g

One-pot Seafood Chowder
Servings: 3 | Cooking Time: 10 Minutes

Ingredients:
- 3 cans coconut milk
- 1 tablespoon garlic, minced
- salt and pepper to taste
- 3 cans clams, chopped
- 2 cans shrimps, canned
- 1 package fresh shrimps, shelled and deveined
- 1 can corn, drained
- 4 large potatoes, diced
- 2 carrots, peeled and chopped
- 2 celery stalks, chopped

Directions:
1. Place all ingredients in a pot and give a good stir to mix everything.
2. Close the lid and turn on the heat to medium.
3. Bring to a boil and allow to simmer for 10 minutes.
4. Place in individual containers.
5. Put a label and store in the fridge.
6. Allow to warm at room temperature before heating in the microwave oven.

Nutrition Info:
- Calories per serving: 532; Carbs: 92.5g; Protein: 25.3g; Fat: 6.7g

Crab Stew
Servings: 2 | Cooking Time: 13 Minutes

Ingredients:
- 1/2 lb lump crab meat
- 2 tbsp heavy cream
- 1 tbsp olive oil
- 2 cups fish stock
- 1/2 lb shrimp, shelled and chopped
- 1 celery stalk, chopped
- 1/2 tsp garlic, chopped
- 1/4 onion, chopped
- Pepper
- Salt

Directions:
1. Add oil into the inner pot of instant pot and set the pot on sauté mode.
2. Add onion and sauté for 3 minutes.
3. Add garlic and sauté for 30 seconds.
4. Add remaining ingredients except for heavy cream and stir well.
5. Seal pot with lid and cook on high for 10 minutes.
6. Once done, release pressure using quick release. Remove lid.
7. Stir in heavy cream and serve.

Nutrition Info:
- Calories 376 Fat 25.5 g Carbohydrates 5.8 g Sugar 0.7 g Protein 48.1 g Cholesterol 326 mg

Easy Broiled Lobster Tails
Servings: 2 | Cooking Time: 10 Minutes

Ingredients:
- 1 6-oz frozen lobster tails
- 1 tbsp olive oil
- 1 tsp lemon pepper seasoning

Directions:
1. Preheat oven broiler.
2. With kitchen scissors, cut thawed lobster tails in half lengthwise.
3. Brush with oil the exposed lobster meat. Season with lemon pepper.
4. Place lobster tails in baking sheet with exposed meat facing up.
5. Place on top broiler rack and broil for 10 minutes until lobster meat is lightly browned on the sides and center meat is opaque.
6. Serve and enjoy.

Nutrition Info:
- Calories per Serving: 175.6; Protein: 3g; Fat: 10g; Carbs: 18.4g

Trout And Tzatziki Sauce
Servings: 4 | Cooking Time: 10 Minutes

Ingredients:
- Juice of ½ lime
- Salt and black pepper to the taste
- 1 and ½ teaspoon coriander, ground
- 1 teaspoon garlic, minced
- 4 trout fillets, boneless
- 1 teaspoon sweet paprika
- 2 tablespoons avocado oil
- For the sauce:
- 1 cucumber, chopped
- 4 garlic cloves, minced
- 1 tablespoon olive oil
- 1 teaspoon white vinegar
- 1 and ½ cups Greek yogurt
- A pinch of salt and white pepper

Directions:
1. Heat up a pan with the avocado oil over medium-high heat, add the fish, salt, pepper, lime juice, 1 teaspoon garlic and the paprika, rub the fish gently and cook for 4 minutes on each side.
2. In a bowl, combine the cucumber with 4 garlic cloves and the rest of the ingredients for the sauce and whisk well.
3. Divide the fish between plates, drizzle the sauce all over and serve with a side salad.

Nutrition Info:
- calories 393, fat 18.5, fiber 6.5, carbs 18.3, protein 39.6

Creamy Curry Salmon
Servings: 2 | Cooking Time: 20 Minutes

Ingredients:
- 2 salmon fillets, boneless and cubed
- 1 tablespoon olive oil
- 1 tablespoon basil, chopped
- Sea salt and black pepper to the taste
- 1 cup Greek yogurt
- 2 teaspoons curry powder
- 1 garlic clove, minced
- ½ teaspoon mint, chopped

Directions:
1. Heat up a pan with the oil over medium-high heat, add the salmon and cook for 3 minutes.
2. Add the rest of the ingredients, toss, cook for 15 minutes more, divide between plates and serve.

Nutrition Info:
- calories 284, fat 14.1, fiber 8.5, carbs 26.7, protein 31.4

Mustard Cod

Servings: 2 | Cooking Time: 20 Minutes

Ingredients:
- 1 tablespoon Dijon mustard
- 2 teaspoons sunflower oil
- 1 white onion, diced
- 1/3 teaspoon minced garlic
- 2 tomatoes, chopped
- ¾ cup black olives, chopped
- 1 teaspoon capers, drained
- 1 tablespoon fresh parsley
- 10 oz cod fillets (5 oz each fish fillet)

Directions:
1. Preheat sunflower oil in the skillet over the medium heat.
2. Then place the fish fillets in the hot oil and roast them for 2 minutes from each side.
3. Transfer the fish in the plate.
4. After this, add diced onion in the skillet.
5. Then add minced garlic, tomatoes, and capers. Mix up well and close the lid.
6. Cook the vegetables for 5 minutes over the medium heat.
7. Then ad roasted cod fillets and stir puttanesca well.
8. Close the lid and cook the meal for 10 minutes over the medium-low heat.
9. Transfer the cooked cod in the serving plates and top with the cooked vegetables.

Nutrition Info:
- Per Servingcalories 285, fat 12.2, fiber 4.7, carbs 13.9, protein 32.6

Garlic Roasted Shrimp With Zucchini Pasta

Servings: 2 | Cooking Time: 10 Minutes

Ingredients:
- 2 medium-sized zucchinis, cut into thin strips or spaghetti noodles
- Salt and pepper to taste
- 1 lemon, zested and juiced
- 2 garlic cloves, minced
- 2 tablespoon ghee, melted
- 2 tablespoon olive oil
- 8 ounces shrimps, cleaned and deveined

Directions:
1. Preheat the oven to 4000F.
2. In a mixing bowl, mix all ingredients except the zucchini noodles. Toss to coat the shrimp.
3. Bake for 10 minutes until the shrimps turn pink.
4. Add the zucchini pasta then toss.

Nutrition Info:
- Calories per Serving: 299; Fat: 23.2g; Protein: 14.3g; Carbs: 10.9g

Delicious Fish Tacos

Servings: 8 | Cooking Time: 8 Minutes

Ingredients:
- 4 tilapia fillets
- 1/4 cup fresh cilantro, chopped
- 1/4 cup fresh lime juice
- 2 tbsp paprika
- 1 tbsp olive oil
- Pepper
- Salt

Directions:
1. Pour 2 cups of water into the instant pot then place steamer rack in the pot.
2. Place fish fillets on parchment paper.
3. Season fish fillets with paprika, pepper, and salt and drizzle with oil and lime juice.
4. Fold parchment paper around the fish fillets and place them on a steamer rack in the pot.
5. Seal pot with lid and cook on high for 8 minutes.
6. Once done, release pressure using quick release. Remove lid.
7. Remove fish packet from pot and open it.
8. Shred the fish with a fork and serve.

Nutrition Info:
- Calories 67 Fat 2.5 g Carbohydrates 1.1 g Sugar 0.2 g Protein 10.8 g Cholesterol 28 mg

Shrimp Scampi

Servings: 6 | Cooking Time: 8 Minutes

Ingredients:
- 1 lb whole wheat penne pasta
- 1 lb frozen shrimp
- 2 tbsp garlic, minced
- 1/4 tsp cayenne
- 1/2 tbsp Italian seasoning
- 1/4 cup olive oil
- 3 1/2 cups fish stock
- Pepper
- Salt

Directions:
1. Add all ingredients into the inner pot of instant pot and stir well.
2. Seal pot with lid and cook on high for 6 minutes.
3. Once done, release pressure using quick release. Remove lid.
4. Stir well and serve.

Nutrition Info:
- Calories 435 Fat 12.6 g Carbohydrates 54.9 g Sugar 0.1 g Protein 30.6 g Cholesterol 116 mg

Salads & Side Dishes Recipes

Salads & Side Dishes Recipes

Garden Salad With Grapes
Servings: 6 | Cooking Time: 0 Minutes

Ingredients:
- ¼ tsp black pepper
- ¼ tsp salt
- ½ tsp stone-ground mustard
- 1 tsp chopped fresh thyme
- 1 tsp honey
- 1 tsp maple syrup
- 2 cups red grapes, halved
- 2 tbsp toasted sunflower seed kernels
- 2 tsp grapeseed oil
- 3 tbsp red wine vinegar
- 7 cups loosely packed baby arugula

Directions:
1. In a small bowl whisk together mustard, syrup, honey and vinegar. Whisking continuously, slowly add oil.
2. In a large salad bowl, mix thyme, seeds, grapes and arugula.
3. Drizzle with the oil dressing, season with pepper and salt.
4. Gently toss to coat salad with the dressing.

Nutrition Info:
- Calories per serving: 85.7; Protein: 1.6g; Carbs: 12.4g; Fat: 3.3g

Tangy Citrus Salad With Grilled Cod
Servings: 2 | Cooking Time: 10 Minutes

Ingredients:
- ½ cup orange segments
- ¾ cup chopped red bell pepper
- 1 ½ cups shredded carrot
- 1 ½ cups shredded kohlrabi
- 1 ½ cups shredded spinach
- 1 ½ tbsp olive oil
- 1 cup grapefruit segments
- 1 cup shredded celery
- 1 tbsp minced garlic
- 1 tbsp shredded fresh basil
- 1 tsp black pepper
- 6-oz baked or broiled cod
- Zest and juice of 1 lemon
- Zest and juice of 1 lime
- Zest and juice of 1 orange

Directions:
1. Grease grill grate with cooking spray and preheat to medium high fire. Once grate is hot, grill cod until flaky, around 5 minutes per side.
2. Meanwhile, mix remaining ingredients, except for citrus pieces, in a large salad bowl and toss well to combine.
3. To serve, evenly divide salad into two plates, top with ½ of grilled cod and garnish with citrus pieces.

Nutrition Info:
- Calories per serving: 381.9; Protein: 22g; Carbs: 47.6g; Fat: 11.5g

Dill Cucumber Salad
Servings: 8 | Cooking Time: 0 Minutes

Ingredients:
- 4 cucumbers, sliced
- 1 cup white wine vinegar
- 2 white onions, sliced
- 1 tablespoon dill, chopped

Directions:
1. In a bowl, mix the cucumber with the onions, vinegar and the dill, toss well and keep in the fridge for 1 hour before serving as a side salad.

Nutrition Info:
- calories 182, fat 3.5, fiber 4.5, carbs 8.5, protein 4.5

Easy Quinoa & Pear Salad
Servings: 6 | Cooking Time: 0 Minutes

Ingredients:
- ¼ cup chopped parsley
- ¼ cup chopped scallions
- ¼ cup lime juice
- ¼ cup red onion, diced
- ½ cup diced carrots
- ½ cup diced celery
- ½ cup diced cucumber
- ½ cup diced red pepper
- ½ cup dried wild blueberries
- ½ cup olive oil
- ½ cup spicy pecans, chopped
- 1 tbsp chopped parsley
- 1 tsp honey
- 1 tsp sea salt
- 2 fresh pears, cut into chunks
- 3 cups cooked quinoa

Directions:
1. In a small bowl mix well olive oil, salt, lime juice, honey, and parsley. Set aside.
2. In large salad bowl, add remaining ingredients and toss to mix well.
3. Pour dressing and toss well to coat.
4. Serve and enjoy.

Nutrition Info:
- Calories per serving: 382; Protein: 5.6g; Carbs: 31.4g; Fat: 26g

Barley And Chicken Salad
Servings: 8 | Cooking Time: 50 Minutes

Ingredients:
- For the salad:
- 1 cup grape tomatoes, halved
- 1 cup pearl barley, uncooked
- 1 teaspoon olive oil
- 1/2 cup yellow bell pepper, cubed
- 1/3 cup feta cheese, reduced-fat
- 1/4 cup Kalamata olives, chopped, pitted
- 1/8 teaspoon kosher salt
- 2 pieces (6-ounce each) chicken breast halves, skinless, boneless
- 2 cups cucumber, seeded, cubed
- 4 cups chicken broth, fat-free, less-sodium, divided
- 3 tablespoons extra-virgin olive oil
- 3 garlic cloves, minced
- 2 tablespoons freshly squeezed lemon juice
- 1/2 teaspoon kosher salt
- 1 teaspoon red wine vinegar
- 1 teaspoon fresh thyme, minced
- 1 teaspoon lemon rind, grated
- 1 tablespoon fresh basil, minced

Directions:
1. For the salad:
2. Sprinkle the chicken with the kosher salt.
3. In a nonstick skillet, heat the olive oil over medium-high heat. Add the chicken, and cook each side for 2 minutes or until browned. Add 1 cup of the broth, cover, reduce the heat, and simmer 10 minutes or until the chicken is cooked. Let cool, discard the broth, and shred the chicken.
4. In a large-sized saucepan, bring the 3 cups of broth to a boil. Add the barley; cover, reduce the heat, and simmer for 35 minutes or until the barley absorbs the liquid. Fluff with the fork; let cool. In a large-sized bowl, combine the barley, chicken, cucumber, tomatoes, bell pepper, feta cheese, and Kalamata olives.
5. For the dressing:
6. Combine all of the ingredients; stirring well. Add the dressing to the barley mixture; toss well to combine. Cover and chill; serve.

Nutrition Info:
- Per Serving: 230 cal., 9.8 g fat (2 g sat. fat, 5.7 g mono fat, 1.1 g poly fat), 18 g protein, 18.3 g carb., 3.2 g fiber, 38 mg chol., 1.2 mg iron, 611 mg sodium, and 38 mg calcium.

Chickpeas, Corn And Black Beans Salad
Servings: 4 | Cooking Time: 0 Minutes

Ingredients:
- 1 and ½ cups canned black beans, drained and rinsed
- ½ teaspoon garlic powder
- 2 teaspoons chili powder
- A pinch of sea salt and black pepper
- 1 and ½ cups canned chickpeas, drained and rinsed
- 1 cup baby spinach
- 1 avocado, pitted, peeled and chopped
- 1 cup corn kernels, chopped
- 2 tablespoons lemon juice
- 1 tablespoon olive oil
- 1 tablespoon apple cider vinegar
- 1 teaspoon chives, chopped

Directions:
1. In a salad bowl, combine the black beans with the garlic powder, chili powder and the rest of the ingredients, toss and serve cold.

Nutrition Info:
- calories 300, fat 13.4, fiber 4.1, carbs 8.6, protein 13

Sweet And Sour Spinach Salad
Servings: 4 | Cooking Time 15 Minutes

Ingredients:
- Red onions - 2, sliced
- Baby spinach leaves - 4
- Sesame oil - 1 2 tsp.
- Apple cider vinegar - 2 tbsp.
- Honey - 1 tsp.
- Sesame seeds - 2 tbsp.
- Salt and pepper - to taste

Directions:
1. Mix together honey, sesame oil, vinegar and sesame seeds in a small bowl to make a dressing. Add in salt and pepper to suit your taste.
2. Add red onions and spinach together in a salad bowl.
3. Pour dressing over the salad and serve while cool and fresh.

Cardamom Apples
Servings: 2 | Cooking Time: 15 Minutes

Ingredients:
- 1 tablespoon honey
- ½ teaspoon ground cardamom
- 2 apples

Directions:
1. Cut the apples into halves and remove the seeds.
2. Then cut the apples into 4 bites more.
3. Place the apple bites in the tray and sprinkle with ground cardamom and honey.
4. Bake apples for 15 minutes at 355F.

Nutrition Info:
- Per Serving calories 149, fat 0.4, fiber 5.6, carbs 39.8, protein 0.7

Cucumber Salad Japanese Style
Servings: 5 | Cooking Time: 0 Minutes

Ingredients:
- 1 ½ tsp minced fresh ginger root
- 1 tsp salt
- 1/3 cup rice vinegar
- 2 large cucumbers, ribbon cut
- 4 tsp white sugar

Directions:
1. Mix well ginger, salt, sugar and vinegar in a small bowl.
2. Add ribbon cut cucumbers and mix well.

Mediterranean Diet Cookbook

3. Let stand for at least one hour in the ref before serving.

Nutrition Info:
- Calories per Serving: 29; Fat: .2g; Protein: .7g; Carbs: 6.1g

Cheesy Barley
Servings: 8 | Cooking Time: 45 Minutes

Ingredients:
- 2 cups of water
- 1 cup barley
- 1 teaspoon salt
- 1 cup Cheddar cheese, shredded
- 1/3 cup Mozzarella cheese, shredded
- 1 cup milk
- 1 tablespoon butter
- 1 tablespoon fresh cilantro, chopped
- 1/3 cup fresh parsley, chopped
- 1 teaspoon ground black pepper
- ½ teaspoon minced garlic
- 2 tablespoons almond flour

Directions:
1. Place barley and water in the pan and bring them to boil.
2. Close the lid and cook the barley for 20 minutes.
3. Meanwhile, combine together Cheddar cheese, Mozzarella cheese, milk, fresh cilantro, parsley, ground black pepper, and minced garlic. Mix up the mixture well.
4. Rub the gratin mold with butter generously.
5. Then make the layer of barley inside it.
6. After this, pour the cheese mixture over the barley and flatten it well with the help of the spatula.
7. Sprinkle the top of the gratin with almond flour.
8. Bake the gratin for 25 minutes at 355F

Nutrition Info:
- Per Servingcalories 212, fat 11, fiber 3.6, carbs 14.9, protein 6.8

Mediterranean-style fish soup
Servings:4 | Cooking Time:20 Minutes

Ingredients:
- 1 can (14.5-ounce) diced tomatoes, no-salt-added, undrained
- 1 can (15-ounce) cannellini beans, rinsed, drained (or other white beans)
- 1 cup whole-wheat pasta, uncooked, medium seashell
- 1 tablespoon fresh oregano, finely chopped
- 1 tablespoon olive oil
- 1/2 cup onion, finely chopped
- 1/3 cup carrot, thinly sliced
- 1/4 cup (about 1 ounce) Parmesan cheese, shaved
- 1/4 teaspoon freshly ground black pepper
- 2 cans (14-ounce each) chicken broth, fat-free, less-sodium
- 2 cups (about 1/2 pound) green beans, cut into 1-inch pieces
- 2 garlic cloves, minced
- 2 tablespoons fresh basil, finely chopped
- 2 tablespoons tomato paste
- 3/4 pound halibut fillets, skinless, cut into 1-inch pieces

Directions:
1. In a Dutch oven, heat the olive oil over medium-high heat. Add the onion and the garlic; sauté for about 5 minutes or until tender. Add the green beans, carrots, broth, beans, and tomatoes; bring the mixture to a boil. When boiling, add the whole-wheat pasta; cover, reduce the heat, and simmer for about 12 minutes or until the pasta is tender.
2. Stir in the oregano, basil, tomato paste, and the lack pepper. Gently stir in the fish; cook for about 3 minutes or until easily flakes when tester using a fork, or until your preferred doneness. Serve with a sprinkle of cheese.

Nutrition Info:
- Per Serving:385 Cal, 8.3 g total fat (2.1 g sat. fat, 4 g mono fat, 1.3 g poly fat), 31.4 g protein, 45.9 g carb, 7.9 g fiber, 32 g chol., 4.2 mg iron, 698 mg sodium, and 218 mg calcium.

Quinoa Salad
Serves: 2 Cups | Cooking Time:20 Minutes

Ingredients:
- 2 cups red quinoa
- 4 cups water
- 1 (15-oz.) can chickpeas, drained
- 1 medium red onion, chopped (1/2 cup)
- 3 TB. fresh mint leaves, finely chopped
- 1/4 cup extra-virgin olive oil
- 3 TB. fresh lemon juice
- 1/2 tsp. salt
- 1/2 tsp. fresh ground black pepper

Directions:
1. In a medium saucepan over medium-high heat, bring red quinoa and water to a boil. Cover, reduce heat to low, and cook for 20 minutes or until water is absorbed and quinoa is tender. Let cool.
2. In a large bowl, add quinoa, chickpeas, red onion, and mint.
3. In a small bowl, whisk together extra-virgin olive oil, lemon juice, salt, and black pepper.
4. Pour dressing over quinoa mixture, and stir well to combine.
5. Serve immediately, or refrigerate and enjoy for up to 2 or 3 days.

Summer Bean Salad And Smoked Trout
Servings:6 | Cooking Time:5 Minutes

Ingredients:
- 1 cup oil-cured black olives, pitted and halved
- 1 cup Greek yogurt, plain
- 1 tablespoon lemon zest, finely grated
- 1/2 cup red onion, finely chopped
- 1/2 cup grapeseed or sunflower seed oil, preferably unfiltered
- 1/2 cup sunflower seeds, toasted
- 1/4 cup fresh curly parsley, chopped, 1 teaspoon reserved for garnish
- 1/4 cup fresh dill, chopped, 1 teaspoon reserved for garnish
- 12 ounces (about 2-3/4 cups) green beans (or an assortment of string beans), string removed if tough, cut into 1/2-inch pieces
- 2 medium cloves garlic, finely chopped
- 1 large or 2 small cucumber, peeled if skin is tough, cut into

1/2-inch dice (about 3 cups)
- 2 tablespoons fresh marjoram leaves, coarsely chopped, 1 teaspoon reserved for garnish
- 3 tablespoons freshly squeezed lemon juice
- 3 tablespoons red wine vinegar
- 4 cups cranberry or cannellini beans, cooked (fresh, dried, or canned)
- 8-10 ounces, smoked trout fillet, skinless
- Kosher or sea salt and freshly ground black pepper

Directions:
1. Cook the green beans in a 12-inch skillet over medium heat for about 1 minute or until they start to sizzle. Add 1 tablespoon water; cover and steam for about 4 minutes or until tender crisp. Transfer to a large-sized bowl; let cook for about 15 minutes or until room temperature.
2. Add the cucumber, cranberry beans, onion, olives, parsley, sunflower seeds, lemon juice, dill, marjoram, vinegar, garlic, and lemon zest; season with salt and pepper to taste and gently mix.
3. Arrange the salad into a large-sized platter; top with dollops of yogurt. Crumble the trout into chunks; scatter over the salad top. Garnish with the reserved herbs and with more black pepper; serve.

Nutrition Info:
- Per Serving:310 cal., 19 g fat (3.5 g sat. fat, 6 g mono fat, 9 g poly fat), 14 g protein, 21 g carb., 8 g fiber, 30 mg chol., and 500 mg sodium.

Chickpea Salad Recipe
Servings: 4 | Cooking Time: 15 Minutes

Ingredients:
- Drained chickpeas: 1 can
- Halved cherry tomatoes: 1 cup
- Sun-dried chopped tomatoes: 1 2 cups
- Arugula: 2 cups
- Cubed pita bread: 1
- Pitted black olives: 1 2 cups
- 1 sliced shallot
- Cumin seeds: 1 2 teaspoon
- Coriander seeds: 1 2 teaspoon
- Chili powder: 1 4 teaspoon
- Chopped mint: 1 teaspoon
- Pepper and salt to taste
- Crumbled goat cheese: 4 oz.

Directions:
1. In a salad bowl, mix the tomatoes, chickpeas, pita bread, arugula, olives, shallot, spices and mint.
2. Stir in pepper and salt as desired to the cheese and stir.
3. You can now serve the fresh Salad.

Quick Arugula Salad
Servings: 4 | Cooking Time: 15 Minutes

Ingredients:
- Roasted red bell peppers - 6, sliced
- Pine nuts - 2 tbsp.
- Dried raisins - 2 tbsp.
- Red onion - 1, sliced
- Arugula - 3 cups
- Balsamic vinegar - 2 tbsp.
- Feta cheese - 4 oz., crumbled
- Extra virgin olive oil – 2 tbsp.
- Feta cheese - 4 oz., crumbled
- Salt and pepper - to taste

Directions:
1. Using a salad bowl, combine vinegar, olive oil, pine nuts, raisins, peppers and onions.
2. Add arugula and feta cheese to the mix and serve.

Fennel Salad With Lemon, Toasted Almonds, And Mint
Servings:4-6 | Cooking Time: 25 Minutes

Ingredients:
- 1/2 cup sliced almonds, toasted
- 1/4 cup extra-virgin olive oil
- 1/4 cup fresh mint leaves, torn
- 2 large (about 4 pounds total) fennel bulbs, stalks trimmed, tough outer layer removed
- 3 tablespoons freshly squeezed lemon juice
- Coarsely ground black pepper
- Kosher salt

Directions:
1. Cut the fennel bulbs lengthwise and core. With a mandoline, shave the bulbs crosswise. You will have about 6 cups at the end. Alternatively, if you don't have a mandolin, cut each bulb into quarters. With a peeler, shave them lengthwise.
2. In a medium-sized bowl, toss the shaved fennel with lemon juice and 1/2 teaspoon salt; let sit for 10 minutes.
3. Add 1/2 of the almonds, 1/2 of the mint, and the olive oil; toss to combine. Transfer the salad into a serving platter or divide between serving plates.
4. Scatter the remaining mint and almonds over the top. Sprinkle with a few grinds of pepper and serve.

Nutrition Info:
- per serving: 220 cal., 15 g fat (1.5 g sat. fat, 2.5 g mono fat, 10 g poly fat), 5 g protein, 10 g carb., 8 g fiber, 0 mg chol., and 210 mg sodium.

Lamb Stew With Apricots And Moroccan Mint Tea
Servings: 6 | Cooking Time:2 Hours

Ingredients:
- 1 can (15-ounces) chickpeas, drained, rinsed
- 1 can (28-ounces) crushed tomatoes
- 1 cinnamon stick
- 1 medium carrot, cut into 1/2-inch dice
- 1 medium yellow onion, cut into 1/2-inch dice
- 1 small rib celery, cut into 1/2-inch dice
- 1 tablespoon dry mustard
- 1 tablespoon finely chopped garlic
- 1 tablespoon grated fresh ginger
- 1 tablespoon ras el hanout
- 1/2 cup fresh mint leaves, chopped, plus whole leaves for

garnish
- 1/2 cup mint tea, preferably Moroccan
- 2 star anise
- 3 cups orange juice, freshly squeezed, strained (about 6 medium oranges)
- 3 tablespoons olive oil, divided
- 4 pieces (3/4-inch-thick each) lamb shoulder chops (about 2 pounds), patted dry
- 6 ounces (1 cup) soft dried apricots, halved
- 6 tablespoons plain yogurt
- Kosher salt and freshly ground black pepper

Directions:
1. In a nonreactive, 2-quart saucepan, bring the orange juice to a simmer over medium heat. Remove the pan from the heat. Add the tea leaves; steep for 3 minutes. Strain through a fine-mesh sieve; press as much liquid as you can and set aside.
2. Season the lamb with salt and generous amount of black pepper.
3. In a flat dish, combine the ras el hanout and mustard; dredge the lamb chops in the mixture.
4. In a 7 to 8-quart heavy-duty pot over medium-high heat, heat 2 tablespoons of the olive oil. Add the lamb chops; cook for about 3 minutes each side, or until all sides are browned. Transfer the lamb chops into a plate; set aside.
5. Into the same pot, add the remaining 1 tablespoon of olive oil, celery, carrot, ginger, garlic, and the remaining ras el hanout and mustard mixture; cook for 5 minutes, stirring often and scraping any browned bits from the pan bottom.
6. Stir in the orange juice, star anise, tomatoes, and cinnamon stick; return the lamb into the pot. Add the apricots; cover and adjust the heat to a gentle simmer. Cook for about 1 to 1 1/2 hours, occasionally turning, until the lamb is tender.
7. Transfer the chops into the cutting board. Bring the sauce to a boil; add the chickpeas and cook for 5 to 10 minutes, stirring occasionally and skimming any fat from the surface, until the sauce is thick. Remove the star anise and the cinnamon stick.
8. Trim the fat and the boned from the lamb; cut the meat into bite-sized pieces and return to the sauce. Stir in the chopped mint.
9. Serve with a dollop of yogurt and sprinkle with the whole mint leaves.

Nutrition Info:
- Per Serving:630 cal., 28 g fat (9 g sat. fat, 4.5 g poly fat, 12 g mono fat), 65 mg chol., 800 mg sodium, 65 g carbs., 11 g fiber, and 33 g protein.

Mediterranean Potato Salad
Servings: 6 | Cooking Time:35 Minutes

Ingredients:
- 2 pounds new potatoes
- ¼ cup chopped parsley
- 2 tablespoons chopped dill
- 1 pinch chili flakes
- 1 lemon, juiced
- 1 tablespoon Dijon mustard
- 2 tablespoons extra virgin olive oil
- 1 teaspoon red wine vinegar
- Salt and pepper to taste

Directions:
1. Place the potatoes in a large pot and cover them with water. Add salt to taste and cook until tender. Drain well then cut into small cubes and place in a salad bowl.
2. Add the parsley, dill and chili flakes.
3. For the dressing, mix the lemon juice, mustard, oil and vinegar in a bowl. Add salt and pepper to taste and mix well.
4. Drizzle the dressing over the potatoes and mix well.
5. Serve the salad fresh.

Nutrition Info:
- Per Serving:Calories:153 Fat:5.0g Protein:3.0g Carbohydrates:25.5g

Tuna-dijon Salad
Servings: 6 | Cooking Time: Minutes

Ingredients:
- 5 whole small radishes, stems removed and chopped
- 3 stalks green onions, chopped
- 1 cup chopped parsley leaves
- ½ cup chopped fresh mint leaves, stems removed
- Six slices heirloom tomatoes for serving
- Pita chips or pita pockets for serving
- 2 1/2 celery stalks, chopped
- 1/2 English cucumber, chopped
- 1/2 medium-sized red onion, finely chopped
- 1/2 cup pitted Kalamata olives, halved
- 3 5-ounce cans Genova tuna in olive oil
- 1 1/2 limes, juice of
- 1/2 tsp crushed red pepper flakes, optional
- 1/2 tsp sumac
- 1/3 cup Early Harvest extra virgin olive oil
- 2 1/2 tsp good quality Dijon mustard
- Pinch of salt and pepper
- Zest of 1 lime

Directions:
1. Make the dressing by mixing all ingredients in a small bowl until thoroughly blended. Set aside to allow flavors to mix.
2. In a large salad bowl, make the salad.
3. Mix well mint leaves, parsley. Olives, chopped veggies, and tuna.
4. Drizzle with vinaigrette and toss well to coat.
5. Put in the fridge for at least half an hour to allow flavors to mix.
6. Toss again. Top with tomatoes.
7. Serve with pita chips on the side and enjoy.

Nutrition Info:
- Calories per Serving: 299; Carbs: 6.6g; Protein: 25.7g; Fats: 19.2g

Tomato-mozzarella With Balsamic Dressing
Servings: 4 | Cooking Time: 5 Minutes

Ingredients:
- 4 pieces fresh mozzarella balls, thickly sliced
- 4 large ripe tomatoes, thinly sliced
- 2 tablespoons extra-virgin olive oil
- 2 tablespoons capers, drained
- 1/2 cup fresh basil leaves
- 1 tablespoon aged balsamic vinegar
- 1 red onion, very thinly sliced

Directions:
1. In a small-sized frying pan, heat the oil over medium heat. Add the capers; cook, tossing, for about 2 to 3 minutes or until crisp. Transfer to a paper towel-line plate to drain.
2. In a small-sized jug, whisk the vinegar and the oil until well combined.
3. In a serving platter, arrange the tomato, the mozzarella, the basil, and the onion. Drizzle with the balsamic dressing, sprinkle with the capers, and serve immediately.

Nutrition Info:
- Per Serving: 51.6 cal, 41 g total fat (21 g sat. fat), 7 g carb, 39 g protein, 7 g sugar, and 707.04mg sodium.

Lime Beans Salad
Servings: 4 | Cooking Time: 0 Minutes

Ingredients:
- 10 ounces canned cannellini beans, drained and rinsed
- 15 ounces canned kidney beans, drained
- Salt and black pepper to the taste
- 1 garlic clove, minced
- 10 ounces corn
- ½ cup olive oil
- 1 red onion, chopped
- 2 tablespoons lime juice
- ½ tablespoon cumin, ground
- ¼ cup cilantro, chopped

Directions:
1. In a bowl, mix the beans with salt, pepper, the garlic and the rest of the ingredients, toss and serve.

Nutrition Info:
- calories 190, fat 11.8, fiber 4.1, carbs 5.4, protein 6.6

Lemony Lentil Salad With Salmon
Servings: 6 | Cooking Time: 0 Minutes

Ingredients:
- ¼ tsp salt
- ½ cup chopped red onion
- 1 cup diced seedless cucumber
- 1 medium red bell pepper, diced
- 1/3 cup extra virgin olive oil
- 1/3 cup fresh dill, chopped
- 1/3 cup lemon juice
- 2 15oz cans of lentils
- 2 7oz cans of salmon, drained and flaked
- 2 tsp Dijon mustard
- Pepper to taste

Directions:
1. In a bowl, mix together, lemon juice, mustard, dill, salt and pepper.
2. Gradually add the oil, bell pepper, onion, cucumber, salmon flakes and lentils.
3. Toss to coat evenly.

Nutrition Info:
- Calories per serving: 349.1; Protein: 27.1g; Carbs: 35.2g; Fat: 11.1g

Healthy Detox Salad
Servings: 4 | Cooking Time: 0 Minutes

Ingredients:
- 4 cups mixed greens
- 2 tbsp lemon juice
- 2 tbsp pumpkin seed oil
- 1 tbsp chia seeds
- 2 tbsp almonds, chopped
- 1 large apple, diced
- 1 large carrot, coarsely grated
- 1 large beet, coarsely grated

Directions:
1. In a medium salad bowl, except for mixed greens, combine all ingredients thoroughly.
2. Into 4 salad plates, divide the mixed greens.
3. Evenly top mixed greens with the salad bowl mixture.
4. Serve and enjoy.

Nutrition Info:
- Calories per serving: 141; Protein: 2.1g; Carbs: 14.7g; Fat: 8.2g

Herbed Tomato-arugula Salad With Chicken
Servings: 4 | Cooking Time: 5 Minutes

Ingredients:
- 1 package (5-ounces) baby arugula
- 1 1/2 tablespoons white wine vinegar
- 1 garlic clove, minced
- Lemon juice, freshly squeezed - 1 tbsp.
- 1 teaspoon dried herbes de Provence
- 1 teaspoon lemon rind, grated
- 1/2 teaspoon Dijon mustard
- 1/2 teaspoon freshly ground black pepper, divided
- 2 cups cherry tomato halves
- 3 tablespoons extra-virgin olive oil, divided
- 3 tablespoons Kalamata olives, halved, pitted
- 3/4 teaspoon salt, divided
- 4 pieces (4-ounces each) chicken breast cutlets
- Cooking spray

Directions:
1. Combine the chicken cutlets, 1 tablespoon olive oil, lemon juice, and lemon rind; let stand for 5 minutes.
2. Over medium-high heat, heat a large-sized skillet. Grease the pan with cooking spray. Evenly sprinkle the chicken with 1/2 teaspoon salt and 1/4 teaspoon pepper; add to the skillet and cook each side for 2 minutes or until done. Remove from

Mediterranean Diet Cookbook

the heat and keep warm.
3. In a large bowl, combine the arugula and the tomatoes.
4. In another bowl, combine the vinegar, mustard, herbes de Provence, remaining 1/4 teaspoon salt, garlic, and remaining 1/4 teaspoon pepper. Constantly stirring the mixture with the whisk, slowly add the remaining 2 tablespoons olive oil.
5. Drizzle the vinaigrette over the salad; gently toss to combine. Evenly divide the salad between 4 plates. Cutting across the grain, cut the cutlets into thin pieces. Arrange 1 sliced cutlet over each salad. Top each serve with about 2 teaspoons olive.

Nutrition Info:
- Per Serving:265 cal., 14.2 g fat (2.1 g sat. fat, 9.5 g mono fat, 1.8 g poly fat), 28 g protein, 6.2 g carb., 1.8 g fiber, 66 mg chol., 1.8 mg iron, 683 mg sodium, and 87 mg calcium.

Parmesan Polenta
Servings: 4 | Cooking Time: 45 Minutes

Ingredients:
- 1 cup polenta
- 1 ½ cup water
- 2 cups chicken stock
- ½ cup cream
- 1/3 cup Parmesan, grated

Directions:
1. Put polenta in the pot.
2. Add water, chicken stock, cream, and Parmesan. Mix up polenta well.
3. Then preheat oven to 355F.
4. Cook polenta in the oven for 45 minutes.
5. Mix up the cooked meal with the help of the spoon carefully before serving.

Nutrition Info:
- Per Servingcalories 208, fat 5.3, fiber 1, carbs 32.2, protein 8

Roasted Eggplant Salad
Servings: 6 | Cooking Time:45 Minutes

Ingredients:
- 3 eggplants, peeled and cubed
- 3 tablespoons extra virgin olive oil
- 1 teaspoon dried oregano
- 1 teaspoon dried basil
- 1 teaspoon dried thyme
- Salt and pepper to taste
- 2 cups cherry tomatoes, halved
- 1 red onion, sliced
- 2 tablespoons chopped parsley

Directions:
1. Season the eggplants with salt, pepper, oregano, basil, thyme and olive oil. Spread in a baking tray lined with parchment paper.
2. Bake in the preheated oven at 350F for 30 minutes then allow to cool down and transfer in a salad bowl.
3. Add the rest of the ingredients and serve the salad fresh.

Nutrition Info:
- Per Serving:Calories: 148 Fat: 7.7g Protein: 3.5g Carbohydrates: 20.5g

Spiced Parsley Salad
Servings: 2 | Cooking Time:15 Minutes

Ingredients:
- 2 cups chopped parsley
- ¼ cup chopped cilantro
- ¼ teaspoon cumin powder
- ¼ teaspoon chili powder
- ¼ teaspoon coriander seeds
- 1 tablespoon red wine vinegar
- Salt and pepper to taste

Directions:
1. Combine the parsley, cilantro, spices and vinegar in a salad bowl.
2. Add salt and pepper to taste and serve the salad as fresh as possible.

Nutrition Info:
- Per Serving:Calories: 26 Fat: 0.6g Protein: 1.9g Carbohydrates: 4.2g

Tabbouleh- Arabian Salad
Servings: 6 | Cooking Time: 0 Minutes

Ingredients:
- ¼ cup chopped fresh mint
- 1 2/3 cups boiling water
- 1 cucumber, peeled, seeded and chopped
- 1 cup bulgur
- 1 cup chopped fresh parsley
- 1 cup chopped green onions
- 1 tsp salt
- 1/3 cup lemon juice
- 1/3 cup olive oil
- 3 tomatoes, chopped
- Ground black pepper to taste

Directions:
1. In a large bowl, mix together boiling water and bulgur. Let soak and set aside for an hour while covered.
2. After one hour, toss in cucumber, tomatoes, mint, parsley, onions, lemon juice and oil. Then season with black pepper and salt to taste. Toss well and refrigerate for another hour while covered before serving.

Nutrition Info:
- Calories per serving: 185.5; Fat: 13.1g; Protein: 4.1g; Carbs: 12.8g

Yogurt Peppers Mix
Servings: 4 | Cooking Time: 15 Minutes

Ingredients:
- 2 red bell peppers, cut into thick strips
- 2 tablespoons olive oil
- 3 shallots, chopped
- 3 garlic cloves, minced
- Salt and black pepper to the taste
- ½ cup Greek yogurt

- 1 tablespoon cilantro, chopped

Directions:
1. Heat up a pan with the oil over medium heat, add the shallots and garlic, stir and cook for 5 minutes.
2. Add the rest of the ingredients, toss, cook for 10 minutes more, divide the mix between plates and serve as a side dish.

Nutrition Info:
- calories 274, fat 11, fiber 3.5, protein 13.3, carbs 6.5

Avocado And Onion Mix
Servings: 4 | Cooking Time: 0 Minutes

Ingredients:
- 4 avocados, pitted, peeled and sliced
- 1 red onion, sliced
- 2 tablespoons olive oil
- 2 tablespoons lime juice
- ¼ cup dill, chopped
- Sea salt and black pepper to the taste

Directions:
1. In a salad bowl, mix the avocados with the onion and the rest of the ingredients, toss and serve as a side dish.

Nutrition Info:
- calories 465, fat 23.5, fiber 14.3, carbs 21.4, protein 5.4

Dill Beets Salad
Servings: 6 | Cooking Time: 0 Minutes

Ingredients:
- 2 pounds beets, cooked, peeled and cubed
- 2 tablespoons olive oil
- 1 tablespoon lemon juice
- 2 tablespoons balsamic vinegar
- 1 cup feta cheese, crumbled
- 3 small garlic cloves, minced
- 4 green onions, chopped
- 5 tablespoons parsley, chopped
- Salt and black pepper to the taste

Directions:
1. In a bowl, mix the beets with the oil, lemon juice and the rest of the ingredients, toss and serve as a side dish.

Nutrition Info:
- calories 268, fat 15.5, fiber 5.1, carbs 25.7, protein 9.6

Warm Shrimp Salad With Feta And Honeydew
Servings:4 | Cooking Time:2 Minutes

Ingredients:
- 1 medium (3-4 pounds) honeydew melon, peeled, seeded, and cut into 1/2-inch dice (about 4 cups)
- 1 medium lime, 1 teaspoon finely grated zest, 4 teaspoon juice
- 1 tablespoon cracked coriander seeds, plus 1 teaspoon
- 1/4 cup extra-virgin olive oil
- 1/4 cup thinly sliced fresh mint
- 1-1/2 lb. extra-jumbo (16-20 per pound) shrimp, peeled (tails left on, if you like) and deveined
- 2 heads frisée (about 1/2 lb.), torn into bite-size pieces
- 2 tablespoons shallots, finely chopped
- 8 ounces feta (about 1-1/2 cups), crumbled
- Freshly ground black pepper
- Kosher salt
- Pinch cayenne

Directions:
1. Lightly season the shrimp with the salt and pepper.
2. Heat 2 tablespoons of olive oil in a 12-inch skillet over medium-high heat until shimmering hot. Add the shrimp; cook for about 1 minute or until 1 side is pink. Flip; add the shallots, 1 teaspoon of lime juice, and the lime zest. Lower the medium; cook for 1 minute or until the shrimp are just opaque through.
3. In a large-sized bowl, whisk the remaining 1 tablespoons lime juice and 2 tablespoons olive oil; season with salt and pepper to taste. Toss the melon and the frisée in the vinaigrette. Divide equally between 4 dinner plates; top with the shrimp, mint, feta, and coriander. Serve.

Nutrition Info:
- Per Serving:530 cal., 29 g fat (11 g sat. fat, 13 g mono fat, 3 g poly fat), 45 g protein, 23 g carb., 4 g fiber, 310 mg chol., and 1210 mg sodium.

Dandelion Greens
Serves: 1 Cup | Cooking Time:50 Minutes

Ingredients:
- 4 cups dandelion greens (2 lb.)
- 14 cups water
- 21/2 tsp. salt
- 1/2 cup extra-virgin olive oil
- 4 large white onions, sliced
- 1 large lemon, cut into quarters

Directions:
1. Thoroughly wash dandelion greens in a large bowl of water three times to remove any dirt, discarding water after each wash. Chop greens into 1-inch pieces.
2. In a large pot over medium-high heat, bring water to a simmer. Add 1 teaspoon salt and dandelion greens, and simmer, stirring occasionally, for 20 minutes. Drain greens, and squeeze out any excess water.
3. Preheat a large skillet over medium heat. Add 1/4 cup extra-virgin olive oil and 1/2 of white onions, and cook, stirring occasionally, for 5 minutes.
4. Add dandelion greens and 1 teaspoon salt to the skillet, reduce heat to low, and cook for 15 more minutes.
5. Transfer dandelion mixture to a serving plate.
6. In the skillet, heat remaining 1/4 cup extra-virgin olive oil. Add remaining 1/2 teaspoon salt and 1/2 of remaining onions, and cook, stirring occasionally, for 20 minutes or until lightly browned.
7. Top dandelion greens with browned onions, squeeze juice of 1/2 lemon on top, and serve with 2 remaining lemon quarters.

Chives Rice Mix

Servings: 4 | Cooking Time: 5 Minutes

Ingredients:
- 3 tablespoons avocado oil
- 1 cup Arborio rice, cooked
- 2 tablespoons chives, chopped
- Salt and black pepper to the taste
- 2 teaspoons lemon juice

Directions:
1. Heat up a pan with the avocado oil over medium high heat, add the rice and the rest of the ingredients, toss, cook for 5 minutes, divide the mix between plates and serve as a side dish.

Nutrition Info:
- calories 236, fat 9, fiber 12.4, carbs 17.5, protein 4.5

Bacon And Tomato Pasta

Servings: 4 | Cooking Time: 20 Minutes

Ingredients:
- 1 egg, beaten
- 4 oz linguine
- 1 oz bacon, chopped
- ½ teaspoon canola oil
- 1 cup cherry tomatoes, halved
- 1 oz Romano cheese, grated
- 1 oz shallot, chopped
- 2 cups of water

Directions:
1. Pour water in the pan and bring to boil.
2. Add linguine and cook it according to the directions of the manufacturer.
3. When the linguine is cooked, drain ½ part of water.
4. Put bacon in the skillet, add canola oil, and roast it for 5 minutes or until crunchy.
5. Add cooked bacon in the linguine.
6. Then add shallot, grated Romano cheese, cherry tomatoes, and beaten egg.
7. Mix up the pasta carefully until it is homogenous and egg is dissolved.
8. Simmer pasta for 3 minutes over the medium-low heat.

Nutrition Info:
- Per Servingcalories 182, fat 7.3, fiber 0.5, carbs 18.9, protein 10.1

Spiced Meat And Rice

Serves: 1 Cup | Cooking Time: 47 Minutes

Ingredients:
- 1/2 lb. ground beef
- 2 cups long-grain rice, rinsed
- 4 cups water
- 1 tsp. seven spices
- 1/2 tsp. cinnamon
- 11/2 tsp. salt
- 1 TB. extra-virgin olive oil

Directions:
1. In a 2-quart pot over medium heat, brown beef for 5 minutes, breaking up chunks with a wooden spoon.
2. Add long-grain rice, stir, and cook for 2 minutes.
3. Add water, seven spices, cinnamon, salt, and extra-virgin olive oil, and stir. Bring to a simmer, cover, reduce heat to low, and cook for 40 minutes.
4. Remove from heat, fluff rice with a fork, cover, and let the rice stand for 10 more minutes.
5. Serve warm.

Spring Soup Recipe With Poached Egg

Servings: 2 | Cooking Time: 20 Minutes

Ingredients:
- 2 eggs
- 2 tablespoons butter
- 4 cups chicken broth
- 1 head of romaine lettuce, chopped
- Salt, to taste

Directions:
1. Boil the chicken broth and lower heat.
2. Poach the eggs in the broth for about 5 minutes and remove the eggs.
3. Place each egg into a bowl and add chopped romaine lettuce into the broth.
4. Cook for about 10 minutes and ladle the broth with the lettuce into the bowls.

Nutrition Info:
- Calories: 264 Carbs: 7g Fats: 18.9g Proteins: 16.1g Sodium: 1679mg Sugar: 3.4g

Minty Cauliflower Mix

Servings: 2 | Cooking Time: 0 Minutes

Ingredients:
- ½ cups walnuts, chopped
- 2 cups cauliflower florets, steamed
- 1 teaspoon ginger, grated
- 1 garlic clove, minced
- 1 tablespoon mint, chopped
- Juice of ½ lemon
- A pinch of sea salt and black pepper

Directions:
1. In a salad bowl, combine the cauliflower with the walnuts and the rest of the ingredients, toss and serve.

Nutrition Info:
- calories 199, fat 5.6, fiber 4.5, carbs 8.4, protein 3.5

Lemon Endives

Servings: 4 | Cooking Time: 35 Minutes

Ingredients:
- Juice of 1 and ½ lemons
- Salt and black pepper to the taste
- 3 tablespoons olive oil
- ¼ cup veggie stock
- 4 endives, halved lengthwise
- 1 tablespoon dill, chopped

Directions:
1. In a roasting pan, combine the endives with the rest of the

ingredients, introduce in the oven and cook at 375 degrees F for 35 minutes.
2. Divide the endives between plates and serve as a side dish.
Nutrition Info:
- calories 221, fat 5.4, fiber 6.4, carbs 15.4, protein 14.3

Tomato Salad With Olives, Feta, And Mint
Servings:6 | Cooking Time: 25 Minutes

Ingredients:
- 1/2 cup Kalamata or niçoise olives (about 15 pieces), pitted, halved
- 1/2 pound cucumber, peeled, seeded, and cut into small dice
- 4 large ripe tomatoes, cut into 1/4-inch slices
- 1/2 pound tomatoes (bite-size, such as pear, cherry, or grape) assorted colors, cut into halves
- 1/2 teaspoon grated lemon zest
- 1/4 cup extra-virgin olive oil
- 1/4 cup fresh mint, chopped, plus sprigs for garnish
- 4 teaspoons fresh lemon juice
- 6 ounces feta cheese
- Freshly ground black pepper
- Kosher salt

Directions:
1. In a small-sized bowl, crumble the feta. Add the mint; toss and set aside.
2. Season the large tomato slices with salt. In a serving platter, arrange them, overlapping them slightly. Sprinkle the cucumber over the tomato layer.
3. Season the bite-sized tomatoes with salt; scatter over the cucumber layer. Sprinkle the olives on top.
4. In a small-sized bowl, whisk the lemon juice, lemon zest, and olive oil together; season with salt and pepper to taste and drizzle over the salad.
5. Scatter the feta over the salad, garnish with the mint sprigs, and serve immediately.

Nutrition Info:
- Per Serving:230 cal., 19 g fat (6 g sat. fat, 10 g mono fat, 2 g poly fat), 6 g protein, 11 g carb., 2 g fiber, 25 mg chol., and 760 mg sodium.

Balsamic Asparagus
Servings: 4 | Cooking Time: 15 Minutes

Ingredients:
- 3 tablespoons olive oil
- 3 garlic cloves, minced
- 2 tablespoons shallot, chopped
- Salt and black pepper to the taste
- 2 teaspoons balsamic vinegar
- 1 and ½ pound asparagus, trimmed

Directions:
1. Heat up a pan with the oil over medium-high heat, add the garlic and the shallot and sauté for 3 minutes.
2. Add the rest of the ingredients, cook for 12 minutes more, divide between plates and serve as a side dish.

Nutrition Info:
- calories 100, fat 10.5, fiber 1.2, carbs 2.3, protein 2.1

Greek Antipasto Salad
Servings: 4 | Cooking Time: 0 Minutes

Ingredients:
- ½ cup artichoke hearts, chipped
- ½ cup olives, sliced
- ½ cup sweet peppers, roasted
- 1 large head romaine lettuce, chopped
- 4 ounces cooked prosciutto, cut into thin strips
- 4 ounces cooked salami, cubed
- Italian dressing to taste

Directions:
1. In a large mixing bowl, add all the ingredients except the Italian dressing. Mix everything until the vegetables are evenly distributed.
2. Add the Italian dressing and toss to combine.
3. Serve chilled.

Nutrition Info:
- Calories per Serving: 425.8; Fat: 38.9 g; Protein: 39.2 g; Carbs: 12.6 g

Anchovy And Orange Salad
Servings: 4 | Cooking Time: 0 Minutes

Ingredients:
- 1 small red onion, sliced into thin rounds
- 1 tbsp fresh lemon juice
- 1/8 tsp pepper or more to taste
- 16 oil cure Kalamata olives
- 2 tsp finely minced fennel fronds for garnish
- 3 tbsp extra virgin olive oil
- 4 small oranges, preferably blood oranges
- 6 anchovy fillets

Directions:
1. With a paring knife, peel oranges including the membrane that surrounds it.
2. In a plate, slice oranges into thin circles and allow plate to catch the orange juices.
3. On serving plate, arrange orange slices on a layer.
4. Sprinkle oranges with onion, followed by olives and then anchovy fillets.
5. Drizzle with oil, lemon juice and orange juice.
6. Sprinkle with pepper.
7. Allow salad to stand for 30 minutes at room temperature to allow the flavors to develop.
8. To serve, garnish with fennel fronds and enjoy.

Nutrition Info:
- Calories per serving: 133.9; Protein: 3.2 g; Carbs: 14.3g; Fat: 7.1g

Other Mediterranean Recipes

Mediterranean Diet Cookbook

Other Mediterranean Recipes

Fresh Gazpacho
Servings: 6 | Cooking Time: 20 Minutes

Ingredients:
- 2 pounds tomatoes, peeled and cubed
- 1 red bell pepper, cored and diced
- 1 celery stalk, sliced
- 2 garlic cloves, chopped
- 2 whole wheat bread slices
- 3 tablespoons extra virgin olive oil
- 1 teaspoon sherry vinegar
- 1 pinch cumin powder
- Salt and pepper to taste
- Chopped cilantro for serving

Directions:
1. Combine the tomatoes, bell pepper, celery, garlic, bread, oil, vinegar and cumin in a blender.
2. Add salt and pepper to taste and puree the soup with an immersion blender or until smooth.
3. Pour the soup into serving bowls right away.

Nutrition Info:
- Per Serving: Calories: 119 Fat: 7.7g Protein: 2.8g Carbohydrates: 11.4g

Buffalo Chicken Crust Pizza
Servings: 6 | Cooking Time: 25 Minutes

Ingredients:
- 1 cup whole milk mozzarella, shredded
- 1 teaspoon dried oregano
- 2 tablespoons butter
- 1 pound chicken thighs, boneless and skinless
- 1 large egg
- ¼ teaspoon black pepper
- ¼ teaspoon salt
- 1 stalk celery
- 3 tablespoons Franks Red Hot Original
- 1 stalk green onion
- 1 tablespoon sour cream
- 1 ounce bleu cheese, crumbled

Directions:
1. Preheat the oven to 400 degrees F and grease a baking dish.
2. Process chicken thighs in a food processor until smooth.
3. Transfer to a large bowl and add egg, ½ cup of shredded mozzarella, oregano, black pepper, and salt to form a dough.
4. Spread the chicken dough in the baking dish and transfer in the oven
5. Bake for about 25 minutes and keep aside.
6. Meanwhile, heat butter and add celery, and cook for about 4 minutes.
7. Mix Franks Red Hot Original with the sour cream in a small bowl.
8. Spread the sauce mixture over the crust, layer with the cooked celery and remaining ½ cup of mozzarella and the bleu cheese.
9. Bake for another 10 minutes, until the cheese is melted

Nutrition Info:
- Calories: 172 Carbs: 1g Fats: 12.9g Proteins: 13.8g Sodium: 172mg Sugar: 0.2g

Mediterranean Father's Day Chicken Burgers
Servings: 4 | Cooking Time: 10-15 Minutes

Ingredients:
- 4 pita breads or your favorite burger buns
- Greek yogurt or labneh
- 1 1/2 pounds ground chicken
- 5 ounces fresh spinach, wilted, squeezed very dry, and then chopped (I set the leaves in a bowl and microwaved them 20 seconds at a time until wilted)
- 2 tablespoons fresh dill, minced
- 2 medium green onions, thinly sliced
- 2 cloves of garlic, micro planed or very finely minced
- 1 teaspoon salt
- 1 tablespoon black pepper
- 1 egg
- 1/2 cup panko crumbs, unseasoned
- 1/2 cup feta cheese crumble
- 1 cup red onion, finely diced
- 1/2 cup flat-leaf parsley, minced
- 1 teaspoon dried oregano
- 1 teaspoon salt
- 1/2 teaspoon black pepper
- 1 tablespoon lemon juice
- 1 tablespoon extra-virgin olive oil
- 2 medium tomatoes, seeded, finely diced

Directions:
1. For the burgers:
2. Put all of the ingredients in a mixing bowl, gently combine until mixed; cover and refrigerate to chill for a couple of hours until the flavors are blended and the mixture is firm.
3. For the tomato relish:
4. Combine all of the relish ingredients together; set aside.
5. To assemble:
6. Form the firmed chicken mixture into 4 patties.
7. Heat the grill to medium and grease the grill with oil. Put the patties on the grill and cook until done or the internal temperature reaches 165F.
8. Spread yogurt on the bottom of each bun or center of each pita. Top the bun or the pita with the burger and then top the burgers with the tomato relish.

Nutrition Info:
- Per Serving: 696 cal., 23.5 g total fat (7.7 g sat. fat), 210 mg

chol., 2001 mg sodium, 1098 mg pot, 54.8 g total carbs., 5.4 g fiber, 6.4 g sugar, 64.9 g protein, 98% vitamin A, 59% vitamin C, 32% calcium, and 44% iron.

Bbq Chicken Pizza

Servings: 4 | Cooking Time: 30 Minutes

Ingredients:
- Dairy Free Pizza Crust
- 6 tablespoons Parmesan cheese
- 6 large eggs
- 3 tablespoons psyllium husk powder
- Salt and black pepper, to taste
- 1½ teaspoons Italian seasoning
- Toppings
- 6 oz. rotisserie chicken, shredded
- 4 oz. cheddar cheese
- 1 tablespoon mayonnaise
- 4 tablespoons tomato sauce
- 4 tablespoons BBQ sauce

Directions:
1. Preheat the oven to 400 degrees F and grease a baking dish.
2. Place all Pizza Crust ingredients in an immersion blender and blend until smooth.
3. Spread dough mixture onto the baking dish and transfer in the oven.
4. Bake for about 10 minutes and top with favorite toppings.
5. Bake for about 3 minutes and dish out.

Nutrition Info:
- Calories: 356 Carbs: 2.9g Fats: 24.5g Proteins: 24.5g Sodium: 396mg Sugar: 0.6g

Parmesan Zucchini Soup

Servings: 6 | Cooking Time: 40 Minutes

Ingredients:
- 2 tablespoons olive oil
- 2 garlic cloves, chopped
- 1 shallot, chopped
- 1 celery stalk, sliced
- 3 zucchinis, sliced
- 2 cups vegetable stock
- 1 cup water
- Salt and pepper to taste
- 1 rosemary sprig
- ½ cup heavy cream
- Grated Parmesan for serving

Directions:
1. Heat the oil in a soup pot and stir in the garlic, shallot and celery. Cook for 5 minutes then add the zucchinis, stock, water and rosemary.
2. Season with salt and pepper and cook for 15 minutes.
3. When done, remove from heat, remove the rosemary and stir in the cream.
4. Puree the soup with an immersion blender and serve the soup fresh, topped with grated Parmesan.

Nutrition Info:
- Per Serving:Calories:110 Fat:9.6g Protein:3.1g Carbohydrates:4.7g

Veal Shank Barley Soup

Servings: 10 | Cooking Time:1 ¼ Hours

Ingredients:
- 3 tablespoons olive oil
- 4 veal shanks, sliced
- 4 cups vegetable stock
- 4 cups water
- 1 sweet onion, chopped
- 2 red bell peppers, cored and diced
- 2 carrots, diced
- 2 celery stalk, sliced
- 2 tomatoes, peeled and diced
- 1 parsnip, diced
- ½ cup barley pearls, rinsed
- Salt and pepper to taste
- Chopped parsley for serving

Directions:
1. Heat the oil in a soup pot and stir in the veal shank slices. Cook for 10 minutes then add the stock and water.
2. Cook for 10 minutes then stir in the rest of the ingredients, except the parsley.
3. Continue cooking for 30 more minutes on low heat, seasoning with salt and pepper.
4. Serve the soup warm, topped with parsley.

Nutrition Info:
- Per Serving:Calories:254 Fat:9.3g Protein:26.5g Carbohydrates:15.3g

Creamy Bell Pepper Soup With Cod Fillets

Servings: 6 | Cooking Time:1 Hour

Ingredients:
- 2 tablespoons olive oil
- 1 shallot, chopped
- 2 garlic cloves, chopped
- 1 jar roasted red bell peppers, sliced
- 2 cups chicken stock
- 2 cups water
- 1 bay leaf
- 1 thyme sprig
- 1 rosemary sprig
- Salt and pepper to taste
- 4 cod fillets, cubed

Directions:
1. Heat the oil in a soup pot and stir in the shallot and garlic. Cook for 2 minutes then add the bell peppers, stock, water and herbs, as well as salt and pepper to taste.
2. Cook for 15 minutes then remove the herbs and puree the soup with an immersion blender.
3. Add the cod fillets and place the soup back on heat.
4. Cook for another 5 minutes.
5. Serve the soup warm and fresh.

Nutrition Info:
- Per Serving:Calories:48 Fat:5.0g Protein:0.4g Carbohydrates:1.3g

Santorini Sunrise
Servings: 1 | Cooking Time: 5 Minutes

Ingredients:
- 2 1/4 cups vodka, unflavored, plus more
- 1 pink grapefruit, sliced
- 1 ounces Campari
- 2 ounce Pink Grapefruit-infused Vodka
- 2 slices pink grapefruit, quartered (8 total pieces)
- 2 teaspoons honey (or Greek honey, if available)
- 3 ounces freshly squeezed pink grapefruit juice
- 4 mint leaves, plus more for garnish

Directions:
1. For the grapefruit-infused vodka:
2. Put the grapefruit in a sterilized 1-quart glass jar, stuffing them tight. Pour the vodka over the grapefruit. Add more vodka, if needed, to submerge the grapefruit completely. Seal the jar with a tight lit; let sit at room temperature for 3 days. After 3 days, strain the infused-vodka through a coffee filter into another sterilized glass jar; store with other spirits for up to 2 months.
3. For the cocktail:
4. In a highball glass, muddle 7 pieces of the quartered grapefruit slices with the honey and mint leaves. Add ice until the glass is filled. Add the vodka, Campari, and grapefruit juice. Stir. Garnish with the remaining 1 grapefruit slice and mint leaves; serve.

Nutrition Info:
- Per Serving: 284 cal., 0.6 g total fat (0 g sat. fat), 0 mg chol., 14 mg sodium, 606 mg pot., 38.3 g total carbs., 6.2 g fiber, 31.4 g sugar, 3.3 g protein, 89% vitamin A, 173% vitamin C, 12% calcium, and 31% iron.

Minty Green Pea Soup
Servings: 6 | Cooking Time: 35 Minutes

Ingredients:
- 2 tablespoons olive oil
- 2 shallots, chopped
- 2 garlic cloves, chopped
- 1 pound green peas
- 4 mint leaves, chopped
- ½ teaspoon dried oregano
- 2 cups vegetable stock
- 1 cup water
- Salt and pepper to taste
- 1 tablespoon lemon juice
- ¼ cup heavy cream

Directions:
1. Heat the oil in a soup pot and stir in the shallots and garlic. Cook for 2 minutes until softened then add the green peas, mint, oregano, stock and water.
2. Add salt and pepper to taste and cook on low heat for 15 minutes.
3. Stir in the lemon juice and cook for 2 additional minutes.
4. When done, remove from heat and stir in the cream.
5. Puree the soup with an immersion blender until creamy and smooth.
6. Serve the soup warm or chilled.

Nutrition Info:
- Per Serving: Calories: 129 Fat: 6.9g Protein: 4.7g Carbohydrates: 13.0g

Curried Veggies And Poached Eggs
Servings: 4 | Cooking Time: 45 Minutes

Ingredients:
- 4 large eggs
- ½ tsp white vinegar
- 1/8 tsp crushed red pepper – optional
- 1 cup water
- 1 14-oz can chickpeas, drained
- 2 medium zucchinis, diced
- ½ lb sliced button mushrooms
- 1 tbsp yellow curry powder
- 2 cloves garlic, minced
- 1 large onion, chopped
- 2 tsps extra virgin olive oil

Directions:
1. On medium high fire, place a large saucepan and heat oil.
2. Sauté onions until tender around four to five minutes.
3. Add garlic and continue sautéing for another half minute.
4. Add curry powder, stir and cook until fragrant around one to two minutes.
5. Add mushrooms, mix, cover and cook for 5 to 8 minutes or until mushrooms are tender and have released their liquid.
6. Add red pepper if using, water, chickpeas and zucchini. Mix well to combine and bring to a boil.
7. Once boiling, reduce fire to a simmer, cover and cook until zucchini is tender around 15 to 20 minutes of simmering.
8. Meanwhile, in a small pot filled with 3-inches deep of water, bring to a boil on high fire.
9. Once boiling, reduce fire to a simmer and add vinegar.
10. Slowly add one egg, slipping it gently into the water. Allow to simmer until egg is cooked, around 3 to 5 minutes.
11. Remove egg with a slotted spoon and transfer to a plate, one plate one egg.
12. Repeat the process with remaining eggs.
13. Once the veggies are done cooking, divide evenly into 4 servings and place one serving per plate of egg.
14. Serve and enjoy.

Nutrition Info:
- Calories per serving: 215; Protein: 13.8g; Carbs: 20.6g; Fat: 9.4g

Cooked Beef Mushroom Egg
Servings: 2 | Cooking Time: 15 Minutes

Ingredients:
- ¼ cup cooked beef, diced
- 6 eggs
- 4 mushrooms, diced
- Salt and pepper to taste
- 12 ounces spinach
- 2 onions, chopped
- A dash of onion powder

Mediterranean Diet Cookbook

- ¼ green bell pepper, chopped
- A dash of garlic powder

Directions:
1. In a skillet, toss the beef for 3 minutes or until crispy.
2. Take off the heat and add to a plate.
3. Add the onion, bell pepper, and mushroom in the skillet.
4. Add the rest of the ingredients.
5. Toss for about 4 minutes.
6. Return the beef to the skillet and toss for another minute.
7. Serve hot.

Nutrition Info:
- Calories per serving: 213; Protein: 14.5g; Carbs: 3.4g; Fat: 15.7g

Tuscan White Bean Soup
Servings: 8 | Cooking Time: 50 Minutes

Ingredients:
- 2 tablespoons olive oil
- 2 shallots, chopped
- 2 carrots, diced
- 2 celery stalks, sliced
- 2 yellow bell peppers, cored and diced
- 2 garlic cloves, chopped
- 1 can white beans, drained
- 1 zucchini, cubed
- 1 thyme sprig
- 1 rosemary sprig
- 1 can diced tomatoes
- 2 cups chicken stock
- 6 cups water
- 2 cups baby spinach
- Salt and pepper to taste

Directions:
1. Heat the oil in a soup pot and stir in the shallots, carrots, celery, peppers and garlic.
2. Cook for 10 minutes on low heat then add the rest of the ingredients and season with salt and pepper.
3. Cook for another 20 minutes.
4. Serve the soup warm and fresh.

Nutrition Info:
- Per Serving: Calories: 146 Fat: 4.1g Protein: 7.4g Carbohydrates: 21.5g

Open Face Egg And Bacon Sandwich
Servings: 1 | Cooking Time: 20 Minutes

Ingredients:
- ¼ oz reduced fat cheddar, shredded
- ½ small jalapeno, thinly sliced
- ½ whole grain English muffin, split
- 1 large organic egg
- 1 thick slice of tomato
- 1-piece turkey bacon
- 2 thin slices red onion
- 4-5 sprigs fresh cilantro
- Cooking spray
- Pepper to taste

Directions:
1. On medium fire, place a skillet, cook bacon until crisp tender and set aside.
2. In same skillet, drain oils, and place ½ of English muffin and heat for at least a minute per side. Transfer muffin to a serving plate.
3. Coat the same skillet with cooking spray and fry egg to desired doneness. Once cooked, place egg on top of muffin.
4. Add cilantro, tomato, onion, jalapeno and bacon on top of egg. Serve and enjoy.

Nutrition Info:
- Calories per Serving: 245; Carbs: 24.7g; Protein: 11.8g; Fat: 11g

Mediterranean-style Lamb Leg With Potatoes
Servings: 4-6 | Cooking Time: 1 Hour 10 Minutes

Ingredients:
- 1 piece (4-5 pounds) lamb leg, bone in, fat trimmed
- 1 teaspoon garlic powder
- 1 teaspoon paprika, plus additional for later
- 1 yellow onion, medium, peeled, cut into wedges
- 2 cups water
- 5 garlic cloves, peeled and sliced; more for later
- 8 gold potatoes, medium, peeled, cut into wedges
- Olive oil, plus additional for later
- Fresh parsley, for garnish, optional
- Salt and pepper
- 1 recipe Lebanese rice, optional
- 1 tablespoon paprika
- 1/2 cup olive oil
- 1/2 tablespoon ground nutmeg
- 15 garlic cloves, peeled
- 2 lemons, juice of
- 2 tablespoon dried mint flakes
- 2 tablespoon dried oregano

Directions:
1. Take the lamb leg out of the fridge; let stand for about 1 hour in room temperature.
2. Meanwhile, prepare the rest of the ingredients and the lamb rub.
3. To make the rub, put all of the ingredients in a food processor; process until smooth and set aside. If you are preparing in advance, refrigerate.
4. When ready to make the lamb roast; pat the leg dry with paper towels. Cut a few slits on both sides of the leg; season with salt and pepper.
5. Preheat the oven broiler.
6. Put the lamb on a wire rack. Put the rack on the top oven rack directly a few inches away from the heat source; broil for about 5-7 minutes per side or until the lamb leg is nicely seared. Remove the rack with the leg from the oven; turn the oven temperature to 375F.
7. When the seared lamb is cool enough to handle; insert the slices of garlic into the slits made earlier. Rub the surface of the seared lamb with the rub; put the lamb on the middle on a

rack in the roasting pan. Add 2 cups water in the roasting pan.
8. Season the onion wedges and the potato with a little salt, garlic powder, and paprika; add to the rack, placing them around the lamb leg.
9. Cover the roasting pan with a large foil piece. Put the roasting pan in the middle rack of the oven; roast covered for 1 hour. Remove the foil tent, return the roasting pan in the oven, and roast for additional 10-15 minutes or until the a meat thermometer reads 140F when inserted in the lam b for medium.
10. Remove the roasting pan from the oven; let rest for at least 20 minutes and serve.
11. If desired, halfway through roasting the leg, cook the rice according to the recipe needed for this dish.
12. Put the lamb leg into a serving platter and surround the potatoes and the wedges around the lamb. If desired, you can serve the lamb over the bed of Lebanese rice. Garnish with parsley.
13. Alternatively, you can carve the leg first, and arrange the lamb slices with the onion wedges and the potatoes over the Lebanese rice.

Nutrition Info:
- per serving: 945 cal., 40 g total fat (10.6 g sat. fat), 272 mg chol., 254 mg sodium, 2340 mg pot., 54 g total carbs., 9.5 g fiber, 5.1 g sugar, 91.3 g protein, 20% vitamin A, 121% vitamin C,13% calcium, and 57% iron.

Eggs Benedict And Artichoke Hearts
Servings: 2 | Cooking Time: 30 Minutes

Ingredients:
- Salt and pepper to taste
- ¾ cup balsamic vinegar
- 4 artichoke hearts
- ¼ cup bacon, cooked
- 1 egg white
- 8 eggs
- 1 tablespoon lemon juice
- ¾ cup melted ghee or butter

Directions:
1. Line a baking sheet with parchment paper or foil.
2. Preheat the oven to 3750F.
3. Deconstruct the artichokes and remove the hearts. Place the hearts in balsamic vinegar for 20 minutes. Set aside.
4. Prepare the hollandaise sauce by using four (4) eggs and separate the yolk from the white. Reserve the egg white for the artichoke hearts. Add the yolks and lemon juice and cook in a double boiler while stirring constantly to create a silky texture of the sauce. Add the oil and season with salt and pepper. Set aside.
5. Remove the artichoke hearts from the balsamic vinegar marinade and place on the cookie sheet. Brush the artichokes with the egg white and cook in the oven for 20 minutes.
6. Poach the remaining four (4) eggs. Turn up the heat and let the water boil. Crack the eggs one at a time and cook for a minute before removing the egg.
7. Assemble by layering the artichokes, bacon and poached eggs.
8. Pour over the hollandaise sauce.
9. Serve with toasted bread.

Nutrition Info:
- Calories per serving: 640; Protein: 28.3g; Carbs: 36.0g; Fat: 42.5g

Spicy Tortilla Soup
Servings: 10 | Cooking Time:1 Hour

Ingredients:
- 3 tablespoons olive oil
- 1 sweet onion, chopped
- 2 garlic cloves, chopped
- ½ teaspoon cumin powder
- ½ teaspoon chili powder
- 1 celery stalk, sliced
- 2 carrots, grated
- 1 can diced tomatoes
- 2 tablespoons tomato paste
- 1 can kidney beans, drained
- 1 cup canned sweet corn, drained
- 4 cups vegetable stock
- 4 cups water
- Salt and pepper to taste
- 1 avocado, peeled and sliced
- ¼ cup chopped parsley
- 1 lime, juiced

Directions:
1. Heat the oil in a soup pot and stir in the onion, garlic, cumin powder, chili powder, celery and carrots.
2. Cook for 5 minutes then add the rest of the ingredients, except the parsley, avocado and lime juice.
3. Continue cooking the soup for 20-25 minutes then add the parsley and avocado slices, as well as lime juice.
4. Serve the soup fresh.

Nutrition Info:
- Per Serving:Calories:174 Fat:8.6g Protein:5.8g Carbohydrates:21.1g

Roasted Vegetable Soup
Servings: 8 | Cooking Time:45 Minutes

Ingredients:
- 2 red onions, halved
- 2 red bell peppers, cored and sliced
- 1 carrot, sliced
- 1 parsnip, sliced
- 1 small butternut squash, peeled and cubed
- 4 tomatoes, cubed
- 4 garlic cloves
- 1 rosemary sprig
- 3 tablespoons olive oil
- 2 cups vegetable stock
- 2 cups water
- Salt and pepper to taste

Directions:
1. Combine the red onions, bell peppers, carrot, parsnip, butternut squash, garlic, tomatoes and rosemary in a baking tray.
2. Season with salt and pepper and drizzle with olive oil.

Mediterranean Diet Cookbook

3. Cook in the preheated oven at 350F for 25-30 minutes or until golden brown.
4. Transfer the vegetables in a soup pot and pour in the stock and water.
5. Cook for another 10 minutes then remove the rosemary from the pot and puree the soup with an immersion blender.
6. Serve the soup warm.

Nutrition Info:
- Per Serving:Calories:104 Fat:5.6g Protein:1.8g Carbohydrates:13.3g

Chicken Green Bean Soup
Servings: 8 | Cooking Time:45 Minutes

Ingredients:
- 3 tablespoons olive oil
- 2 chicken breasts, cubed
- 1 shallot, chopped
- 1 garlic clove, chopped
- 1 red bell pepper, cored and diced
- 1 celery stalk, diced
- 2 carrots, diced
- 1 pound green beans, sliced
- 3 cups vegetable stock
- 4 cups water
- 1 bay leaf
- 1 thyme sprig
- 1 can diced tomatoes
- Salt and pepper to taste

Directions:
1. Heat the oil in a soup pot and stir in the chicken. Cook for 5 minutes then add the shallot, garlic, bell pepper, celery and carrots.
2. Cook for 5 more minutes then stir in the green beans, stock, water, bay leaf, thyme sprig and tomatoes.
3. Add salt and pepper and cook for 25 minutes.
4. Serve the soup warm and fresh.

Nutrition Info:
- Per Serving:Calories:149 Fat:8.1g Protein:11.9g Carbohydrates:8.2g

Leek And Potato Soup
Servings: 8 | Cooking Time:1 Hour

Ingredients:
- 3 tablespoons olive oil
- 3 leeks, sliced
- 4 garlic cloves, chopped
- 6 potatoes, peeled and cubed
- 2 cups vegetable stock
- 2 cups water
- 1 thyme sprig
- 1 rosemary sprig
- Salt and pepper to taste

Directions:
1. Heat the oil in a soup pot and stir in the leeks. Cook for 15 minutes until slightly caramelized.
2. Add the garlic and cook for 2 more minutes.
3. Add the rest of the ingredients and season with salt and pepper.
4. Cook on low heat for 20 minutes then remove the herb sprigs and puree the soup with an immersion blender.
5. Serve the soup fresh.

Nutrition Info:
- Per Serving:Calories:179 Fat:5.5g Protein:3.4g Carbohydrates:30.6g

Breakfast Egg On Avocado
Servings: 6 | Cooking Time: 15 Minutes

Ingredients:
- 1 tsp garlic powder
- 1/2 tsp sea salt
- 1/4 cup Parmesan cheese (grated or shredded)
- 1/4 tsp black pepper
- 3 medium avocados (cut in half, pitted, skin on)
- 6 medium eggs

Directions:
1. Prepare muffin tins and preheat the oven to 350oF.
2. To ensure that the egg would fit inside the cavity of the avocado, lightly scrape off 1/3 of the meat.
3. Place avocado on muffin tin to ensure that it faces with the top up.
4. Evenly season each avocado with pepper, salt, and garlic powder.
5. Add one egg on each avocado cavity and garnish tops with cheese.
6. Pop in the oven and bake until the egg white is set, about 15 minutes.
7. Serve and enjoy.

Nutrition Info:
- Calories per serving: 252; Protein: 14.0g; Carbs: 4.0g; Fat: 20.0g

Mediterranean Dip
Servings: 8-12 | Cooking Time: 20 Minutes

Ingredients:
- 8 ounces garlic hummus
- 6 ounces marinated artichoke hearts, drained and then chopped; reserve the liquid
- 3/4 cup carrot, shredded
- 1/2 cup sour cream
- 1/2 cup Kalamata olive, sliced
- 1/2 cup green onion, sliced
- 1 cup feta, crumbled
- Pita chips, 1-2 boxes, for serving

Directions:
1. In a medium-sized bowl, combine the hummus and sour cream, mixing well. Spread the mix into a plate or into a serving container of similar size.
2. Sprinkle the olives, the feta, the artichoke hearts, the green onions, and the carrots, layering them in order; drizzle the top with the reserved artichoke marinade.
3. Cover and then refrigerate for at least1 hour up to 12 hours before serving with pita crackers.

Nutrition Info:
- per serving: 153 cal., 10.7 g total fat (5.2 g sat. fat), 23 mg chol., 426 mg sodium, 227 mg pot., 9.7 g total carbs., 3.5 g fiber, 1.7 g sugar, 6.3 g protein, 40% vitamin A, 7% vitamin C, 14% calcium, and 8% iron.

Neufchatel Cheese Mediterranean Dip
Servings:12 | Cooking Time: 10 Minutes

Ingredients:
- 1 package (8 ounces) PHILADELPHIA Neufchatel Cheese, softened
- 1 plum tomato, chopped
- 1/2 cup seedless cucumbers, chopped
- 2 tablespoons KRAFT Greek Vinaigrette Dressing
- 2 tablespoons red onions, finely chopped

Directions:
1. In a 9-inch pie plate, spread the cheese evenly in the bottom.
2. Mix all the remaining ingredients; spoon over the cheese layer. Serve.

Nutrition Info:
- Per Serving:62 cal., 4 g total fat (0.8 g sat. fat), 0 mg chol., 1 mg sodium, 81 mg pot., 7.2 g total carbs., 1.3 g fiber, 5.5 g sugar, 0.8 g protein, 0% vitamin A, 0% vitamin C, 1% calcium, and 3% iron.

Potato Rosti
Servings: 4 | Cooking Time: 15 Minutes

Ingredients:
- ½ pound russet potatoes, peeled and grated roughly
- Salt and freshly ground black pepper, to taste
- 3.5 ounces smoked salmon, cut into slices
- k1 teaspoon olive oil
- 1 tablespoon chives, chopped finely
- 2 tablespoons sour cream

Directions:
1. Preheat the Airfryer to 360 degrees F and grease a pizza pan with the olive oil.
2. Add chives, potatoes, salt and black pepper in a large bowl and mix until well combined.
3. Place the potato mixture into the prepared pizza pan and transfer the pizza pan in an Airfryer basket.
4. Cook for about 15 minutes and cut the potato rosti into wedges.
5. Top with the smoked salmon slices and sour cream and serve.

Nutrition Info:
- Calories: 91 Carbs: 9.2g Fats: 3.6g Proteins: 5.7g Sodium: 503mg Sugar: 0.7g

Italian Vegetable Soup
Servings: 8 | Cooking Time:1 Hour

Ingredients:
- 2 tablespoons olive oil
- 1 sweet onion, chopped
- 1 garlic clove, chopped
- 1 celery stalk, sliced
- 1 small fennel bulb, sliced
- 1 leek, sliced
- 1 carrot, diced
- 2 tomatoes, peeled and diced
- 2 tablespoons tomato paste
- 2 potatoes, peeled and cubed
- 4 cups chicken stock
- 4 cups water
- Salt and pepper to taste

Directions:
1. Heat the oil in a soup pot and stir in the onion, garlic, celery and fennel, as well as leek and carrot.
2. Cook for 5 minutes then add the potatoes, stock, water, salt and pepper.
3. Cook on low heat for 25 minutes.
4. Serve the soup warm and fresh.

Nutrition Info:
- Per Serving:Calories:101 Fat:4.0g Protein:2.2g Carbohydrates:15.4g

Jew's Mallow Stew (mulukhiya)
Serves: 1 Cup | Cooking Time:2 Hours

Ingredients:
- 2 whole chicken thighs, including drumstick
- 1 (2-in.) cinnamon stick
- 2 bay leaves
- 8 cups water
- 2 tsp. salt
- 1/2 cup extra-virgin olive oil
- 6 cups rehydrated Jew's mallow leaves, drained
- 1 large yellow onion, chopped
- 6 TB. minced garlic
- 1 cup fresh cilantro, finely chopped
- 1/2 tsp. cayenne
- 1/2 cup fresh lemon juice

Directions:
1. In a large pot over medium heat, combine chicken thighs, cinnamon stick, bay leaves, water, and 1 teaspoon salt. Cook for 30 minutes. Skim off any foam that comes to the top.
2. Meanwhile, in another large pot over medium heat, heat 1/4 cup extra-virgin olive oil. Add Jew's mallow leaves, and cook, tossing leaves, for 10 minutes. Remove leaves, and set aside.
3. Reduce heat to medium-low. Add remaining 1/4 cup extra-virgin olive oil, yellow onion, and 3 tablespoons garlic, and cook for 5 minutes.
4. Return Jew's mallow leaves to onions. Add 8 cups chicken broth strained to the first pot to onions and Jew's mallow leaves in the second pot. Add remaining 1 teaspoon salt, and cook for 1 hour.
5. Meanwhile, separate chicken meat from bones. Discard bones and remaining contents of first pot.
6. After leaves have been cooking for 1 hour, add chicken, cilantro, cayenne, and remaining 3 tablespoons garlic, and cook for 20 more minutes.
7. Add lemon juice, and cook for 10 more minutes.
8. Serve with brown rice.

Mediterranean Diet Cookbook

Breakfast Egg-artichoke Casserole
Servings: 8 | Cooking Time: 35 Minutes

Ingredients:
- 16 large eggs
- 14 ounce can artichoke hearts, drained
- 10-ounce box frozen chopped spinach, thawed and drained well
- 1 cup shredded white cheddar
- 1 garlic clove, minced
- 1 teaspoon salt
- 1/2 cup parmesan cheese
- 1/2 cup ricotta cheese
- 1/2 teaspoon dried thyme
- 1/2 teaspoon crushed red pepper
- 1/4 cup milk
- 1/4 cup shaved onion

Directions:
1. Lightly grease a 9x13-inch baking dish with cooking spray and preheat the oven to 350oF.
2. In a large mixing bowl, add eggs and milk. Mix thoroughly.
3. With a paper towel, squeeze out the excess moisture from the spinach leaves and add to the bowl of eggs.
4. Into small pieces, break the artichoke hearts and separate the leaves. Add to the bowl of eggs.
5. Except for the ricotta cheese, add remaining ingredients in the bowl of eggs and mix thoroughly.
6. Pour egg mixture into the prepared dish.
7. Evenly add dollops of ricotta cheese on top of the eggs and then pop in the oven.
8. Bake until eggs are set and doesn't jiggle when shook, about 35 minutes.
9. Remove from the oven and evenly divide into suggested servings. Enjoy.

Nutrition Info:
- Calories per serving: 302; Protein: 22.6g; Carbs: 10.8g; Fat: 18.7g

Light Tartar Dill Sauce
Servings:6 | Cooking Time: 3 Minutes

Ingredients:
- 1 1/2 tablespoons capers, minced
- 1 cup light sour cream (you can use fat free)
- 1 tablespoon fresh parsley, minced
- 1/2 lemon, juice
- 1/4 teaspoon salt
- 2 tablespoons honey Dijon mustard
- 3 tablespoons fresh dill, minced
- Pinch pepper

Directions:
1. Mix all of the ingredients in a bowl; serve.

Nutrition Info:
- Per Serving:58 cal., 4.3 g total fat (2.5 g sat. fat), 13.4 mg chol., 235.8 mg sodium, 3.7 g total carbs., 0.5 g fiber, 0.3 g sugar, 1.7 g protein, 5% vitamin A, 9% vitamin C, 6% calcium, and 2% iron.

Yogurt Fish Soup
Servings: 4 | Cooking Time:35 Minutes

Ingredients:
- 2 tablespoons olive oil
- 2 garlic cloves, chopped
- 1 red pepper, chopped
- 1 shallot, finely chopped
- 2 cups vegetable stock
- 1 cup Greek yogurt
- 4 cod fillets
- Salt and pepper to taste

Directions:
1. Heat the oil in a soup pot and stir in the garlic, red pepper and shallot. Cook for 2 minutes then add the stock.
2. Cook for 5 minutes then stir in the yogurt.
3. Add the cod fillets and season with salt and pepper.
4. Continue cooking for another 10 minutes on low heat, with a lid on.
5. Serve the soup warm and fresh.

Nutrition Info:
- Per Serving:Calories:114 Fat:8.2g Protein:5.7g Carbohydrates:5.2g

Spiced Lentil Stew
Servings: 8 | Cooking Time:45 Minutes

Ingredients:
- 2 tablespoons extra virgin olive oil
- 2 shallots, chopped
- 2 garlic cloves, chopped
- 2 red bell peppers, cored and diced
- 2 carrots, diced
- 1 celery stalk, diced
- ½ teaspoon mustard seeds
- ½ teaspoon cumin seeds
- 1 can crushed tomatoes
- 3 cups vegetable stock
- 3 cups water
- 1 cup green lentils
- Salt and pepper to taste
- Yogurt for serving

Directions:
1. Heat the oil in a soup pot and stir in the shallots and garlic. Cook for 2 minutes then add the rest of the ingredients.
2. Adjust the taste with salt and pepper and cook on low heat for 30 minutes.
3. Serve the soup warm and fresh, topped with plain yogurt or freshly chopped parsley.

Nutrition Info:
- Per Serving:Calories:143 Fat:4.0g Protein:7.3g Carbohydrates:20.2g

Lentil And Swiss Chard Soup
Serves: 2 Cups | Cooking Time:1 Hour

Ingredients:
- 12 cups water
- 2 tsp. salt
- 1 1/2 cups brown or green lentils, picked over and rinsed
- 6 medium garlic cloves, finely chopped
- 2 lb. Swiss chard (about 2 bunches), washed and chopped
- 2 medium yellow onions, chopped
- 4 TB. extra-virgin olive oil
- 1 large potato, peeled and diced
- 1/2 tsp. ground black pepper
- 1/4 cup fresh lemon juice

Directions:
1. In a large pot over medium heat, combine water, 1 teaspoon salt, and brown lentils. Simmer for 30 minutes.
2. Add remaining 1 teaspoon salt, garlic, Swiss chard, and half of onions; stir; and simmer for 20 minutes.
3. In a small pan over medium heat, heat extra-virgin olive oil. Add remaining yellow onions, and sauté for 5 minutes. Add onions to the large pot.
4. Add potato, black pepper, and lemon juice to the pot, and simmer for 5 minutes.
5. Serve warm.

St. Valentine's Mediterranean Pancakes
Servings: 2 | Cooking Time:20 Minutes

Ingredients:
- 4 eggs, preferably organic
- 2 pieces banana, peeled and then cut into small pieces
- 1/2 teaspoon extra-virgin olive oil (for the pancake pan)
- 1 tablespoon milled flax seeds, preferably organic
- 1 tablespoon bee pollen, milled, preferably organic

Directions:
1. Crack the eggs into a mixing bowl. Add in the banana, flax seeds, and bee pollen. With a hand mixer, blend the ingredients until smooth batter inn texture.
2. Put a few drops of the olive oil in a nonstick pancake pan over medium flame or heat. Pour some batter into the pan; cook for about 2 minutes, undisturbed until the bottom of the pancake is golden and can be lifted easily from the pan. With a silicon spatula, lift and flip the pancake; cook for about 30seconds more and transfer into a plate.
3. Repeat the process with the remaining batter, oiling the pan with every new batter.
4. Serve the pancake as you cook or serve them all together topped with vanilla, strawberry, pine nuts jam.

Nutrition Info:
- Per Serving:272 cal.,11.6 g total fat (3 g sat. fat), 327 mg chol., 125 mg sodium, 633 mg pot., 32.7 g total carbs., 4.5 g fiber, 17.3 g sugar, 13.3 g protein, 10% vitamin A, 20% vitamin C, 6% calcium, and 12% iron

Okra Stew (bamya)
Serves: 1 Cup | Cooking Time:40 Minutes

Ingredients:
- 4 TB. extra-virgin olive oil
- 1 lb. boneless skinless chicken breast, cut into 1/2-in. cubes
- 4 cups fresh or frozen baby okra
- 1 large yellow onion, chopped
- 3 TB. garlic, minced
- 1 (16-oz.) can plain tomato sauce
- 2 cups water
- 1 1/2 tsp. salt
- 1 tsp. ground black pepper
- 1/2 tsp. cayenne
- 1 cup fresh cilantro, chopped

Directions:
1. In a 3-quart pot over medium heat, heat 2 tablespoons extra-virgin olive oil. Add chicken, and cook for 5 minutes. Remove chicken to a plate, and set aside.
2. Add remaining 2 tablespoons extra-virgin olive oil to the pot. Add okra and yellow onion, and cook for 7 minutes.
3. Add garlic, and cook for 3 minutes.
4. Return chicken to the pot, and add tomato sauce, water, salt, black pepper, and cayenne. Cook for 20 minutes.
5. Stir in cilantro, and cook for 15 more minutes.
6. Serve warm with brown rice.

French Baked Brie Recipe With Figs, Walnuts And Pistachios
Servings: 6 To 8 | Cooking Time:10 Minutes

Ingredients:
- 13 ounces French brie
- 4 tablespoons fig jam or preserves, divided
- 1/3 cup walnut hearts, roughly chopped
- 1/3 cup pistachios, shelled and roughly chopped
- 1/3 cup dried mission figs, sliced

Directions:
1. Preheat the oven to 375F.
2. Place the fig preserves or jam in a microwavable dish; microwave for 30 seconds or until soft.
3. In a small-sized bowl, combine the nuts and the dried figs. Add in 1/2 of the softened fig preserve; mix well until well combined.
4. Place the brie into a small-sized ovenproof dish or a cast-iron skillet. With a knife, coat the brie with remaining 1/2 of the softened fig preserve/jam.
5. Top the brie with the nut and fig mixture.
6. Place the dish or the skillet in the oven and bake for 10 minutes at 375F or until the brie starts to ooze, but not melt.
7. Serve warm with your favorite crackers.

Nutrition Info:
- Per Serving:330 cal.,22.8 g total fat (11.1 g sat. fat), 61 mg chol., 410 mg sodium, 250 mg pot., 18.1 g total carbs., 2 g fiber, 12.3 g sugar, 15.5 g protein, 7% vitamin A, 2% vitamin C, 14% calcium, and 5% iron

Mediterranean Diet Cookbook

Egg And Ham Breakfast Cup
Servings: 12 | Cooking Time: 12 Minutes

Ingredients:
- 2 green onion bunch, chopped
- 12 eggs
- 6 thick pieces nitrate free ham

Directions:
1. Grease a 12-muffin tin and preheat oven to 400oF.
2. Add 2 hams per muffin compartment, press down to form a cup and add egg in middle. Repeat process to remaining muffin compartments.
3. Pop in the oven and bake until eggs are cooked to desired doneness, around 10 to 12 minutes.
4. To serve, garnish with chopped green onions.

Nutrition Info:
- Calories per serving: 92; Protein: 7.3g; Carbs: 0.8g; Fat: 6.4g

Spicy Red Lentil Soup
Servings: 8 | Cooking Time: 45 Minutes

Ingredients:
- 2 tablespoons olive oil
- 1 shallot, chopped
- 3 garlic cloves, chopped
- 1 chili pepper, chopped
- ¼ teaspoon cumin powder
- ½ teaspoon turmeric powder
- 1 cup red lentils
- 2 cups chicken stock
- 2 cups water
- 1 cup diced tomatoes
- 1 bay leaf
- 1 thyme sprig
- 1 teaspoon sherry vinegar
- Salt and pepper to taste

Directions:
1. Heat the oil in a soup pot and stir in the shallot, garlic, chili pepper, cumin powder and turmeric.
2. Cook for 5 minutes then add the lentils, stock, water, tomatoes, bay leaf, thyme and sherry vinegar.
3. Add salt and pepper to taste and cook on low heat for 15 minutes.
4. Serve the soup warm and fresh.

Nutrition Info:
- Per Serving:Calories:125 Fat:4.0g Protein:6.7g Carbohydrates:16.3g

Arrabbiata White Bean Soup
Servings: 8 | Cooking Time:1 Hour

Ingredients:
- 2 tablespoons olive oil
- 2 carrots, diced
- 1 sweet onion, chopped
- 2 garlic cloves, chopped
- ½ teaspoon chili flakes
- 1 can diced tomatoes
- 1 can white beans, drained
- 4 cups chicken stock
- 4 cups water
- 1 bay leaf
- Salt and pepper to taste

Directions:
1. Heat the oil in a soup pot and stir in the carrots, onion, garlic and chili flakes.
2. Cook for 5 minutes then add the tomatoes, beans, stock, water and bay leaf, as well as salt and pepper.
3. Cook on low heat for 25 minutes.
4. Serve the soup warm and fresh.

Nutrition Info:
- Per Serving:Calories:135 Fat:4.0g Protein:6.7g Carbohydrates:19.3g

Veggie Hash
Servings: 8 | Cooking Time: 55 Minutes

Ingredients:
- 2 medium onions, chopped
- 2 teaspoons dried thyme, crushed
- 4 teaspoons butter
- 1 green bell pepper, seeded and chopped
- 3 pounds russet potatoes, peeled and cubed
- Salt and freshly ground black pepper, to taste
- 10 eggs

Directions:
1. Preheat the Airfryer to 395 degrees F and grease the Airfryer pan with butter.
2. Add bell peppers and onions and cook for about 5 minutes.
3. Add the herbs, potatoes, salt and black pepper and cook for about 30 minutes.
4. Heat a greased skillet on medium heat and add beaten eggs.
5. Cook for about 1 minute on each side and remove from the skillet.
6. Cut it into small pieces and add egg pieces into Airfryer pan.
7. Cook for about 5 more minutes and dish out.

Nutrition Info:
- Calories: 229 Carbs: 31g Fats: 7.6g Proteins: 10.3g Sodium: 102mg Sugar: 4.3g

Easy Butternut Squash With Quinoa And Lentils

Servings: 4 To 6 | Cooking Time:15 Minutes

Ingredients:
- 1 cup quinoa, cooked
- 1 cup small brown lentils, steamed or cooked
- 1 teaspoon cumin, divided
- 1 teaspoon ground cinnamon, divided
- 1/2 butternut squash, seeded, peeled, and chopped into 1/2-inch cubes
- 1/2 lime, juiced
- 1/2 teaspoon hot paprika
- 1/3 cup almonds, slivered, browned or toasted stove-top
- 1/4 head radicchio lettuce
- 2 green onions, washed, dried, and halved
- 4 fresh garlic cloves
- Olive oil

Directions:
1. Preheat the oven to 425F.
2. Prepare the ingredients as directed above.
3. Grease the baking sheet. Place the butternut squash, radicchio, green onions, and the garlic into the baking sheet. Sprinkle with salt, 1/2 teaspoon cinnamon, 1/2 teaspoon cumin, and 1/2 teaspoon hot paprika. Drizzle with the olive oil and roast for 1bout 15 minutes at 425F until the veggies are browned and tender, tossing halfway through roasting. When the veggies are roasted, remove from the oven and let cool slightly.
4. Chop the roasted radicchio with the garlic and the green onions.
5. Combine the cooked lentils and the quinoa; season with the salt and the remaining cinnamon and cumin. Add the roasted butter nut squash with the chopped radicchio mixture; toss to combine. Squeeze the lemon juice; toss to combine. Mix in the almonds.

Nutrition Info:
- Per Serving:283 cal.,5.1 g total fat (0.5 g sat. fat), 0 mg chol., 24 mg sodium, 983 mg pot., 46.1 g total carbs., 14.7 g fiber, 3.8 g sugar, 15.8 g protein, 9% vitamin A, 51% vitamin C, 9% calcium, and 27% iron

Pink Lady Mediterranean Drink

Servings:1 | Cooking Time: 5 Minutes

Ingredients:
- 1 1/2 ounces London dry gin,
- 1 large egg white
- 1/2 ounce Cointreau
- 1/2 ounce freshly squeezed lemon juice
- 1/4 ounce Campari
- 1/4 ounce limoncello
- 3-4 lemon zest, thin strips, for garnish
- Ice

Directions:
1. Except for the ice and garnish, combine all the ingredients in a cocktail shaker; shake well. Add the ice; shake again. Strain the drink into a chilled coupe. Garnish with the strips of lemon zest.

Nutrition Info:
- Per Serving:163 cal., 0.2 g total fat (0 g sat. fat), 0 mg chol., 39 mg sodium, 72 mg pot., 0.5 g total carbs., 0 g fiber, 0.5 g sugar, 3.7g protein, 0% vitamin A, 11% vitamin C, 1% calcium, and 0% iron.

Toasted Bagels

Servings: 6 | Cooking Time: 10 Minutes

Ingredients:
- 6 teaspoons butter
- 3 bagels, halved

Directions:
1. Preheat the Airfryer to 375 degrees F and arrange the bagels into an Airfryer basket.
2. Cook for about 3 minutes and remove the bagels from Airfryer.
3. Spread butter evenly over bagels and cook for about 3 more minutes.

Nutrition Info:
- Calories: 169 Carbs: 26.5g Fats: 4.7g Proteins: 5.3g Sodium: 262mg Sugar: 2.7g

Mediterranean Last-minute Feta Cheese Dip

Servings:6 | Cooking Time:5 Minutes

Ingredients:
- 8-10 ounces feta cheese, crumbled
- 1 1/2 tablespoon chives, chopped
- 3/44 cup sundried tomato bits
- 3 ounces cream cheese, softened, at room temperature
- 10 fresh basil leaves, torn
- 1 teaspoon honey
- 1 Persian cucumber (about ½ cup), chopped or ¼ English cucumber
- 1 jalapeno, chopped
- Olive oil

Directions:
1. In a large-sized mixing bowl, put the feta cheese, cream cheese, honey, and 1 tablespoon olive oil. Using the back of spoon, press the mixture until cheeses are soft and everything is well combined.
2. Add the remaining ingredients 2 tablespoons olive oil; gently combine. Transfer the dip into a serving bowl and serve with pita chips or pita bread.

Nutrition Info:
- Per Serving:163 cal., 13.1 g total fat (8.8 g sat. fat), 49 mg chol., 478 mg sodium, 145 mg pot., 5.2 g total carbs., 0 g fiber, 3.7 g sugar, 6.9 g protein, 10% vitamin A, 5% vitamin C, 21% calcium, and 4% iron.

Mediterranean Diet Cookbook

Sweet And Sour Rhubarb Lentil Soup

Servings: 6 | Cooking Time: 45 Minutes

Ingredients:
- 2 tablespoons olive oil
- 1 shallot, chopped
- 1 garlic clove, chopped
- 1 green bell pepper, cored and diced
- 1 yellow bell pepper, cored and diced
- 1 carrot, diced
- 1 celery stalk, diced
- 1 cup green lentils
- 4 rhubarb stalks, sliced
- 2 cups vegetable stock
- 6 cups water
- ½ cup diced tomatoes
- Salt and pepper to taste
- 1 thyme sprig
- 1 oregano sprig

Directions:
1. Heat the oil in a soup pot and stir in the shallot, garlic, bell peppers, carrot and celery.
2. Cook for 5 minutes until softened then add the lentils, rhubarb, stock and water, as well as tomatoes.
3. Season with salt and pepper and add the thyme and oregano sprig.
4. Cook on low heat for 20 minutes.
5. Serve the soup warm or chilled.

Nutrition Info:
- Per Serving: Calories: 184 Fat: 5.3g Protein: 9.4g Carbohydrates: 25.6g

Tomato Haddock Soup

Servings: 6 | Cooking Time: 30 Minutes

Ingredients:
- 2 tablespoons olive oil
- 1 shallot, chopped
- 2 garlic cloves, minced
- 1 celery stalk, diced
- 4 tomatoes, peeled and diced
- 2 cups vegetable stock
- 2 cups water
- 1 teaspoon sherry vinegar
- 4 haddock fillets, cubed
- 1 thyme sprig
- 1 bay leaf
- ½ teaspoon dried oregano
- Salt and pepper to taste

Directions:
1. Heat the oil in a soup pot and stir in the shallot and garlic. Cook for 2 minutes until fragrant.
2. Add the celery, tomatoes, stock, water, vinegar, thyme and bay leaf, as well as oregano, salt and pepper.
3. Cook for 15 minutes then add the haddock and cover the pot with a lid.
4. Cook for another 10 minutes on low heat.
5. Serve the soup warm and fresh.

Nutrition Info:
- Per Serving: Calories: 172 Fat: 5.8g Protein: 25.2g Carbohydrates: 4.3g

Kale Gazpacho

Servings: 6 | Cooking Time: 20 Minutes

Ingredients:
- 2 whole wheat bread slices
- 4 tomatoes, peeled and diced
- 2 cucumbers
- 4 kale leaves
- 2 garlic cloves
- 1 shallot, chopped
- 2 tablespoons olive oil
- 1 pinch cayenne pepper
- 1 teaspoon sherry vinegar
- ¼ cup chopped parsley
- Salt and pepper to taste
- 1 cup water
- 4 ice cubes

Directions:
1. Combine all the ingredients in a blender.
2. Season with salt and pepper and pulse until the soup is smooth.
3. Serve the soup as fresh as possible.

Nutrition Info:
- Per Serving: Calories: 119 Fat: 5.3g Protein: 4.1g Carbohydrates: 16.1g

Dessert Recipes

Dessert Recipes

Lime Grapes And Apples
Servings: 2 | Cooking Time: 25 Minutes

Ingredients:
- ½ cup red grapes
- 2 apples
- 1 teaspoon lime juice
- 1 teaspoon Erythritol
- 3 tablespoons water

Directions:
1. Line the baking tray with baking paper.
2. Then cut the apples on the halves and remove the seeds with the help of the scooper.
3. Cut the apple halves on 2 parts more.
4. Arrange all fruits in the tray in one layer, drizzle with water, and bake for 20 minutes at 375F.
5. Flip the fruits on another side after 10 minutes of cooking.
6. Then remove them from the oven and sprinkle with lime juice and Erythritol.
7. Return the fruits back in the oven and bake for 5 minutes more.
8. Serve the cooked dessert hot or warm.

Nutrition Info:
- Per Servingcalories 142, fat 0.4, fiber 5.7, carbs 40.1, protein 0.9

Mediterranean Doughnuts
Serves: 1 Doughnut | Cooking Time: 15 Minutes

Ingredients:
- 1 TB. active dry yeast
- 1 cup warm water
- 3 TB. sugar
- 1 large potato, boiled, peeled, and mashed
- 2 cups all-purpose flour
- 1 tsp. cinnamon
- 8 cups vegetable oil
- 4 cups Simple Syrup (recipe in Chapter 21)

Directions:
1. In a large bowl, combine yeast, warm water, and sugar. Set aside for 5 minutes.
2. Add mashed potato, all-purpose flour, and cinnamon, and stir to combine. Cover with plastic wrap, and let sit for 1 hour.
3. In a large pot over medium heat, bring vegetable oil to 365°F.
4. Pour Simple Syrup in a large bowl.
5. Spoon up about 2 tablespoons dough mixture, drop into hot oil, and fry for 2 or 3 minutes or until dark brown.
6. Spoon out fried doughnuts from oil, and drop into Simple Syrup to soak for about 5 minutes.
7. Spoon out doughnuts from Simple Syrup, and place on a plate. Serve at room temperature.

Five Berry Mint Orange Infusion
Servings: 12 | Cooking Time: 10 Minutes

Ingredients:
- ½ cup water
- 3 orange pekoe tea bags
- 3 sprigs of mint
- 1 cup fresh strawberries
- 1 cup fresh golden raspberries
- 1 cup fresh raspberries
- 1 cup blackberries
- 1 cup fresh blueberries
- 1 cup pitted fresh cherries
- 1 bottle Sauvignon Blanc
- ½ cup pomegranate juice, natural
- 1 teaspoon vanilla

Directions:
1. In a saucepan, bring water to a boil over medium heat. Add the tea bags, mint and stir. Let it stand for 10 minutes.
2. In a large bowl, combine the rest of the ingredients.
3. Put in the fridge to chill for at least 3 hours.

Nutrition Info:
- Calories per serving: 140; Carbs: 32.1g; Protein: 1.2g; Fat: 1.5g

Shredded Phyllo And Sweet Cheese Pie (knafe)
Serves: 1/8 Pie | Cooking Time: 30 Minutes

Ingredients:
- 1 lb. pkg. shredded phyllo (kataifi dough)
- 1 cup butter, melted
- 1/2 cup whole milk
- 2 TB. semolina flour
- 1 lb. ricotta cheese
- 2 cups mozzarella cheese, shredded
- 2 TB. sugar
- 1 cup Simple Syrup (recipe later in this chapter)

Directions:
1. 1 cup Simple Syrup (recipe later in this chapter)
2. In a food processor fitted with a chopping blade, pulse shredded phyllo and butter 10 times. Transfer mixture to a bowl.
3. In a small saucepan over low heat, warm whole milk.
4. Stir in semolina flour, and cook for 1 minute.
5. Rinse the food processor, and to it, add ricotta cheese, mozzarella cheese, sugar, and semolina mixture. Blend for 1 minute.
6. Preheat the oven to 375°F.
7. In a 9-inch-round baking dish, add 1/2 of shredded phyllo mixture, and press down to compress. Add cheese mixture, and spread out evenly. Add rest of shredded phyllo mixture,

spread evenly, and gently press down. Bake for 40 minutes or until golden brown.
8. Let pie rest for 10 minutes before serving with Simple Syrup drizzled over top.

Peach Tart
Servings:6 | Cooking Time: 40 Minutes

Ingredients:
- ½ cup Erythritol
- 1/3 cup butter, softened
- 1 cup wheat flour
- ½ cup peaches, sliced
- 1 teaspoon baking powder
- 1 teaspoon ground cinnamon
- 1 tablespoon almond meal

Directions:
1. Sprinkle the round springform pan with almond meal.
2. Then place the sliced peaches and sprinkle them with all Erythritol.
3. Make the dough: mix up together butter, wheat flour, baking powder, and cinnamon.
4. With the help of the cooking machine knead the dough.
5. Then put the dough over the peaches and flatten it carefully with the help of the fingertips.
6. Bake the tart for 40 minutes at 365F.
7. When the tart is cooked, remove it from the heat and turn it over to get the peaches on the tart surface.
8. Cut it into the servings.
9. It is recommended to serve tart Tatin hot.

Nutrition Info:
- Per Servingcalories 179, fat 11, fiber 1.1, carbs 38, protein 2.6

Cinnamon Pear Jam
Servings: 12 | Cooking Time: 4 Minutes

Ingredients:
- 8 pears, cored and cut into quarters
- 1 tsp cinnamon
- 1/4 cup apple juice
- 2 apples, peeled, cored and diced

Directions:
1. Add all ingredients into the inner pot of instant pot and stir well.
2. Seal pot with lid and cook on high for 4 minutes.
3. Once done, allow to release pressure naturally. Remove lid.
4. Blend pear apple mixture using an immersion blender until smooth.
5. Serve and enjoy.

Nutrition Info:
- Calories 103 Fat 0.3 g Carbohydrates 27.1 g Sugar 18 g Protein 0.6 g Cholesterol 0 mg

Apple Dates Mix
Servings: 4 | Cooking Time: 15 Minutes

Ingredients:
- 4 apples, cored and cut into chunks
- 1 tsp vanilla
- 1 tsp cinnamon
- 1/2 cup dates, pitted
- 1 1/2 cups apple juice

Directions:
1. Add all ingredients into the inner pot of instant pot and stir well.
2. Seal pot with lid and cook on high for 15 minutes.
3. Once done, allow to release pressure naturally for 10 minutes then release remaining using quick release. Remove lid.
4. Stir and serve.

Nutrition Info:
- Calories 226 Fat 0.6 g Carbohydrates 58.6 g Sugar 46.4 g Protein 1.3 g Cholesterol 0 mg

Minty Tart
Servings:6 | Cooking Time: 30 Minutes

Ingredients:
- 1 cup tart cherries, pitted
- 1 cup wheat flour, whole grain
- 1/3 cup butter, softened
- ½ teaspoon baking powder
- 1 tablespoon Erythritol
- ¼ teaspoon dried mint
- ¾ teaspoon salt

Directions:
1. Mix up together wheat flour and cutter.
2. Add baking powder and salt. Knead the soft dough.
3. Then place the dough in the freezer for 10 minutes.
4. When the dough is solid, remove it from the freezer and grate with the help of the grater. Place ¼ part of the grated dough in the freezer.
5. Sprinkle the springform pan with remaining dough and place tart cherries on it.
6. Sprinkle the berries with Erythritol and dried mint and cover with ¼ part of dough from the freezer.
7. Bake the cake for 30 minutes at 365F. The cooked tart will have a golden brown surface.

Nutrition Info:
- Per Servingcalories 177, fat 10.4, fiber 0.9, carbs 21, protein 2.4

Greek Raisins And Vanilla Cream
Servings: 4 | Cooking Time: 0

Ingredients:
- 1 cup heavy cream
- 2 cups Greek yogurt
- 3 tablespoons stevia
- 2 tablespoons raisins
- 2 tablespoons lime juice

Directions:

1. In a blender, combine the cream with the yogurt and the rest of the ingredients, pulse well, divide into cups and keep in the fridge for 2 hours before serving.

Nutrition Info:
- calories 192, fat 6.5, fiber 3.4, carbs 9.5, protein 5

Spiced Cookies
Servings:6 | Cooking Time: 30 Minutes

Ingredients:
- 1 egg, beaten
- 1 teaspoon vanilla extract
- ½ teaspoon ground cinnamon
- 1 teaspoon ground turmeric
- 1 tablespoon butter, softened
- 1 cup wheat flour
- 1 teaspoon baking powder
- 4 tablespoons pumpkin puree
- 1 tablespoon Erythritol

Directions:
1. Put all ingredients in the mixing bowl and knead the soft and non-sticky dough.
2. After this, line the baking tray with baking paper.
3. Make 6 balls from the dough and press them gently with the help of the spoon.
4. Arrange the dough balls in the tray.
5. Bake the cookies for 30 minutes at 355F.
6. Chill the cooked cookies well and store them in the glass jar.

Nutrition Info:
- Per Servingcalories 111, fat 2.9, fiber 1.1, carbs 20.2, protein 3.2

Vanilla Apple Pie
Servings:8 | Cooking Time: 50 Minutes

Ingredients:
- 3 apples, sliced
- ½ teaspoon ground cinnamon
- 1 teaspoon vanilla extract
- 1 tablespoon Erythritol
- 7 oz yeast roll dough
- 1 egg, beaten

Directions:
1. Roll up the dough and cut it on 2 parts.
2. Line the springform pan with baking paper.
3. Place the first dough part in the springform pan.
4. Then arrange the apples over the dough and sprinkle it with Erythritol, vanilla extract, and ground cinnamon.
5. Then cover the apples with remaining dough and secure the edges of the pie with the help of the fork.
6. Make the small cuts in the surface of the pie.
7. Brush the pie with beaten egg and bake it for 50 minutes at 375F.
8. Cool the cooked pie well and then remove from the springform pan.
9. Cut it on the servings.

Nutrition Info:
- Per Servingcalories 139, fat 3.6, fiber 3.1, carbs 26.1, protein 2.8

Yogurt Mousse With Sour Cherry Sauce
Servings: 6 | Cooking Time:1 Hour

Ingredients:
- 1 ½ cups Greek yogurt
- 1 teaspoon vanilla extract
- 4 tablespoons honey
- 1 ½ cups heavy cream, whipped
- 2 cups sour cherries
- ¼ cup white sugar
- 1 cinnamon stick

Directions:
1. Combine the yogurt with vanilla and honey in a bowl.
2. Fold in the whipped cream then spoon the mousse into serving glasses and refrigerate.
3. For the sauce, combine the cherries, sugar and cinnamon in a saucepan. Allow to rest for 10 minutes then cook on low heat for 10 minutes.
4. Cool the sauce down then spoon it over the mousse.
5. Serve it right away.

Nutrition Info:
- Per Serving:Calories:245 Fat:12.1g Protein:5.8g Carbohydrates:29.7g

Grapes Stew
Servings: 4 | Cooking Time: 10 Minutes

Ingredients:
- 2/3 cup stevia
- 1 tablespoon olive oil
- 1/3 cup coconut water
- 1 teaspoon vanilla extract
- 1 teaspoon lemon zest, grated
- 2 cup red grapes, halved

Directions:
1. Heat up a pan with the water over medium heat, add the oil, stevia and the rest of the ingredients, toss, simmer for 10 minutes, divide into cups and serve.

Nutrition Info:
- calories 122, fat 3.7, fiber 1.2, carbs 2.3, protein 0.4

Healthy Zucchini Pudding
Servings: 4 | Cooking Time: 10 Minutes

Ingredients:
- 2 cups zucchini, shredded
- 1/4 tsp cardamom powder
- 5 oz half and half
- 5 oz almond milk
- 1/4 cup Swerve

Directions:
1. Add all ingredients except cardamom into the instant pot and stir well.
2. Seal pot with lid and cook on high for 10 minutes.
3. Once done, allow to release pressure naturally for 10 minutes then release remaining using quick release. Remove lid.

4. Stir in cardamom and serve.

Nutrition Info:
- Calories 137 Fat 12.6 g Carbohydrates 20.5 g Sugar 17.2 g Protein 2.6 g Cholesterol 13 mg

Watermelon Cream
Servings: 2 | Cooking Time: 0 Minutes

Ingredients:
- 1 pound watermelon, peeled and chopped
- 1 teaspoon vanilla extract
- 1 cup heavy cream
- 1 teaspoon lime juice
- 2 tablespoons stevia

Directions:
1. In a blender, combine the watermelon with the cream and the rest of the ingredients, pulse well, divide into cups and keep in the fridge for 15 minutes before serving.

Nutrition Info:
- calories 122, fat 5.7, fiber 3.2, carbs 5.3, protein 0.4

Chocolate Cups
Servings: 6 | Cooking Time: 0 Minutes

Ingredients:
- ½ cup avocado oil
- 1 cup, chocolate, melted
- 1 teaspoon matcha powder
- 3 tablespoons stevia

Directions:
1. In a bowl, mix the chocolate with the oil and the rest of the ingredients, whisk really well, divide into cups and keep in the freezer for 2 hours before serving.

Nutrition Info:
- calories 174, fat 9.1, fiber 2.2, carbs 3.9, protein 2.8

Banana Cinnamon Cupcakes
Servings: 4 | Cooking Time: 20 Minutes

Ingredients:
- 4 tablespoons avocado oil
- 4 eggs
- ½ cup orange juice
- 2 teaspoons cinnamon powder
- 1 teaspoon vanilla extract
- 2 bananas, peeled and chopped
- ¾ cup almond flour
- ½ teaspoon baking powder
- Cooking spray

Directions:
1. In a bowl, combine the oil with the eggs, orange juice and the other ingredients except the cooking spray, whisk well, pour in a cupcake pan greased with the cooking spray, introduce in the oven at 350 degrees F and bake for 20 minutes.
2. Cool the cupcakes down and serve.

Nutrition Info:
- calories 142, fat 5.8, fiber 4.2, carbs 5.7, protein 1.6

Yogurt Parfait
Servings:1 | Cooking Time: 0 Minutes

Ingredients:
- 1 oz blueberries
- 2 tablespoons Plain yogurt
- ½ teaspoon vanilla extract

Directions:
1. Mix up together Plain yogurt and vanilla extract.
2. Then put ½ oz of blueberries in the glass.
3. Cover the berries with ½ part of Plain Yogurt.
4. Then add the layer of berries.
5. Top parfait with remaining Plain yogurt.

Nutrition Info:
- Per Servingcalories 44, fat 0.5., fiber 0.7, carbs 6.5, protein 2

Peanut Banana Yogurt Bowl
Servings: 4 | Cooking Time: 15 Minutes

Ingredients:
- 4 cups Greek yogurt
- 2 medium bananas, sliced
- ¼ cup creamy natural peanut butter
- ¼ cup flax seed meal
- 1 teaspoon nutmeg

Directions:
1. Divide the yogurt between four bowls and top with banana, peanut butter, and flax seed meal.
2. Garnish with nutmeg.
3. Chill before serving.

Nutrition Info:
- Calories per serving: 370; Carbs: 47.7g; Protein: 22.7g; Fat: 10.6g

Cinnamon Banana And Semolina Pudding
Servings: 6 | Cooking Time: 7 Minutes

Ingredients:
- 2 cups semolina, ground
- 1 cup olive oil
- 4 cups hot water
- 2 bananas, peeled and chopped
- 1 teaspoon cinnamon powder
- 4 tablespoons stevia

Directions:
1. Heat up a pan with the oil over medium high heat, add the semolina and brown it for 3 minutes stirring often.
2. Add the water and the rest of the ingredients except the cinnamon, stir, and simmer for 4 minutes more.
3. Divide into bowls, sprinkle the cinnamon on top and serve.

Nutrition Info:
- calories 162, fat 8, fiber 4.2, carbs 4.3, protein 8.4

Lime Vanilla Fudge
Servings: 6 | Cooking Time: 0 Minutes

Ingredients:
- 1/3 cup cashew butter
- 5 tablespoons lime juice
- ½ teaspoon lime zest, grated
- 1 tablespoons stevia

Directions:
1. In a bowl, mix the cashew butter with the other ingredients and whisk well.
2. Line a muffin tray with parchment paper, scoop 1 tablespoon of lime fudge mix in each of the muffin tins and keep in the freezer for 3 hours before serving.

Nutrition Info:
- calories 200, fat 4.5, fiber 3.4, carbs 13.5, protein 5

Cranberries And Pears Pie
Servings: 4 | Cooking Time: 40 Minutes

Ingredients:
- 2 cup cranberries
- 3 cups pears, cubed
- A drizzle of olive oil
- 1 cup stevia
- 1/3 cup almond flour
- 1 cup rolled oats
- ¼ avocado oil

Directions:
1. In a bowl, mix the cranberries with the pears and the other ingredients except the olive oil and the oats, and stir well.
2. Grease a cake pan with the a drizzle of olive oil, pour the pears mix inside, sprinkle the oats all over and bake at 350 degrees F for 40 minutes.
3. Cool the mix down, and serve.

Nutrition Info:
- calories 172, fat 3.4, fiber 4.3, carbs 11.5, protein 4.5

Delicious Apple Pear Cobbler
Servings: 4 | Cooking Time: 12 Minutes

Ingredients:
- 3 apples, cored and cut into chunks
- 1 cup steel-cut oats
- 2 pears, cored and cut into chunks
- 1/4 cup maple syrup
- 1 1/2 cups water
- 1 tsp cinnamon

Directions:
1. Spray instant pot from inside with cooking spray.
2. Add all ingredients into the inner pot of instant pot and stir well.
3. Seal pot with lid and cook on high for 12 minutes.
4. Once done, release pressure using quick release. Remove lid.
5. Sere and enjoy.

Nutrition Info:
- Calories 278 Fat 1.8 g Carbohydrates 66.5 g Sugar 39.5 g Protein 3.5 g Cholesterol 0 mg

Warm Peach Compote
Servings: 4 | Cooking Time: 1 Minute

Ingredients:
- 4 peaches, peeled and chopped
- 1 tbsp water
- 1/2 tbsp cornstarch
- 1 tsp vanilla

Directions:
1. Add water, vanilla, and peaches into the instant pot.
2. Seal pot with lid and cook on high for 1 minute.
3. Once done, allow to release pressure naturally. Remove lid.
4. In a small bowl, whisk together 1 tablespoon of water and cornstarch and pour into the pot and stir well.
5. Serve and enjoy.

Nutrition Info:
- Calories 66 Fat 0.4 g Carbohydrates 15 g Sugar 14.1 g Protein 1.4 g Cholesterol 0 mg

Pasta Flora Or Greek Tart With Apricot Jam
Servings: 6-8 | Cooking Time: 45 Minutes

Ingredients:
- 300 grams apricot jam
- 3/4 cup sugar
- 280 grams butter, melted
- 250 grams whole-wheat flour
- 250 grams all-purpose flour
- 2 teaspoons baking powder
- 2 eggs

Directions:
1. Whisk the butter, the eggs, and the sugar together. Slowly add the flours and the baking powder, making a soft dough. Refrigerate the dough for about 30 minutes to rest.
2. Preheat the oven to 350F or 180C.
3. Butter well a 25-cm diameter tart pan. Roll out 2/3 of the dough into the buttered tart pan, placing all the way around the raised sides of the pan and gently pressing to evenly cover and join with the base.
4. Roll out the remaining 1/3 dough into 1/2-cm thickness and then cut into strips.
5. Spread the jam evenly over the dough in the pan and cover the jam with the strips of dough.
6. Bake the tart for about 45 minutes.

Nutrition Info:
- Per Serving:656 cal., 30.2 g total fat (18.4 g sat. fat), 116 mg chol., 234 mg sodium, 245 mg pot, 91.3 g total carbs, 1.8 g fiber, 35.3 g sugar, and 8.4 g protein.

Hazelnut Pudding
Servings: 8 | Cooking Time: 40 Minutes

Ingredients:
- 2 and ¼ cups almond flour
- 3 tablespoons hazelnuts, chopped
- 5 eggs, whisked
- 1 cup stevia
- 1 and 1/3 cups Greek yogurt
- 1 teaspoon baking powder
- 1 teaspoon vanilla extract

Directions:
1. In a bowl, combine the flour with the hazelnuts and the other ingredients, whisk well, and pour into a cake pan lined with parchment paper,
2. Introduce in the oven at 350 degrees F, bake for 30 minutes, cool down, slice and serve.

Nutrition Info:
- calories 178, fat 8.4, fiber 8.2, carbs 11.5, protein 1.4

Cocoa Yogurt Mix
Servings: 2 | Cooking Time: 0 Minutes

Ingredients:
- 1 tablespoon cocoa powder
- ¼ cup strawberries, chopped
- ¾ cup Greek yogurt
- 5 drops vanilla stevia

Directions:
1. In a bowl, mix the yogurt with the cocoa, strawberries and the stevia and whisk well.
2. Divide the mix into bowls and serve.

Nutrition Info:
- calories 200, fat 8, fiber 3.4, carbs 7.6, protein 4.3

Red Wine Poached Pears
Servings: 8 | Cooking Time: 1 Hour

Ingredients:
- 6 peaches
- 2 cups red wine
- 2 cups water
- ½ cup white sugar
- 1 star anise
- 1 cinnamon stick
- 2 whole cloves
- 2 cardamom pods
- 1 orange peel
- 1 lemon peel

Directions:
1. Combine the wine, water, sugar and spices in a saucepan and bring to a boil.
2. In the meantime, carefully peel the pears and core them. Choose pears that are ripe, but still firm.
3. When the syrup begins boiling, place the pears in the hot oil.
4. Lower the heat and cover with a lid.
5. Cook on low heat for 30 minutes then allow the pears to cool down in the syrup.
6. Remove the pears on serving plates.
7. Continue cooking the wine syrup until it's reduced by half – it will take about 20 minutes.
8. Cool the syrup down in a bowl with iced water and pour it over the pears.
9. Serve right away.

Nutrition Info:
- Per Serving:Calories:132 Fat:0.4g Protein:0.9g Carbohydrates:23.0g

Almond Tea Biscuits
Servings: 10 | Cooking Time: 1 ¼ Hours

Ingredients:
- ½ cup butter, softened
- ½ cup white sugar
- 1 teaspoon orange flower water
- 1 teaspoon vanilla extract
- 2 eggs
- 2 tablespoons sesame seeds
- ¼ cup almond slices
- 2 cups all-purpose flour
- 1 teaspoon baking powder
- ¼ teaspoon salt

Directions:
1. Mix the butter and sugar in a bowl until creamy and pale.
2. Stir in the orange flower, vanilla and eggs and mix well.
3. Add the sesame seeds, almond slices, flour, salt and baking powder and form a dough that's easy to work with.
4. Form small balls of dough and place them on a baking tray lined with baking paper.
5. Bake in the preheated oven at 350F for 10-12 minutes.
6. Allow to cool in the pan then serve.

Nutrition Info:
- Per Serving:Calories:234 Fat:11.2g Protein:4.1g Carbohydrates:29.9g

Baklava
Serves: 1 Piece | Cooking Time: 31 Minutes

Ingredients:
- 1 cup walnuts
- 1/2 tsp. ground cinnamon
- 1/2 tsp. ground nutmeg
- 1/4 cup sugar
- 1/4 tsp. salt
- 25 (8×8-in.) sheets phyllo dough
- 1/2 cup butter, melted
- 1 cup Simple Syrup (recipe in Chapter 21), at room temperature

Directions:
1. Preheat the oven to 350ºF.
2. In a food processor fitted with a chopping blade, blend walnuts, cinnamon, nutmeg, sugar, and salt for 30 seconds.
3. In an 8×8-inch pan, begin to layer phyllo dough. Add 10 sheets, buttering each sheet as you lay it in the pan. Then sprinkle phyllo dough with 1/2 of nut mixture. Layer next 5

phyllo sheets, brushing each sheet with butter. Sprinkle rest of nut mixture over top, and add remaining 10 layers of phyllo, again brushing each sheet with butter.
4. Using a sharp knife, cut baklava into 12 equal pieces. Bake for 20 to 25 minutes or until phyllo turns golden brown.
5. Pour Simple Syrup over baklava, and let it soak for at least 2 hours before serving.

Mediterranean Stuffed Custard Pancakes
Servings: 10 | Cooking Time: 20 Minutes

Ingredients:
- 2 cups flour
- 1/2 cup whole-wheat flour
- 2 cups milk
- 1 cup water
- 1 teaspoon yeast
- 1 teaspoon baking powder
- 1 teaspoon sugar
- 2 cups whole milk
- 2 cups fat-free milk or 2 % milk
- 1 cup heavy cream
- 3 tablespoons sugar
- 1/2 cup cornstarch
- 1/2 cup water
- 7 pieces medium-sized white bread, crust removed
- 1 tablespoon rose water
- 1 tablespoon orange blossom water
- 1 cup pistachio
- 1 tablespoon honey or simple syrup

Directions:
1. For the custard:
2. In a medium-sized pot, pour in the milks, heavy cream, cornstarch, and sugar; heat the mixture, stirring.
3. Cut the bread into pieces and add into the pot; stir until the mixture starts to thicken. Add the orange and rose water; stir until the custard is very thick. Remove from the heat and then pour into a bowl; let cool for 1 hour, stirring every 15 minutes. Cover with saran wrap and then refrigerate to completely cool.
4. For the batter:
5. Mix all of the batter ingredients in a mixing bowl, stirring until well combined; let sit for 20 minutes.
6. Over medium-low flame or heat, heat a nonstick pan. Pour 1/4 cup-worth of the batter to make a 3-inch diameter pancake; cook for about 30 seconds or until the top of the batter is bubbly and no longer wet and the bottom is golden brown. Transfer into a dish to cool. Repeat the process with the remaining batter.
7. To assemble:
8. Take out the bowl of custard from the refrigerator. Transfer the chilled custard into a piping bag.
9. Fold a pancakes together, pinching the edges to make a pocket. Pipe the custard into the pancake pocket, filling it. Repeat the process with the remaining pancakes and custard. Top each filled pocket with the ground pistachio. Refrigerate until ready to serve. To serve, transfer the custard-filled pancakes into a serving plate; drizzle with honey or simple syrup.

Nutrition Info:
- Per Serving: 450 cal., 19 g total fat (8 g sat. fat), 42.9 mg chol., 241.5 mg sodium, 60 g total carbs., 2.8 g fiber, 16.6 g sugar, 13 g protein, 10.3% vitamin A, 2% vitamin C, 31.2% calcium, and 11.5% iron.

Cinnamon Pears
Servings: 4 | Cooking Time: 25 Minutes

Ingredients:
- 2 pears
- 1 teaspoon ground cinnamon
- 1 tablespoon Erythritol
- 1 teaspoon liquid stevia
- 4 teaspoons butter

Directions:
1. Cut the pears on the halves.
2. Then scoop the seeds from the pears with the help of the scooper.
3. In the shallow bowl mix up together Erythritol and ground cinnamon.
4. Sprinkle every pear half with cinnamon mixture and drizzle with liquid stevia.
5. Then add butter and wrap in the foil.
6. Bake the pears for 25 minutes at 365F.
7. Then remove the pears from the foil and transfer in the serving plates.

Nutrition Info:
- Per Servingcalories 96, fat 4, fiber 3.6, carbs 16.4, protein 0.4

Almond Peaches Mix
Servings: 4 | Cooking Time: 10 Minutes

Ingredients:
- 1/3 cup almonds, toasted
- 1/3 cup pistachios, toasted
- 1 teaspoon mint, chopped
- ½ cup coconut water
- 1 teaspoon lemon zest, grated
- 4 peaches, halved
- 2 tablespoons stevia

Directions:
1. In a pan, combine the peaches with the stevia and the rest of the ingredients, simmer over medium heat for 10 minutes, divide into bowls and serve cold.

Nutrition Info:
- calories 135, fat 4.1, fiber 3.8, carbs 4.1, protein 2.3

Honey Fruit Compote
Servings: 4 | Cooking Time: 3 Minutes

Ingredients:
- 1/3 cup honey
- 1 1/2 cups blueberries
- 1 1/2 cups raspberries

Directions:
1. Add all ingredients into the instant pot and stir well.
2. Seal pot with lid and cook on high for 3 minutes.
3. Once done, allow to release pressure naturally. Remove lid.

4. Serve and enjoy.

Nutrition Info:
- Calories 141 Fat 0.5 g Carbohydrates 36.7 g Sugar 30.6 g Protein 1 g Cholesterol 0 mg

Almond Pudding
Servings:3 | Cooking Time: 7 Minutes

Ingredients:
- ½ cup organic almond milk
- ½ cup milk
- 1/3 cup semolina
- 1 tablespoon butter
- ¼ teaspoon cornstarch
- ½ teaspoon almond extract

Directions:
1. Pour almond milk and milk in the saucepan.
2. Bring it to boil and add semolina and cornstarch.
3. Mix up the ingredients until homogenous and simmer them for 1 minute.
4. After this, add almond extract and butter. Stir well and close the lid.
5. Remove the pudding from the heat and leave for 10 minutes.
6. Then mix it up again and transfer in the serving ramekins.

Nutrition Info:
- Per Servingcalories 201, fat 7.9, fiber 1.1, carbs 25.7, protein 5.8

Blackberry Pie
Servings:6 | Cooking Time: 35 Minutes

Ingredients:
- 1 cup wheat flour, whole grain
- 1 cup blackberries
- 1/3 cup Erythritol
- ½ teaspoon ground clove
- ½ cup rolled oats
- 1/3 cup butter, softened

Directions:
1. In the mixing bowl combine together blackberries, Erythritol, and ground clove.
2. Then take another bowl and put rolled oats, butter, and wheat flour inside.
3. Mix up the ingredients until it is crumbly.
4. Line the round springform pan with baking paper.
5. Put the blackberry mixture inside the springform pan and flatten it with the help of the spoon.
6. After this, top the berries with all crumbly mixture.
7. Bake the crumble for 35 minutes at 365F.
8. Cook the crumble for 15 minutes before serving.

Nutrition Info:
- Per Servingcalories 203, fat 11, fiber 2.6, carbs 36.3, protein 3.5

Cherry Compote
Servings:4 | Cooking Time: 30 Minutes

Ingredients:
- 2 peaches, pitted, halved
- 1 cup cherries, pitted
- ½ cup grape juice
- ½ cup strawberries
- 1 tablespoon liquid honey
- 1 teaspoon vanilla extract
- 1 teaspoon ground cinnamon

Directions:
1. Pour grape juice in the saucepan.
2. Add vanilla extract and ground cinnamon. Bring the liquid to boil.
3. After this, put peaches, cherries, and strawberries in the hot grape juice and bring to boil.
4. Remove the mixture from heat, add liquid honey, and close the lid.
5. Let the compote rest for 20 minutes.
6. Carefully mix up the compote and transfer in the serving plate.

Nutrition Info:
- Per Servingcalories 80, fat 0.3, fiber 2.1, carbs 19.1, protein 1

Cocoa Brownies
Servings: 8 | Cooking Time: 20 Minutes

Ingredients:
- 30 ounces canned lentils, rinsed and drained
- 1 tablespoon honey
- 1 banana, peeled and chopped
- ½ teaspoon baking soda
- 4 tablespoons almond butter
- 2 tablespoons cocoa powder
- Cooking spray

Directions:
1. In a food processor, combine the lentils with the honey and the other ingredients except the cooking spray and pulse well.
2. Pour this into a pan greased with cooking spray, spread evenly, introduce in the oven at 375 degrees F and bake for 20 minutes.
3. Cut the brownies and serve cold.

Nutrition Info:
- calories 200, fat 4.5, fiber 2.4 carbs 8.7, protein 4.3

Mango And Honey Cream
Servings:6 | Cooking Time: 30 Minutes

Ingredients:
- 2 cups coconut cream, chipped
- 6 teaspoons honey
- 2 mango, chopped

Directions:
1. Blend together honey and mango.
2. When the mixture is smooth, combine it with whipped cream and stir carefully.

Mediterranean Diet Cookbook

3. Put the mango-cream mixture in the serving glasses and refrigerate for 30 minutes.

Nutrition Info:
- Per Servingcalories 272, fat 19.5, fiber 3.6, carbs 27, protein 2.8

Blueberry Muffins
Servings:4 | Cooking Time: 25 Minutes

Ingredients:
- 1 cup whole wheat flour
- 1 teaspoon baking powder
- ¼ cup blueberries
- 1 teaspoon vanilla extract
- 1 tablespoon butter, softened
- ¾ cup sour cream
- 1 tablespoon Erythritol
- Cooking spray

Directions:
1. In the mixing bowl combine together wheat flour and baking powder.
2. Then add sour cream, vanilla extract, butter, and Erythritol.
3. Stir the mixture well until smooth. You should get a thick batter. Add more sour cream if needed.
4. After this, add blueberries and carefully stir the batter.
5. Spray the muffin molds with the cooking spray.
6. Fill ½ part of every muffin mold with batter.
7. Preheat the oven to 365F.
8. Place the muffins in the prepared oven and cook them for 25 minutes.
9. The cooked muffins will have a golden color surface.

Nutrition Info:
- Per Servingcalories 241, fat 12.3, fiber 1.1, carbs 31.5, protein 4.7

Mandarin Cream
Servings: 8 | Cooking Time: 0 Minutes

Ingredients:
- 2 mandarins, peeled and cut into segments
- Juice of 2 mandarins
- 2 tablespoons stevia
- 4 eggs, whisked
- ¾ cup stevia
- ¾ cup almonds, ground

Directions:
1. In a blender, combine the mandarins with the mandarins juice and the other ingredients, whisk well, divide into cups and keep in the fridge for 20 minutes before serving.

Nutrition Info:
- calories 106, fat 3.4, fiber 0, carbs 2.4, protein 4

Beetroot Apple Smoothie
Servings: 3 | Cooking Time: 5 Minutes

Ingredients:
- 1 boiled beetroot, peeled
- 2 teaspoons minced ginger
- 1 tablespoon lemon juice
- 1 apple, peeled and cored
- 1 carrot, peeled and sliced
- 1 pear, peeled and cored
- 1 cup ice

Directions:
1. Place all Ingredients: in a blender.
2. Blend until smooth.
3. Pour in a glass container.
4. Serve immediately.

Nutrition Info:
- Calories per serving: 187; Carbs: 29.9g; Protein: 2.6g; Fat: 6.9g

Papaya Cream
Servings: 2 | Cooking Time: 0 Minutes

Ingredients:
- 1 cup papaya, peeled and chopped
- 1 cup heavy cream
- 1 tablespoon stevia
- ½ teaspoon vanilla extract

Directions:
1. In a blender, combine the cream with the papaya and the other ingredients, pulse well, divide into cups and serve cold.

Nutrition Info:
- calories 182, fat 3.1, fiber 2.3, carbs 3.5, protein 2

Raw Truffles
Servings: 6 | Cooking Time:30 Minutes

Ingredients:
- ½ pound dates, pitted
- ½ cup water, hot
- 2 tablespoons raw honey
- ½ teaspoon vanilla extract
- 2 tablespoons cocoa powder
- 1 cup shredded coconut
- 1 tablespoon chia seeds
- 1 oz. candied orange, diced
- Extra cocoa powder for coating

Directions:
1. Combine the hot water, dates, honey and vanilla in a food processor and pulse until well mixed.
2. Add the rest of the ingredients and mix well.
3. Form small balls and roll them through cocoa powder.
4. Serve right away.

Nutrition Info:
- Per Serving:Calories:196 Fat:4.8g Protein:1.7g Carbohydrates:41.3g

Recipe

From the kicthen of ....

Serves .... Prep time .... Cook time ....

☐ Difficulty   ☐ Easy   ☐ Medium   ☐ Hard

Ingredient

Directions

Mediterranean Diet Cookbook

Date: _____

MY SHOPPING LIST

Appendix A: Measurement Conversions

BASIC KITCHEN CONVERSIONS & EQUIVALENTS

DRY MEASUREMENTS CONVERSION CHART

3 TEASPOONS = 1 TABLESPOON = 1/16 CUP

6 TEASPOONS = 2 TABLESPOONS = 1/8 CUP

12 TEASPOONS = 4 TABLESPOONS = 1/4 CUP

24 TEASPOONS = 8 TABLESPOONS = 1/2 CUP

36 TEASPOONS = 12 TABLESPOONS = 3/4 CUP

48 TEASPOONS = 16 TABLESPOONS = 1 CUP

METRIC TO US COOKING CONVERSIONS

OVEN TEMPERATURES

120 °C = 250 °F

160 °C = 320 °F

180° C = 350 °F

205 °C = 400 °F

220 °C = 425 °F

LIQUID MEASUREMENTS CONVERSION CHART

8 FLUID OUNCES = 1 CUP = 1/2 PINT = 1/4 QUART

16 FLUID OUNCES = 2 CUPS = 1 PINT = 1/2 QUART

32 FLUID OUNCES = 4 CUPS = 2 PINTS = 1 QUART

= 1/4 GALLON

128 FLUID OUNCES = 16 CUPS = 8 PINTS = 4 QUARTS = 1 GALLON

BAKING IN GRAMS

1 CUP FLOUR = 140 GRAMS

1 CUP SUGAR = 150 GRAMS

1 CUP POWDERED SUGAR = 160 GRAMS

1 CUP HEAVY CREAM = 235 GRAMS

VOLUME

1 MILLILITER = 1/5 TEASPOON

5 ML = 1 TEASPOON

15 ML = 1 TABLESPOON

240 ML = 1 CUP OR 8 FLUID OUNCES

1 LITER = 34 FL. OUNCES

US TO METRIC COOKING CONVERSIONS

1/5 TSP = 1 ML

1 TSP = 5 ML

1 TBSP = 15 ML

1 FL OUNCE = 30 ML

1 CUP = 237 ML

1 PINT (2 CUPS) = 473 ML

1 QUART (4 CUPS) = .95 LITER

1 GALLON (16 CUPS) = 3.8 LITERS

1 OZ = 28 GRAMS

1 POUND = 454 GRAMS

BUTTER

1 CUP BUTTER = 2 STICKS = 8 OUNCES = 230 GRAMS = 8 TABLESPOONS

WHAT DOES 1 CUP EQUAL

1 CUP = 8 FLUID OUNCES

1 CUP = 16 TABLESPOONS

1 CUP = 48 TEASPOONS

1 CUP = 1/2 PINT

1 CUP = 1/4 QUART

1 CUP = 1/16 GALLON

1 CUP = 240 ML

WEIGHT

1 GRAM = .035 OUNCES

100 GRAMS = 3.5 OUNCES

500 GRAMS = 1.1 POUNDS

1 KILOGRAM = 35 OUNCES

BAKING PAN CONVERSIONS

1 CUP ALL-PURPOSE FLOUR = 4.5 OZ

1 CUP ROLLED OATS = 3 OZ 1 LARGE EGG = 1.7 OZ

1 CUP BUTTER = 8 OZ 1 CUP MILK = 8 OZ

1 CUP HEAVY CREAM = 8.4 OZ

1 CUP GRANULATED SUGAR = 7.1 OZ

1 CUP PACKED BROWN SUGAR = 7.75 OZ

1 CUP VEGETABLE OIL = 7.7 OZ

1 CUP UNSIFTED POWDERED SUGAR = 4.4 OZ

BAKING PAN CONVERSIONS

9-INCH ROUND CAKE PAN = 12 CUPS

10-INCH TUBE PAN = 16 CUPS

11-INCH BUNDT PAN = 12 CUPS

9-INCH SPRINGFORM PAN = 10 CUPS

9 X 5 INCH LOAF PAN = 8 CUPS

9-INCH SQUARE PAN = 8 CUPS

Mediterranean Diet Cookbook

Appendix B: Recipes Index

A

All-Purpose Flour
Multipurpose Dough 31
Pasta Flora Or Greek Tart With Apricot Jam 131
Almond Tea Biscuits 132

Almond
Fennel Salad With Lemon, Toasted Almonds, And Mint 106
Mandarin Cream 135

Almond Flour
Paprika 'n Cajun Seasoned Onion Rings 50
Cheese And Broccoli Balls 56
Hazelnut Pudding 132

Almond Milk
Blueberries Quinoa 21
Almond Pudding 134

Apple
Breakfast Salad From Grains And Fruits 75
Cardamom Apples 104
Healthy Detox Salad 108
Lime Grapes And Apples 127
Apple Dates Mix 128
Vanilla Apple Pie 129
Delicious Apple Pear Cobbler 131

Artichoke
Artichokes And Cheese Omelet 19
Instant Pot Artichoke Hearts 51
Garlic Parmesan Artichokes 52
Eggs Benedict And Artichoke Hearts 118
Mediterranean Dip 119
Breakfast Egg-artichoke Casserole 121

Asparagus
Herbed Quinoa And Asparagus 19
Lemon Peas Quinoa Mix 23
Cheesy Asparagus 53
Lemon Asparagus Risotto 71
Pasta Primavera Without Cream 71
Fruity Asparagus-quinoa Salad 72
Orange, Dates And Asparagus On Quinoa Salad 74
Balsamic Asparagus 112

Avocado
Avocado Baked Eggs 24
Avocado Toast 25
Avocado And Onion Mix 110
Breakfast Egg On Avocado 119

B

Bacon
Stuffed Figs 21

Bagel
Toasted Bagels 124

Baguette
Feta And Roasted Red Pepper Bruschetta 33

Banana
St. Valentine's Mediterranean Pancakes 122
Banana Cinnamon Cupcakes 130
Peanut Banana Yogurt Bowl 130
Cinnamon Banana And Semolina Pudding 130

Bean
Breakfast Tostadas 25
Kalamata Hummus 28
Garbanzo And Kidney Bean Salad 69
Kidney Bean And Parsley-lemon Salad 71
Italian White Bean Soup 72

Cilantro-dijon Vinaigrette On Kidney Bean Salad 76
Goat Cheese 'n Red Beans Salad 77
Feta On Tomato-black Bean 77
Escarole And Cannellini Beans On Pasta 79
Bean And Toasted Pita Salad 79
Chickpeas, Corn And Black Beans Salad 104
Summer Bean Salad And Smoked Trout 105
Lime Beans Salad 108
Spicy Tortilla Soup 118
Chicken Green Bean Soup 119

Beef
Mediterranean-style Nachos Recipe 32
Carrot Mushroom Beef Roast 37
Tender Beef In Tomato-artichoke Stew 38
Flavorful Beef Bourguignon 39
Rosemary Beef Eggplant 39
Beef With Beets And Broccoli 40
Artichoke Beef Roast 41
Thyme Ginger Garlic Beef 43
Beef And Zucchini Skillet 43
Light Beef Soup 43
Stuffed Squash Casserole 44
Italian Beef 45
Spanish Rice Casserole With Cheesy Beef 72
Filling Macaroni Soup 76
Baked Parmesan And Eggplant Pasta 77
Parsley Beef Stew 82
Herbed Beef And Tomato Soup 84
Bean And Beef Chili 87
Beef Stuffed Bell Peppers 89
Spiced Meat And Rice 111
Cooked Beef Mushroom Egg 116

Beef Steak
Steaks And Greek Yogurt Mix 43

Beet
Vinegar Beet Bites 32
Beets Salad 81
Dill Beets Salad 110

Beetroot
Beetroot Apple Smoothie 135

Bell Pepper
Creamy Pepper Spread 34
Quick Arugula Salad 106

Yogurt Peppers Mix 109
Veal Shank Barley Soup 115
Spiced Lentil Stew 121
Sweet And Sour Rhubarb Lentil Soup 125

Berry
Five Berry Mint Orange Infusion 127
Honey Fruit Compote 133

Black Mussel
Garlic Butter Seafood 89

Black Olives
Cheesy Olives Bread 25

Blackberry
Blackberry Pie 134

Blueberry
Nutty And Fruity Amaranth Porridge 73
Easy Quinoa & Pear Salad 103
Yogurt Parfait 130

Bread
Crispy Pollock And Gazpacho 84

Brie
French Baked Brie Recipe With Figs, Walnuts And Pistachios 122

Broccoli
Broccoli And Leek Soup 47
Vegetarian Bowtie Veggie Pasta 52
Chilli Broccoli 55

Brussels Sprout
Roasted Brussels Sprouts And Pecans 49

Butternut Squash
Hot Squash Wedges 31
Pomegranate, Squash In Quinoa Stew 48
Veggie And Pasta Soup 89
Roasted Vegetable Soup 118
Easy Butternut Squash With Quinoa And Lentils 124

C

Cabbage
Savoy Cabbage With Coconut Cream Sauce 48

Calamari Ring
Leeks And Calamari Mix 95
Dill Calamari 98

Carrot
Shrimp And Vegetable Rice 42
Sweet And Savory Couscous 53

Cashew
Lime Vanilla Fudge 131

Cauliflower
Cheesy Thyme Waffles 23
Mushroom-cauliflower Risotto 56
Minty Cauliflower Mix 111

Cauliflower Rice
Cauliflower Hash Brown Breakfast Bowl 22

Cranberry
Cranberry And Dates Squares 21
Fruits And Pistachios 23

Cheddar Cheese
Cheddar Bites 30
Creamy Eggplants 49

Cheese
Cheesy Barley 105
Pesto Dip 34
Mediterranean Diet Styled Stuffed Peppers 50
Refreshing Greek Salad 52
Italian Mac & Cheese 78
Mediterranean Last-minute Feta Cheese Dip 124
Shredded Phyllo And Sweet Cheese Pie (knafe) 127
Caramelized Onion Pasta 81

Cherry
Tomato Salad With Olives, Feta, And Mint 112
Minty Tart 128
Yogurt Mousse With Sour Cherry Sauce 129
Cherry Compote 134

Cherry Tomato
Olives And Cheese Stuffed Tomatoes 32
Chickpea Salad Recipe 106
Tomato And Palm Salad 55
Chipotle Turkey And Tomatoes 59
Bacon And Tomato Pasta 111

Chicken
Pita Chicken Burger With Spicy Yogurt 40
Greek Chicken Stew 41
Ancestral Roasted Chicken 42
Greek Chicken Bites 58
Balsamic Chicken Tortillas 59
Chicken And Lemongrass Sauce 60
Chicken And Parsley Sauce 60
Chicken And Olives Bowls 61
Chili Chicken Fillets 61
Chicken And Rice 63
Chicken Roulade 63
Chicken Salad And Mustard Dressing 65
Honey Roasted Chicken With Rosemary Potatoes 81
Parmesan Penne 87
Garlicky Roasted Chicken 87
Layered Potato Chicken Casserole 88
Herbed Tomato-arugula Salad With Chicken 108
Mediterranean Father's Day Chicken Burgers 114
Bbq Chicken Pizza 115

Chicken Breast
Couscous With Artichokes, Sun-dried Tomatoes And Feta 20
Creamy Chicken-spinach Skillet 39
Curry Chicken, Artichokes And Olives 58
Creamy Coriander Chicken 58
Sage And Nutmeg Chicken 59
Slow Cooked Chicken And Capers Mix 60
Chicken And Olives 60
Chicken And Sweet Potatoes 60
Chicken With Artichokes And Beans 61
Paprika Chicken And Pineapple Mix 62
Turmeric Baked Chicken Breast 62
Chicken With Peas 62
Garlic Chicken And Endives 62
Chicken Pilaf 63
Chicken Skewers 64
Creamy Chicken And Mushrooms 64
Oregano Chicken And Zucchini Pan 64
Bbq Chicken Mix 65
Chicken And Greens Salad 65
Stuffed Chicken 66
Belly-filling Cajun Rice & Chicken 69
Chicken Breasts Mediterranean-style With Avocado Tapenade 83
Mint Chicken Soup 86

Quinoa Chicken Casserole 87
Barley And Chicken Salad 104
Okra Stew (bamya) 122

Chicken Drumstick
Grilled Chicken On The Bone 58

Chicken Liver
Chicken Liver 23

Chicken Thighs
Balsamic Chicken With Roasted Tomatoes 37
Kumquat And Chicken Tagine 45
Tomato Chicken And Lentils 64
Buffalo Chicken Crust Pizza 114
Jew's Mallow Stew (mulukhiya) 120

Chicken Wing
Balsamic Wings 30
Chicken Wings And Dates Mix 65

Chickpea
Marinated Chickpeas 33
Chickpeas Salsa 33
Sun-dried Tomatoes And Chickpeas 70
Saffron Green Bean-quinoa Soup 79

Chili
Lavash Chips 29

Chocolate
Chocolate Cups 130

Chorizo
Creamy Chorizo Bowls 26

Cod Fillet
Kale, Beets And Cod Mix 93
Fish And Orzo 94
Creamy Bacon-fish Chowder 96
Warm Caper Tapenade On Cod 99
Mustard Cod 101
Tangy Citrus Salad With Grilled Cod 103
Creamy Bell Pepper Soup With Cod Fillets 115
Yogurt Fish Soup 121

Crab Meat
Crab Stew 100

Cream
Parmesan Polenta 109
Watermelon Cream 130
Papaya Cream 135

Cremini Mushroom
Appetizing Mushroom Lasagna 75

Cucumber
Cucumber Sandwich 30
Cucumber Roll Ups 34
Lime Yogurt Dip 35
Cold Cucumber Soup 55
Dill Cucumber Salad 103
Cucumber Salad Japanese Style 104
Tabbouleh- Arabian Salad 109
Neufchatel Cheese Mediterranean Dip 120
Kale Gazpacho 125

D

Date
Raw Truffles 135

Duck Leg
Duck And Tomato Sauce 61

E

Egg
Parmesan Omelet 22
Herbed Muffins 23
Oregano Muffins 24
Basil Rice Soup 86
Egg And Ham Breakfast Cup 123
Pink Lady Mediterranean Drink 124
Spiced Cookies 129

Eggplant
Chickpeas And Eggplant Bowls 28
Creamy Eggplant Dip 28
Eggplant Chips 30
Delicious Eggplant Caponata 35
Chili Eggplant 47
Stir Fried Eggplant 49
Eggplant With Olives 52
Ratatouille Pasta Style 52

Ratatouille Spaghetti 82
Stuffed Eggplants 83
Tomato Topped Eggplant Pie 84
Roasted Eggplant Salad 109

Endive
Lemon Endive Bites 33
Lemon Endives 111

English Muffin
Open Face Egg And Bacon Sandwich 117

F

Firm Tofu
Cold Veggie Udon 47

Fish
Anchovy And Orange Salad 112
Baked Sea Bass 93
Avocado Peach Salsa On Grilled Swordfish 96
Tomato Haddock Soup 125
Easy Fish Curry 98
Lemon Swordfish 99
Puttanesca Style Bucatini 78

Flour
Olive And Milk Bread 26
Peach Tart 128

Fruit
Santorini Sunrise 116

G

Greek Yogurt
Cheesy Yogurt 25
Shanklish Cheese 25
Greek Raisins And Vanilla Cream 128
Cocoa Yogurt Mix 132

Green Onion
Raw Tomato Sauce & Brie On Linguine 74

Ground Chuck
Meatball Gyro Pita Sandwich 41

H

Halibut
Mediterranean Flounder 89

Honey Halibut 92
Lemon-garlic Baked Halibut 94
Mediterranean-style fish soup 105

I

Italian Sausage
Chicken And Sausage Mix 66

J

Jumbo Shrimp
Crazy Saganaki Shrimp 96

K

Kale
Creamy Kale And Mushrooms 50
Braised Kale And Carrots 51
Chickpea-crouton Kale Caesar Salad 78

L

Lamb
Bulgur Lamb Meatballs 29
Sweet Chili Lamb 39
Upside-down Rice (makloubeh) 40
Chili Lamb Meatballs 42
Lamb And Zucchini Mix 45

Lamb Chop
Lamb Chops 38
Pistachio Crusted Lamb Chops 84

Lamb Leg
Mediterranean-style Lamb Leg With Potatoes 117

Lamb Loin
Cherry Stuffed Lamb 38

Lamb Shank
Cherry Braised Lamb Shanks 83

Lamb Shoulder
Raisin Stuffed Lamb 90
Lamb Stew With Apricots And Moroccan Mint Tea 106

Leek
Summer Vegetables 48
Leek, Bacon And Pea Risotto 70

Lentil
Tomato And Lentils Salad 21
Celery Carrot Brown Lentils 47
Lentil Tabbouleh And Haloumi 83
Spicy Red Lentil Soup 123
Cocoa Brownies 134

Lettuce
Orange Lettuce Salad 55
Spring Soup Recipe With Poached Egg 111
Greek Antipasto Salad 112

Lobster Tail
Easy Broiled Lobster Tails 100

M

Mango
Mango And Honey Cream 134

Milk
Overnight Oats With Nuts 22

Mussel
Mediterranean Diet Pasta With Mussels 70
Chorizo Broiled Mussels 85
Mussels And Shrimp In Wine Sauce And Garlic Crostini 90
Stewed Mussels & Scallops 97

Mushroom
Curried Veggies And Poached Eggs 116

N

Nut
Popcorn-pine Nut Mix 31

O

Oatmeal
Baked Oatmeal With Cinnamon 19
Pumpkin Oatmeal With Spices 22

Onion
Cheese Onion Spread 54
Dandelion Greens 110

P

Pea
Minty Green Pea Soup 116

Peach
Peach Skewers 29
Red Quinoa Peach Porridge 69
Warm Peach Compote 131
Red Wine Poached Pears 132
Almond Peaches Mix 133

Pear
Cinnamon Pear Jam 128
Cranberries And Pears Pie 131
Cinnamon Pears 133

Penne Pasta
Vegan Olive Pasta 78

Pita Bread
Fig And Prosciutto Pita Bread Pizza 86

Pork
Italian Pork Spareribs 37
Italian Pork And Mushrooms 39
Pork Shanks And Wine Sauce 41
Pork Kebabs 43
Pork And Tomato Meatloaf 44
Pork Fennel Meatballs 85
Sage Pork And Beans Stew 88

Pork Chop
Pork Chops And Cherries Mix 37
Yogurt Marinated Pork Chops 82

Pork Loin
Pork And Parsley Spread 37
Hot Pork Meatballs 45

Pork Loin Chop
Baked Pork Chops 38

Pork Rib
Sweet Pork Ribs 44

Pork Sausage
Feta, Eggplant And Sausage Penne 68

Portobello Mushroom
Cheesy Caprese Style Portobellos Mushrooms 21
Thyme Mushrooms 54

Potato
Quinoa And Potato Bowl 19
Herbed Potatoes And Eggs 20
Creamy Potato Spread 29
Perfect Italian Potatoes 30
Lentils Stuffed Potato Skins 34
Rosemary Sweet Potato 50
Mushroom And Potato Mix 53
Indian Bell Peppers And Potato Stir Fry 53
Sweet Potatoes Oven Fried 54
Rice And Chickpea Stew 74
Fish Parcels 88
Mediterranean Potato Salad 107
Leek And Potato Soup 119
Potato Rosti 120
Italian Vegetable Soup 120
Veggie Hash 123
Mediterranean Doughnuts 127

Prosciutto
Plum Wraps 32

Pumpkin Seed
Roasted Seeds 35

Q

Quinoa
Cinnamon Quinoa Bars 76
Quinoa Salad 105

R

Radish
Tuna-dijon Salad 107

Rice
Lime-cilantro Rice Chipotle Style 73
Cucumber Olive Rice 77
Chives Rice Mix 111

S

Salmon
Lemon Salmon Rolls 33
Mediterranean-style Salmon Fillet 86
Salmon And Zucchini Rolls 93
Fried Salmon 93
Parmesan Salmon Balls 95
Salmon And Peach Pan 96
Salmon And Green Beans 97
Leftover Salmon Salad Power Bowls 98
Walnut Salmon Mix 99
Creamy Curry Salmon 100
Lemony Lentil Salad With Salmon 108

Sardine
Minty Sardines Salad 98

Scallop
Seafood Paella With Couscous 69

Shrimp
Corn And Shrimp Salad 19
Grilled Shrimp Kabobs 34
Seafood And Veggie Pasta 75
Fettuccine With Spinach And Shrimp 81
Shrimp Pancakes 82
Shrimp And Yogurt Sauce 92
Dijon Mustard And Lime Marinated Shrimp 93
Shrimp And Calamari Mix 94
Shrimp And Lemon Sauce 98
One-pot Seafood Chowder 99
Garlic Roasted Shrimp With Zucchini Pasta 101
Shrimp Scampi 101
Warm Shrimp Salad With Feta And Honeydew 110

Smoked Trout

Smoked Trout Tartine 95
Greek Trout Spread 97

Sour Cream
Goat Cheese And Chives Spread 30
Mediterranean Dip Duo 35
Light Tartar Dill Sauce 121
Blueberry Muffins 135

Spanish Chorizo
Chorizo-kidney Beans Quinoa Pilaf 73

Spinach
Breakfast Spanakopita 24
Mediterranean Omelet 24
Endives, Fennel And Orange Salad 26
Slow Cooked Cheesy Artichoke Dip 28
Ricotta And Spinach Ravioli 68
Cucumber And Tomato Salad 79
Kalamata Olives Penne 88
Sweet And Sour Spinach Salad 104
Tuscan White Bean Soup 117

Squash
Flavors Basil Lemon Ratatouille 51

Swiss Chard
Lentil And Swiss Chard Soup 122

T

Tilapia Fillet
Baked Tilapia 92
Salsa Fish Fillets 97
Delicious Fish Tacos 101

Tomato
Menemen 20
Cold Watermelon Gazpacho 56
Pecorino Pasta With Sausage And Fresh Tomato 68
Tomato Roasted Feta 86
Italian Tuna Pasta 95
Tomato-mozzarella With Balsamic Dressing 108
Fresh Gazpacho 114

Trout
Trout And Tzatziki Sauce 100

Tuna
Tuna Risotto 94

Turkey
Sesame Turkey Fillets With Fresh Greens 85
Turkey Fritters And Sauce 85

Turkey Breast
Herbed Almond Turkey 59
Turkey And Chickpeas 61
Turkey And Cranberry Sauce 62
Turkey And Salsa Verde 63
Turkey And Asparagus Mix 65
Lemony Turkey And Pine Nuts 66

W

Walnut
Baklava 132

White Bass Fillet
Orange Herbed Sauced White Bass 92

White Bean
Arrabbiata White Bean Soup 123

White Bread
Mediterranean Stuffed Custard Pancakes 133

Z

Zucchini
Zucchini Oats 20
Zucchini Cakes 29
Stuffed Zucchinis 31
Zucchini Fritters 49
Vegetarian Cabbage Rolls 50
Instant Pot Fried Veggies 51
Mushroom And Zucchini Pie 54
Ginger Vegetable Stir Fry 55
Delicious Pasta Primavera 73
Parmesan Zucchini Soup 115
Healthy Zucchini Pudding 129

Printed in Great Britain
by Amazon